NATION-BUILDING

A Reference Handbook

Other Titles in ABC-CLIO's
CONTEMPORARY
WORLD ISSUES
Series

Books in the Contemporary World Issues series address vital issues in today's society such as terrorism, sexual harassment, homelessness, AIDS, gambling, animal rights, and air pollution. Written by professional writers, scholars, and nonacademic experts, these books are authoritative, clearly written, up-to-date, and objective. They provide a good starting point for research by high school and college students, scholars, and general readers, as well as by legislators, businesspeople, activists, and others.

Each book, carefully organized and easy to use, contains an overview of the subject; a detailed chronology; biographical sketches; facts and data and/or documents and other primary-source material; a directory of organizations and agencies; annotated lists of print and nonprint resources; a glossary; and an index.

Readers of books in the Contemporary World Issues series will find the information they need in order to better understand the social, political, environmental, and economic issues facing the world today.

NATION-BUILDING

A Reference Handbook

Cynthia A. Watson

**CONTEMPORARY
WORLD ISSUES**

A B C ☰ C L I O

Santa Barbara, California • Denver, Colorado • Oxford, England

Library of Congress Cataloging-in-Publication Data

Watson, Cynthia Ann.
  Nation-building : a reference handbook / Cynthia A. Watson.
     p. cm.—(Contemporary world issues)
  Includes bibliographical references and index.

  ISBN 1-85109-594-2 (hardcover : alk. paper)
  ISBN 1-85109-599-3 (e-book)

1. United States—Foreign relations—1989– 2. United States—Foreign relations—1945–1989. 3. Intervention (International law) 4. Economic development. 5. Peacekeeping forces. 6. International relations. 7. United States—Foreign relations—Developing countries. 8. Developing countries—Foreign relations—United States. I. Title. II. Series.

  E840.W38 2004
  327.73'009'045—dc22

                                    2004003048

08   07   06   05   04   10   9   8   7   6   5   4   3   2   1

This book is also available on the World Wide Web as an eBook. Visit abc-clio.com for details.

ABC-CLIO, Inc.
130 Cremona Drive, P.O. Box 1911
Santa Barbara, California 93116-1911

This book is printed on acid-free paper ∞ .
Manufactured in the United States of America.

For Janet Ballantyne, Carole Palma, and Carla Klausner—nation-builders all

Contents

Foreword

Three weeks before I submitted this manuscript, I was asked to engage in nation-building by helping rebuild the higher education system in Iraq. Although my role would be negligable, that slight engagement caused me to reconsider the concept of helping other countries redo their systems. Much of my early life was indirectly tied to nation-building because my father worked for the U.S. Agency for International Development, and I approach the world somewhat differently than most people because I have seen how the world works outside of the United States. I am also profoundly aware that actions too often have unintended and unanticipated consequences. I have no idea how the higher education system of Iraq will look thirty-five years from now, but I do know that the evolution will have many unplanned stops and starts and successes and failures; that is the nature of the endeavor.

At the risk of slighting some people, I want to mention several individuals who have lent me support in this project. Mildred "Mim" Vasan persuaded me to do this book for ABC-CLIO, and I have learned a great deal in the process. One of the joys of teaching at the National War College is the necessity of exploring ideas, institutions, and linkages that are not always obvious or familiar. Not long after agreeing to write this book, a colleague, Captain Craig Rankin, U.S. Navy, and I noticed in semiannual oral evaluations of students that they were unsure of what nation-building meant to them as national security strategists. I laud and thank Mim and ABC-CLIO for working to fill that hole in the national debate while stimulating me to rethink how I address it in my own teaching at the college.

There are many other people to thank, and I apologize in

advance for any I have forgotten. Maurie Negrin and Sharon Murphy have both been important friends. My colleagues at the National War College and the National Defense University have been their usual supportive, giving selves. Carolyn Turner, Bruce Thornlow, Rosemary Dzuik, Dawn Humphrey, and Julie Arighetti of our world-class library showed me things I could only dream existed and have helped me considerably. The Institute for National Strategic Studies, especially Dr. Steve Flanagan and Dr. Jim Schear, allowed me to use an office across from that wonderful library. Gina Zondorak or ABC- CLIO was always cheerful, patient, and easy to answer.

Each of us approaches work differently, but several National War College faculty members have been particularly helpful and generous with that finite commodity—time. Rear Admiral Richard Jaskot, U.S. Navy, had enthusiasm for this project as soon as he walked in the door as commandant of the college. Col. Jimmy Rabon, U.S. Army, has shared his methodology as well as his experiences in Iraq, both of which were illuminating. Ambassador Ryan Crocker, literally just back from Baghdad, has been gracious, patient, and extremely informative; he helped me a great deal. Thank goodness there are practitioners like Ryan in this field, many of whom share their wisdom by teaching at the college. Col. Dave Lamm, U.S. Army, was extremely helpful. Dr. Paul Godwin may have taken his long and prestigious China background with him into retirement in Chico, California, but his willingness to burn electrons and to have marvelous debates over the phone lines makes it feel as if he hasn't left. Paul's careful analysis of where an expansion here or there would lead proved crucial to keeping me on track. Capt. Keith Johnson, U.S. Coast Guard, brings a refreshing honesty and irreverence that I will miss when he goes back to Seattle. Dr. Mel "Moshe" Goodman, with incredible passion in all he does, keeps all of us mindful that questions always need to be asked in a democracy and in an educational facility. Susan Sherwood was a patient listener and often had immediately practical suggestions.

I dedicate this volume to three women, two of whom have been on the front lines of nation-building throughout their prestigious careers at the U.S. Agency for International Development. I met both of these women as they graced the classrooms of the National War College with dry wit, scholarly rigor, and tremendous toughness. Dr. Janet C. Ballantyne came to us straight out of some of the most contentious years of reform and nation-building in Russia. Before that, she had years of experiences in Central and

South America, Nepal, and Morocco. It was a great loss seeing her leave government service to go into the private sector. Similarly, Dr. Carole Palma negotiated with the Afghan warlords after the Soviet defeat to get food and medical supplies to that tense, fragmented area of the world before people understood its strategic relevance. She also battled malaria and took on different warlords in several African states. I was incredibly impressed, as were National War College students, that she included seeing the effects of HIV/AIDS in Africa when she took students there—talk about a teacher. At the same time, both of these women know how to laugh, and each keeps life in perspective when the rest of us would melt down. The third woman, Dr. Carla Klausner, taught me thirty years ago that women could do whatever they want but it requires grace, skill, persistence, and juggling; I consider this an equal form of nation-building. I hope my daughter, Bonnie Lesley, will have the same confidence to take on some sort of important building in life, here or abroad.

Scott and Bonnie have been and remain incredibly resilient at such tender ages. I can only tell them how proud I am of them and how they have so much to offer others, especially if they do not take the path of least resistance.

Bud Cole has taught me many more lessons over the past decade than I ever expected to learn. From each of these lessons I have grown a great deal. His patient editing, his willingness to offer significant improvements, and his overall gift of time have helped each and every piece of mine that he has read. I appreciate and thank him profoundly and look forward to each and every day of knowing him.

I would like to point out that the views I present here are my views only, not those of the National War College or any part of the U.S. government.

1

Introduction

A s this volume is being concluded, the United States is recognizing that the task ahead in Afghanistan and Iraq is more daunting than originally envisioned by the Bush administration. Before the war began in 2003, many in the administration had argued that the conflict would be rapidly concluded and that U.S. forces would receive heroes' welcomes as they instituted a post-Saddam Iraq. Instead, in the months following President Bush's declaration on 1 May that major combat operations had concluded, U.S. and coalition forces in Iraq face daily guerrilla attacks, along with increasingly frequent car bombings aimed at undermining attempts to stabilize the new environment. Increasingly, in the United States, the situation in Iraq is seen as significantly more complicated and less hopeful than when war began. In Afghanistan, more than two years after the Taliban government was ousted, NATO forces in charge of the operations find themselves increasingly retracing their steps to pursue Taliban forces. President Hamid Karzai has little control over much of the country outside of Kabul itself. Afghanistan, like Iraq, appears to be a much more intractable problem than originally envisioned.

At the same time, the Bush administration began a low-level involvement in a civil war in the West African country of Liberia. President Bush sent in just over a thousand Marines in July 2003, and UN Secretary General Kofi Annan later requested 15,000 peacekeepers to secure the country—a dramatic difference. As the nation in Africa with which the United States has the longest ties, Liberia has suffered through at least two decades of virtually constant upheaval that has caused destabilization of its neighbors as well as its own society.

For U.S. forces being called upon to engage in peacekeeping, government- and institution-building, and an array of other activities that are broadly termed nation-building, the list of tasks appears endless. As noted by Karin von Hippel, this concept of "nation-building" has evolved dramatically over the past fifty years since MacArthur did it in Japan and the Marshall Plan paid for it in Europe: "Nation building, which really means state building, has over the years signified an effort to construct a government that may or may not be democratic, but preferably is stable. Today, nation building normally implies the attempt to create democratic and secure states. Thus democratization efforts are part of the larger and more comprehensive nation-building campaign, but democratization can also occur in places where the state is secure and does not need to be rebuilt, such as with electoral reform in Mexico" (2000, 96). In many of the locations where these efforts must occur, the most visible immediate problem is providing the basic security that will allow states to change political systems. The lessons of the past decade, after the ideological battle of the cold war ended, is that the development of democratic institutions is a far greater challenge than anyone had realized.

Ironically, the United States came late to nation-building compared with the rest of the developed world. Because much of Western Europe had a much longer and more extensive history of colonial rule, it was more accustomed to the idea of intervention in a state to prevent civil unrest or to promote a form of government. The United States, with its long history of advocating self-determination, came slowly to the idea that it was benefiting the world if it engaged in actions to stop domestic conflicts. Additionally, the U.S. preference to selectively engage in foreign actions, often misnamed isolationism, prior to World War II left the public disinclined to focus on the needs of other states in developing state institutions.

For the U.S. public, the notion that the United States must take the lead, financially and on the ground, in Bosnia, Kosovo, Afghanistan, Colombia, Iraq, and then Liberia is an intimidating and seemingly limitless proposition. The possibility that North Korea, Syria, and Iran might be on the horizon is frustrating and worrisome. Questions arise about why the United States must carry so much of the burden. Can these efforts somehow backfire, promoting attacks on the nation instead of the peace and goodwill that the United States so earnestly anticipates when answering the call to reestablish peace and stability in some other land?

Are these actions masquerading as nation-building or are they indeed empire-building, something that the United States has prided itself on *not* doing with very few exceptions in its history?

The United States has chosen the theme of nation-building, or rebuilding, as a major course for U.S. policy for the initial years of the twenty-first century, with the assumption that by helping to create a world of democratic, free market states, the attacks resulting from the hatred of nineteen terrorists on 11 September 2001 will be prevented from recurring. The belief that the United States offers the rest of the world a model of freedom, hope, ethics, and equality is not new; it has been woven throughout our history. But the 2001 tragedies called for a more draconian approach by the United States. The idea that we could trust no one else to defend our security and nation-building became a crucial piece of U.S. strategy.

Once derided by politicians on the political right, as George W. Bush did in his 2000 presidential campaign, nation-building's utility in preserving U.S. dominance of the international community is now recognized and heralded. The political left in the United States, long comfortable with aspirations to make the world more liberal and democratic in our image, has continued to support various aspects of the goal. Individuals across the U.S. political spectrum differ basically only in their focus. All accept the basic premise that a nation can be strengthened from the outside.

The war against terrorism in Afghanistan began with grand aspirations to retaliate against those who brought the horror of terrorism to U.S. shores in September 2001, but the war gradually became more focused on rebuilding wild, exotic Afghanistan into a trustworthy member of the international community. Roughly two years after the initial retaliation against the Taliban for support of Osama Bin Laden and the September 11 attacks, many fear that the tide is turning in favor of the Taliban because the nation-building process has been too hasty. Critics charge that the United States simply did not do enough, in a sustained enough manner, to alter Afghanistan fundamentally enough, to preclude the Taliban from returning. Some would argue this cannot be done because democracy and nation-building must be internally driven, not externally imposed, as the United States has so often attempted.

The movement, however, to get other states to behave as the United States desires is not new, dating back at least to the beginning of the twentieth century, when Theodore Roosevelt proclaimed that the United States would operate in the Caribbean Basin with "a big stick." The idea that an outside entity could construct a nation within set national boundaries may offend some but has been an important component of U.S. foreign policy and national power for many generations.

This issue has attracted more recent interest because of Afghanistan and Iraq. The Bush administration, entering office at the beginning of the new millennium, campaigned on a platform of disdain for the United States trying to use its powerful military for nation-building enterprises. The campaign accused the outgoing Clinton administration of naively wasting U.S. resources—financial, military, and political—in the unrealistic expectation of creating societies more like us—and hence less likely to threaten us.

It was not long after the September 11 shocks that the Bush administration began realizing that it, too, had to contemplate nation-building as part of the strategy to prevent another such attack. Accounts of the discussions leading up to and into the U.S. action in Afghanistan in early October 2001 reveal the gradual rethinking of the Bush administration, and the president himself, to seeing a central role for nation-building in trying to create a stable, pro-Western, anti-Taliban regime in Kabul.

After the fairly easy success in overturning the Taliban regime, the United States and the world had to face the daunting task of achieving nation-building in a country where that has not been achieved before, in spite of many attempts. Afghanistan remains, months after the initial U.S. intervention, a country with competing tribal leaders who would be termed "warlords" in other places around the world. The tasks necessary to build meaningful, enduring institutions in Afghanistan are numerous and complex. Although this may be an extreme example, it points to the challenges that creating a nation from outside will provide.

Additionally, the Bush administration has had to come to grips with the various aspects of nation-building in ousting a dictator and creating a viable democratic system in Iraq. Although the period leading up to the conflict focused on the question of whether the international community faced a genuine threat to its security from weapons of mass destruction under Baghdad's control, many analysts immediately recognized that creating a new political system to preclude the return to a Saddam Hussein–type regime were complicated by the many years of Hussein's rule. Bush administration officials increasingly allowed their arguments for war against Saddam to target regime change, much to the dissatisfaction of the global community who feared that this personalization was a bad move.

Much of the debate about the war ignored discussion of the possible costs involved. In March 2003, some estimates had indicated that the nation-building process for Iraq might cost in the tens of millions of dollars and be multiple-year commitments to maintaining U.S. ground troops (Shinseki 2003). This prognostication attracted considerable skepticism on the part of the administration, but on 7 September 2003 President Bush asked the country to provide $87 billion for these efforts, on top of the amount already budgeted. These are significant sums of money, many argue, because domestic needs are great and the United States is anticipating a budget deficit of $455 billion by the end of 2003.

For many in the U.S. national security community, as well as some in the international community, nation-building remained an amorphous topic in the years after the Berlin Wall collapsed, something done by "somebody else." The post-Soviet states largely emerged on their own from the former empire, and the world ignored the many pleas from these new states for sovereign status. Some of these areas then provided painful and bloody examples that history had not ended, as blithely predicted by Francis Fukuyama (1992), nor had conflict subsided. The anticipated "peace dividend" so widely expected in the first Bush administration (1989–1993) proved a chimera, and the world nervously looked for someone to solve the problems of Haiti, Bosnia-Herzegovina, Rwanda, Burundi, Kosovo, East Timor, and Afghanistan. Iraq was last on the list. Each of these had unique characteristics, but all required the creation of the basic institutions of civil society, inherent in the birth of a new entity, as demonstrated in the former Yugoslav republics of the Balkans or some of the post-Soviet states in Central Asia and the Caucasus. Some required the recrafting of society to promote more representative or less threatening governments. Some were failed states, such as Rwanda and Burundi, which had perpetrated horrific brutalities on a portion of their own populations, and clearly needed societal alterations to prevent such abuse from recurring. Many would-be nation-states obviously required international support and guidance to ensure the security of their citizens.

In the early twenty-first century, two U.S. military campaigns caused the Bush administration to engage in massive nation-building campaigns. Afghanistan had been a Taliban-controlled country that treated women as noncitizens. Historically, warlord control in the remote areas of its geographical spread was the norm, in the absence of a unified, representational state. But the U.S. government pledged its intention to preclude a similarly repressive government by growing an Afghan democracy. Iraq, governed for more than a quarter of a century by Saddam Hussein, practiced some of history's grossest human rights abuses against its own citizens. Both these regimes were seen by Washington as unacceptable.

Weeks after the September 11 attacks on New York City and Washington, D.C., Taliban shelter given to the Al Qaeda terrorist network became the justification for removing the regime. Eighteen months later, the administration entered Iraq with the stated intention of eradicating the weapons of mass destruction program, a position that much of the international community questioned. After a swift move into the petroleum-rich country, preventing a return to dictatorship through creating a democratic system in Iraq again indicated that the Bush administration understood the need to engage in something it had derided during the 2000 presidential election campaign: the Global War on Terrorism required strong nation-building efforts.

What constitutes nation-building depends on the builder. Various activities are considered essential by some and not by others. The term implies starting from scratch, but, as an example, this is not the way the Bush administration approached Iraq. The administration initially intended to use judges and policy from the Ba'athist regime but later decided to reject members of the odious government party, only to reverse course again to reinstate some Ba'athists as the June 2004 deadline for government power transfer approached. For other analysts and practitioners, nation-building constitutes complete creation of a structure, set of values, and system of loyalty, ideology, and culture. It is perhaps this lack of clarity or this difference of opinion that makes nation-building so tough for decision makers and implementers alike.

No debate about the likelihood of further nation-building exists, however, as the United States and the world community evaluate the threats facing them in the twenty-first century. As shown in Iraq, the level of U.S. involvement is the greater issue. Many individuals were struck by the difference between the reactions of UN Security Council members in the debates over whether to authorize the use of force against Saddam Hussein's government (prior to March 2003) and the mid-May 2003 unanimous vote to allow the lifting of sanctions against Iraq. The discussions prior to use of force were divisive and caused ill feelings between the United States and France, as well as Germany, for example. Although the United States and Britain anticipated being the primary actors in the reconstruction or nation-building, the final Security Council Resolution of 22 May 2003 added United Nations involvement as a means of curtailing U.S. influence.

John Owen argues that the data he has accumulated on 198 attempts by outsiders to use force to impose democratic institutions between 1500 and 2000 is not encouraging (2002, 375–409). Indeed, it appears that the resiliency of existing institutions is often considerably stronger than generally thought before the use of force. The decision to attempt to improve national security through altering the form of government is not unique to the United States. Although U.S. actions attract more attention in this age of international media concentration in the United States, countries have tried to take steps toward what we now consider nation-building for generations. In 1500, France acted to alter the government of Scotland, for instance, far predating the United States first engaging in this behavior in 1899 when it intervened in the newly independent Cuba. The United States then moved to alter domestic institutions in dozens of states in the century after the Cuban intrusion, although its concern focused on Latin American states with geographic proximity to the United States. In today's world where international travel is common and even the types of threats—now including cyberthreats to the economic, commercial, and information infrastructure—are closer to home, the reasons for altering institutions appear to have become even more urgent. The decision to use force to change the domestic political institutions of another state is not an inconsequential one, however, and there have actually been few nation-building commitments.

This volume is heavily weighted toward the actions of the United States in the post–World War II, and especially the recent, period. Although this list is not exhaustive, nation-building in the post–World War II world has included Germany (1945), the Marshall Plan (1947) in Western Europe, Japan (1945), South Korea (1953), Colombia (1998 to the present), Palestine (1993 to the present), Somalia (1993), Haiti (1993 and 2004), Cambodia (1988 to 1995), El Salvador and Nicaragua (1980s), East Timor (1999 to the present), Liberia (2003), Zimbabwe (1980 to the present), Afghanistan (2001 to the present), Former Republic of Yugoslavia (1996 to the present), Iraq (2003), and Liberia (2003).

References

Ackerman, Spencer. 2002. "Drop Zone—Remember Afghanistan?" *New Republic*, 9 September, p. 10.

Bacevich, Andrew J. 2003. *American Empires: The Realities and Consequences of U.S. Diplomacy*. Cambridge: Harvard University Press.

Barnett, Michael. 2002. "Nation Building's New Face." *Foreign Policy* (November–December): 98.

Crocker, Chester A., Fen Osler Hampson, and Pamela Aall, eds. 2001. *Turbulent Peace*. Washington, DC: U.S. Institute of Peace.

Fukuyama, Francis. 1992. *The End of History*. New York: Free Press.

Kagan, Robert, and William Kristol. 2000. *Present Dangers: Crisis and Opportunities in American Foreign and Defense Policy*. New York: Encounter.

Ottaway, Marina. 2002. "Think Again: Nation Building." *Foreign Policy* (September–October): 16–22.

Owen, John. 2002. "The Foreign Imposition of Domestic Institutions." *International Organization* 56, no. 2 (spring): 375–409.

Shinseki, General Eric K. 2003. Testimony before the Senate Armed Services Committee on FY 2004 Defense Budget, 25 February.

Von Hippel, Karin. 2000. "Democracy by Force: A Renewed Commitment to Nation Building." *Washington Quarterly* 23, no. 1 (winter): 95–112.

Zeller, Tom. 2003. "Building Democracy Is Not a Science." *New York Times*, 26 April, Section 4, 2.

2

Enduring Questions in Nation-Building

The issue of nation-building is as multifaceted and complex as any current public policy issue. The Romans, like the Greeks before them, engaged in nation-building, but probably could not fathom the tasks facing L. Paul Bremer as he worked to pull Iraq together in the postconflict period. The British and French, as the great colonialists of the modern era, created entities that achieved independence in the mid-twentieth century, but their task was also quite different from that of the contemporary period.

For the purposes of this volume, nation-building is defined as "ending military conflict and rebuilding economic and political infrastructures, along with basic services, to include the armed forces, police, government, banks, transportation networks, communications, health and medical care, schools, and the other basic infrastructure." This is my definition, but the term has increasingly come to encompass an expectation of building democratic systems as well (see von Hippel 2000, 95, on this subject). But there may be large differences of interpretation within that definition. Note that this definition does not explicitly include rebuilding social systems, a point often lost in the contentious discussions about different cultures and societies coming into conflict through nation-building. U.S. policy does not include rebuilding social systems in Afghanistan and Iraq, but it is that very notion that alarms some in both parts of the world.

What Is Included in Nation-Building?

In the United States, presidential candidates frequently campaign, as did George W. Bush in 2000, that they will not put U.S. forces into the position of nation-building; yet they often end up doing so by the end of their terms. This is not hypocrisy as much as it is misunderstanding the term, construing it too narrowly, or finding their options limited. The U.S. military, similarly, has long argued that its role is to "win the nation's wars, not build institutions" (the military slang is "kill people and break things," not build institutions), but this is a shortsighted view of the military's role in carrying out national security strategy. Humanitarian organizations, on the other hand, often believe that the U.S. government's role includes reconstituting neglected sectors of foreign societies. These different ideas of nation-building complicate the coordination of efforts by the United States to carry out such tasks.

Nation-building is generally seen as stopping violence against the population of a country and then constructing a society supported by institutions based upon the rule of law and various other norms that will make it function autonomously and to the benefit of its population. Nation-building may involve outside intervention for a variety of reasons: peacekeeping, preemption, humanitarian relief, institution-building, conflict avoidance, liberation, or revenge. To a great extent, nation-building is limited only in the goals of the state advocating it. The differences in perspectives is not limited to political views within the United States. European visions of nation-building are generally more interventionist and less military-based than those in the United States.

Can Nation-Building Be Brought to a People or Does It Need to Be Home Grown?

In many ways, this is the fundamental question of nation-building. Whether a state can institutionalize all of the changes to its society that are basic to nation-building is crucial to sustainment of those changes. A program that cannot stay the course fails. Much of the evidence of the twentieth century indicates that it is virtually impossible for nation-building to be imposed on a people. The United States has attempted to bring governmental change to Haiti, Somalia, Bosnia, Japan, Germany, Afghanistan, Iraq, Colombia, and the Philippines, and it is arguable that only in Japan and Germany has the effort been successful. This record supports the conclusion that foreign attempts at government resurrection most often fail. France and Britain also pursued nation-building in their former colonial territories, for more than a century in some cases. In an overwhelming number of those cases, nation-building failed to sustain institutionalization of the stable, democratic systems the colonial powers sought.

This raises the question as to whether democracy will take hold in certain cultures. Islamic societies are frequently considered in this light; some analysts believe that cultural and religious laws, *Shari'a*, make these cultures incompatible with western-style democracy. The same possibility has been raised about Russia and other Slavic societies, with their histories of strong, central authoritarian control. Similarly, Latin America with its cultural acceptance of the role of the state in people's lives, has been seen as incompatible with democracy and the free market.

Many U.S. observers maintain that democracy has thrived in the United States because of the culture of entrepreneurship and suspicion of government in people's lives, along with optimism and the melding of nationalities, that characterize the nation's history. Most importantly, the United States appears to have developed this commitment to democracy because it was a system developed from within. Once independence was achieved, the United States began its political process with little outside intervention. The political philosophies of great thinkers were studied, but Britain was the only state with the power to intervene, and it gradually, particularly after 1812, began turning its attention to colonial holdings in South Asia. This indigenous political growth may be the reason for democracy's success in the United States.

In Latin America, democracy has been something the United States has sought to promote for most of the twentieth century. Particularly in the period from 1960 through the present, the United States, through the *Alianza para el Progreso*, the U.S. Agency for International Development, education assistance, military and diplomatic missions, and various incentives, has tried to help Latin America commit to the democratic path. Instead, each and every country has a flawed democracy for reasons largely related to each nation's history.

Is Nation-Building a Military Operation or Is It a Civilian Activity?

This question is at the heart of many controversies in western democratic states. U.S. armed forces have always prided themselves on being involved in external issues that guarantee the defense of the United States. Defense most often was seen as destroying an opponent or defeating a threat from outside the country. Seen in this way, the reasons for military opposition to being involved in nation-building is obvious and unambiguous. Nation-building, with its nuances and stops and starts, has traditionally been seen by the military as a civilian responsibility.

In the aftermath of the cold war, and especially after the attacks of September 11, the military is being used to solidify regimes that have pro-Western, democratic orientations, because liberal, free market democracies are too often viewed as the sole model of success in the international system following the collapse of the Soviet Union. But one could certainly point to Singapore, as it is strongly authoritarian and has been since its separation from Malaysia in the 1960s. And China's tremendous economic growth under a far-from-democratic regime raises another challenge to the widely held view that democracy, free market economics, and success go hand in hand.

The military is seen as more efficient, more effective, and better funded for these nation-building activities. The resulting tensions between civilian leadership and military commanders have been significant, because each side believes it needs to control the situation for success. Additionally, some have argued that the military, which receives a significant portion of the budget, must be used in some capacity because it absorbs so many resources.

At the same time, the U.S. way of warfare has always made a distinction between military and civilian activities. The concept of *posse comitatus*, dating to the late nineteenth century, strictly limits military actions in the civil sector. The military has only taken on police functions in the most extreme national emergencies, and there is great reluctance in both spheres to alter that pattern. Negotiating the differences remains a feature in even the most stable of democratic systems, and this is even more difficult where the political system is in flux.

Does Outside Intervention Thwart Nation-Building?

This question has been particularly relevant since the end of the cold war in 1990, especially in the former Yugoslavia. The independence of Bosnia-Herzegovina could not be sustained without outside intervention to prevent the Serbs from engaging in ethnic cleansing. In Kosovo, the Kosovars, ethnic Albanians living in this area of the former Yugoslavia, were being killed by the Serbs, even though the territory was not formally independent.

In Iraq, however, one must consider whether outside intervention after the removal of Saddam Hussein is creating a situation conducive or detrimental to nation-building, because it appears to be inciting resistance. The same question can be asked of Colombia, a state that has been sovereign for almost two centuries.

How Much of Nation-Building Relates to Democratization and How Much to the Free Market? Is Nation-Building an Exploitation of Lesser-Developed States?

This highly charged question has been especially important in the Iraqi case, where petroleum is involved. Many critics outside of the U.S. government, including foreigners, have charged that U.S. intervention in Iraq was really about exploiting petroleum and the Iraqi economy—and had little to do with concern for the Iraqi people. These critics have charged that the Bush and Blair administrations only retroactively called the action nation-building and made the assumption that people live better under democratic, free market systems. The view that intervention in Iraq was in fact exploitation to gain control of a resource the United States needs remains high, particularly outside of the United States. The handling of contracts for the rebuilding of Iraq, particularly when those contracts go to the company previously run by Vice President Richard B. Cheney, only reinforces doubts about the nature of U.S. motives.

Iraq is not the first place where questions about nation-building's true goals have been raised. During the rebuilding after World War II, many critics questioned whether the Marshall Plan was really an attempt to bring European democracies into the U.S. orbit through economic assistance, rather than allowing those states to pursue their own courses of development. In Japan and Korea in the decade after 1945, questions arose about whether the United States truly cared about the form of government or was simply expanding its market share at the expense of others. In Vietnam during the 1960s and Central America two decades later, similar charges were made that the United States sought to rebuild in its own image to further economic exploitation. The point here is that nation-building has long been the focus of concerns about the true nature of any state's intentions when it violates the sovereignty of another state and then works to create a new form of government.

In any case, nation-building is a complicated endeavor with unanticipated twists and turns. Few if any states can afford the tasks of nation-building without outside financial assistance, particularly if there has been domestic armed conflict. This situation by itself indicates the need for outside intervention in the form of financial aid. At the same time, outsiders invariably have different views, cultures, concerns, and orientations, so their understanding of the particular conditions in any state undergoing nation-building is imperfect at best.

How Does Nation-Building Relate to Peacekeeping Operations, Humanitarian Operations, or "Operations Other Than War"?

The complexity of nation-building is reflected in this question because it illustrates the interaction of various stages as well as groups of actors. Humanitarian operations are generally seen as the least invasive type of activity, the goal being to alleviate an emergency often caused by a physical disaster. Providing food to Somalia in late 1992 was a humanitarian operation because people were starving after warlords restricted the distribution of food by outside groups. Peacekeeping operations, by contrast, indicate that an armed conflict has occurred and is in the process of being ended and that a neutral force, usually foreign, providing a buffer is acceptable to all sides in the conflict. As peacekeeping operations developed over the 1990s, however, it became obvious that peacekeepers often had to become peacemakers. "Operations other than war" was the term used for military activities, which included peace operations of all types, humanitarian operations, and anything less than full-fledged warfare. A problem with this term is that its definition differs depending upon whether one is on the giving or the receiving end of the operation.

Nation-building is broader than any of these terms because it implies and almost invariably includes a broader list of participants such as the military, the humanitarian nongovernmental operations sector, and civilian agents such as diplomats and foreign assistance cadres. A difficulty with these terms, however, is that specialists often distinguish among them, while politicians and other policymakers tend to use them interchangeably.

How Do Civil Affairs and Psychological Operations Fit into Nation-Building?

These are two important aspects to the military's work in any nation-building effort, but they are not necessarily seen in that light by those who live in the society being affected. In particular, psychological operations ("psy ops") has a negative image because of fear that some Machiavellian manipulation of the population's will is the goal. Democracy, after all, is the will of the majority in a representative system of elections, negotiations, and peace. Psy ops and civil affairs, often associated with the same campaigns in which the United States was accused of such actions as undermining duly elected governments during the cold war (such as in Guatemala in 1954 or Chile in 1970 to 1973, and in continuing actions against Fidel Castro in the more than four decades since his seizure of power in 1959), has left some observers questioning the motives under which the United States and other nation-builders operate. In far too many cases, Washington is suspected of acting in corporate interests rather than in the interests of the nations being rebuilt.

Civil affairs, however, is seen by its practitioners as an essential part of nation-building because so much of the activity involves the everyday aspects of putting a society back on its feet or, in some cases, building functioning twenty-first-century societies virtually from scratch. Controversy arises from different views of the appropriate starting and stopping points for the nation-builders. U.S. efforts in Afghanistan are sometimes viewed as an attempt to create a new state based on Western, free market democracy. To the warlords who have held sway in that country for at least twenty-five years, the resulting loss of power, influence, and economic benefits is an unappealing result.

What Is the Role of the United Nations (and Other Supranational Organizations) and the International Community in Nation-Building?

On this question, the United States generally stands apart from much of the rest of the world because of its tradition of not trusting supranational organizations. The United States prefers remaining in control of its troops, its funding, and its overall goals. In the case of Iraq, the Bush administration remains convinced that the United Nations is incapable of dealing realistically with the issues.

This distrust of the United Nations results from traditional U.S. fear of concentration of political and military power (the latter an irony in today's world), along with an unwillingness to put U.S. military forces under the command of a foreign officer of any organization. Some have accused Washington of being simply unwilling to share the economic gains likely to result in Iraq from petroleum exports. Concerns also relate to the widely held perceptions that the United Nations is too bureaucratic to cope with serious needs of a state like Iraq emerging from thirty years of authoritarian rule.

The question of burden sharing is always a relevant one. During the decision making that led to NATO intervention in Kosovo in 1999, the idea that the United States was the most able and had paid the most for the forces to wage war for Kosovo's population defense was important to the debate. With deterioration of conditions in Iraq at the end of April 2004, many in the world have called for a significantly greater UN role than was true earlier. Even within the United States, UN assumption of the job is becoming more palatable. The issues of cost, efficiency, and some of the overarching fundamental doubts about the efficacy of the United Nations' approach still outrides the U.S. concerns about its role in Iraq; but the concerns about whether the United States can accomplish what it originally believed so easy remain and appear growing daily.

One of the ironies in these discussions is the tendency for states to ask the rest of the world to provide financial resources but not to share the decision making in nation-building efforts. This frequently creates tension, and this tendency is likely to increase.

How Do Nongovernmental Organizations Relate to U.S. Government Operations?

In the post–cold war period, foreign assistance has been dramatically reduced and nongovernmental actors have stepped in to fill the breach. These nongovernmental organizations (NGOs) almost never, however, have the logistical ability to get into places where their assistance is required and must, therefore, work with the U.S. government and especially the armed forces, which do have the capability of getting the people to the places of greatest need. The NGO community, however, is often ideologically uncomfortable with the military, and tensions over chain-of-command questions often result. The tensions between these two not traditionally allied constituencies are important and likely to continue even as nongovernmental groups will face more association with the military as nation-building expands around the world.

At What Point Is Belligerency Over and Nation-Building Beginning?

Some observers believe that nation-building cannot start until all hostilities have come to a complete halt, while others believe that peace operations may most importantly mean peace*making*. But the dangers and difficulties of nation-building rise extraordinarily during the periods of open hostilities. Some observers discuss

nation-building as part of a broader period called "peace maintenance operations." Over the past decade, examples of peace*making* (Kosovo, 1999), peace maintenance (Sinai since 1978), and
peace*keeping* (Bosnia-Herzegovina, 1995 to the present) have all
existed. This is one of the harder concepts upon which the international community must find agreement.

What Are the Measures of Success in Nation-Building?

How can whether a state has completed its nation-building
process be determined? This appears to be a simple question but
is, in fact, quite complicated. If nation-building enables a country
to choose its own path, the result can could be quite different
from that of a stable, traditional democracy such as France, the
United States, or Britain. The temptation, however, is to "mirror
image" from one society to another, thus dragging out the experience. In Iraq, the United States has had to fight the temptation
to say that everything must be perfect before the Iraqi nation is
completely rebuilt. Some observers fear that this attitude will preclude the United States from ever leaving. Seasoned practitioners
of nation-building as frequently express serious reservations
about this problem as any other. Nation-building is difficult because there is no easily identifiable way to know that success is
being reached.

How Much Resistance Does Any Leader Tolerate from His Population in Trying to Accomplish These Goals?

For many U.S. citizens over the age of forty, popular opposition
to one nation-building effort—Vietnam—remains a red flag about
the political, military, and cultural quagmire that can result.
People recall the street protests accompanying the continued deployment of half-a-million U.S. forces in Southeast Asia in the late
1960s and early 1970s. Presidents since Lyndon Johnson and
Richard Nixon have been leery of actions overseas for fear of the

"body bag" phenomenon: the daily casualty counts on news programs that were so important to raising public doubts about the wisdom of nation-building in Southeast Asia. President Reagan withdrew U.S. marines from Lebanon in the 1980s after attacks on U.S. forces there, as did President Clinton from Somalia a decade later. Many analysts fear that this image of U.S. forces being thwarted in their nation-building efforts will affect popular support for presidents; others say that U.S. resolve is so strong in most cases that the "body bag" issue is nonexistent. President George W. Bush's nation-building in Iraq, where daily attacks on U.S. forces have led to doubts about the conflict there, has led many to raise this question of long-term U.S. support for efforts in that country.

Summary

Nation-building is as complicated as any other public-policy question facing any state. For each decision taken, trade-offs are made as well. The perspective of what is "best" or "worst" largely lies in the eye of the beholder rather than in some empirical "best" answer to a tough question. Although history is no guarantee of the future, in general, nation-building has been successful only when done from within because the challenges facing outsiders in any culture or society are so vast. Undoubtedly, however, nation-building appears one of the predominant challenges facing the world in this decade, if not this century.

References

Ignatieff, Michael. 2003. "A Mess of Intervention." *New York Times Magazine* (7 September): 38–43, 71, 72, 85.

Rice, Condoleezza. 2000. "Promoting the National Interest." *Foreign Affairs* 79, no. 1 (January–February): 45–63.

Rock, Michael T. 1993. "'Twenty-Five Years of Economic Development' Revisited." *World Development* 21, no. 11 (November): 1787–1802.

Schneider, William. 2001. "Not Exactly a Bush Flip-Flop." *Atlantic Online*, 31 October. Available at http://www.theatlantic.com/politics/nj/schneider2001-10-31.htm (accessed 16 January 2004).

Tharoor, Shashi. 2003. "Why America Still Needs the United Nations." *Foreign Affairs* 82, no. 5 (September–October): 67–80.

Traub, James. 2000. "Inventing East Timor." *Foreign Affairs* 79, no. 4 (July–August): 74–89.

Von Hippel, Karin. 2000. "Democracy by Force: A Renewed Commitment to Nation Building." *Washington Quarterly* 23, no. 1 (winter): 95–112.

Woodward, Susan. 1997. "Bosnia." *Brookings Review* 15, no. 2 (spring): 29–31.

3

Chronology

1898   The Spanish-American War leads to Cuban independence and the Philippines coming under U.S. colonial control after four hundred years of Spanish colonization.

1900   The overwhelming majority of the international community is made up of states under colonial domination.

1918   World War I ends with the fall of the Russian, Austro-Hungarian, Ottoman, and German empires. Britain and France are on the side of victory, but both are undergoing economic, demographic, and social declines that contribute to World War II. Numerous new states are created from the fallen empires.

1931   The Japanese seize the northeast province of China, rename it Manchukuo, and begin a process that today would be termed nation-building. The Japanese maintain control until the end of the war fourteen years later.

1945   The United States leads the coalition to victory over the Axis powers and recognizes that massive reconstruction will be necessary in Japan and Germany. This reconstruction, tailored to each situation, is considered highly successful. Both states become democratic within a decade, although the nation-building lasts until about 1952. In Germany, roughly 1.6 million U.S. troops are used, versus about 300,000 in Japan.

21

1945
(cont.)
This is the beginning of the cold war, and Soviet expansionism is a concern.

Indonesia becomes independent in August from Dutch colonial control.

The political need for reconstruction throughout the rest of Europe becomes obvious.

1946
India and Pakistan are partitioned from the former British Raj into sovereign states with tremendous sectarian violence resulting.

President Truman declares that the United States will help democracies under siege, referring specifically to Greece and Turkey but with greater application around the world. The Truman Doctrine establishes that the United States would protect democracies under threat.

1947
General George C. Marshall, the secretary of state, proposes what becomes known as the Marshall Plan to reconstruct Europe.

1948
Israel and Jordan are created from the Palestine Mandate, which the British controlled for the international community. The first of the Arab-Israeli wars ensues, but Israel's victory allows it to remain sovereign. Thousands of Palestinians go into exile in refugee camps and are rarely treated well by the Arab states that contain them.

1954
The French are defeated at Dien Bien Phu after a long siege, leading to the end of French colonialism in Southeast Asia. President Eisenhower is skeptical about the United States stepping in to fill the gap against Ho Chi Minh's goal of putting all of Vietnam under Hanoi's control. The Paris Peace Accords partition Vietnam into north and south.

The United States covertly supports the overthrow of elected government of Jacobo Arbenz Guzman in

Guatemala on grounds of anticommunist goals, leading to four decades of turmoil, some of which are considered nation-building.

1956   President Eisenhower does not respond to Hungarian pleas for assistance when Soviet tanks move in to crush an autonomous movement.

1958   President Eisenhower sends U.S. marines to Lebanon to help with what would today be described as nation-building.

1960   Most of Africa becomes independent.

1965   President Johnson escalates U.S. involvement in nation-building in Vietnam, ultimately failing by 1975.

1979   Long-time dictator Anastacio Somoza Debayle, second generation leader in Nicaragua, is ousted by the *Frente Sandinista de Liberacion Nacional* headed by the Ortega brothers. The Carter administration reacts with caution.

1981   The newly inaugurated Reagan administration increasingly accuses the Sandinista government in Managua of being a Soviet proxy. It initiates actions to oust them through arming *contrarevolucionarios,* who become known as the Contras. Similar concerns about Cuban and Soviet activity in nearby El Salvador, which still has a pro-U.S. government, spur massive spending to build up democracy and defeat the *Farabundo Marti Liberacion Nacional* movement.

1982   President Reagan sends U.S. marines into Lebanon to act as peacekeepers.

1983   On 23 October, more than two hundred U.S. marines are killed in the marine barracks bombing.

President Reagan sends U.S. forces to rescue students and other citizens in Granada after the overthrow of a leader and subsequent fear that the island was coming under Soviet expansionism under the Cuban proxy.

1984   President Reagan withdraws U.S. marines from Lebanon.

1986   President Ferdinand Marcos, longtime dictator of the Philippines, is overthrown by a popular movement led by the widow of assassinated political opponent, Corazon Aquino.

Dictator Jean "Baby Doc" Duvalier is overthrown by Haitian military officers as the absolute corruption of the regime arouses public protests.

1989   Civil war begins in Liberia, nominally ending with Charles Taylor's removal in 2003.

Soviet bloc collapses in Eastern Europe and states there must consider how to develop their post-Soviet governing systems

People's Liberation Army forces are called in to quell domestic protests in order to keep the Communist Party in power in China, paralyzing the political system.

1991   Gulf War I lasts six weeks—as an air campaign, beginning 16 January, and then a ground campaign for ninety-six hours in the last week in February. Saddam Hussein signs an armistice but is not removed from office.

Slovenia achieves independence from Yugoslavia, and Croatia begins a war to achieve a similar statehood.

Elected Haitian president Jean-Bertrand Aristide, a priest leading the *Lavalas* movement advocating social justice for this chronically destitute country, is overthrown by the Haitian military.

On the last day of the calendar year, the Soviet Union disintegrates into fifteen republics, including several states in Central Asia and the Caucasus as well as the Baltic Republics. There, states all face institution-building along with nation-building.

1992   Croatia achieves independence from Yugoslavia.

Secretary of Defense Dick Cheney is asked to explain a Pentagon policy that appears to advocate that no state become a peer of the United States, including close allies.

Haitian "boat people" wash ashore in Florida, an incident that is probably tied to candidate Clinton's position that the Bush administration is mistreating these "economic refugees."

Clinton defeats President George H. W. Bush in the latter's reelection attempt.

President Bush decides to send U.S. troops to Somalia where warlord violence and a drought are causing massive starvation. At the same time, the United States does not intervene in the former Yugoslavia.

1993   A terrorist bomb explodes in the parking lot below the World Trade Center in Manhattan, killing several people but not causing major structural damage to the building.

During the summer, the mission for U.S. forces in Somalia, initially Operation CONTINUE HOPE, becomes more explicit bringing peace rather than food to Somalia, as the United Nations alters the mission. In October, U.S. forces in this mission are ambushed in Mogadishu and eighteen Rangers are killed. One is dragged through the streets as a symbol of Somalis defeating the United States. President Clinton orders U.S. forces out of Somalia, which occurs by 1994.

A U.S. warship trying to assist with stabilization efforts in Haiti is greeted by an angry crowd on the pier in Port-au-Prince, and U.S. forces withdraw.

1993
(cont.)

Operation PROVIDE HOPE III, to assist the former republics of the Soviet Union, goes into effect to provide
humanitarian aid.

The United States enforces a no-fly zone in Bosnia and
Herzegovina, called Operation DENY FLIGHT, through
1995.

During the same period, the U.S. navy conducts Sharp
Guard, an operation through 1995 in the Adriatic Sea
to enforce sanctions against the former republic of Yugoslavia.

1994

The assassination of several government leaders in
Rwanda leads to sectarian violence between Hutus
and Tutsis. Estimates are that more than a million
people died in one hundred days. U.S. citizens are
evacuated from Rwanda under Operation DISTANT
RUNNER. After the extent of the murders becomes
known, Operation QUIET RESOLVE / SUPPORT HOPE is conducted to provide assistance after the genocide.

Haiti becomes the target of U.S. concern as the United
States seeks to restore the democratically elected
regime of Jean-Bertrand Aristide with the support of
the Organization of American States, which traditionally objects to violation of sovereignty of any states in
the hemisphere. This action is known as Uphold
Democracy and Restore Democracy. Nation-building
lasts roughly through 1995 but little affects the deso-
late condition of Haiti.

Operation STEADY STATE to stem drug production and
trafficking in Peru and Colombia begins, lasting for
two years. In Colombia alone, numerous drug labora-
tories are destroyed in Operation SELVA VERDE, which
continues to the present.

Concerns about troop activity in southern Iraq cause
U.S. forces to hold exercises in Kuwait under the Operation VIGILANT WARRIOR.

Operation PROVIDE HOPE IV, to continue humanitarian assistance to the republics of the former Soviet Union, is carried out by U.S. forces.

Boat people from Cuba and Haiti are helped through a U.S. humanitarian operation called SEA SIGNAL, which lasts sporadically for more than two years.

Fearing the spread of conflict and ethnic cleansing to another former Yugoslav republic, Macedonia, the United States assists the United Nations in Operation ABLE SENTRY, which still carries on. Deterioration of conditions for ethnic minorities in enclaves of Bosnia-Herzegovina continues.

1995   Operation UNITED SHIELD is conducted to remove UN peacekeepers and humanitarian assistance workers from Somalia.

Extra forces monitor Iraqi behavior near Kuwait between 1995 and 1997 under Operation VIGILANT SENTINEL/VIGILANT WARRIOR II. Joint operations with the Kuwaiti military are carried out under Operation INSTRINIC ACTION between 1995 and 1999.

Operation ZORRO II begins and lasts through 1996, a counter-drug operation in Mexico.

After Ecuador and Peru fight over a long-standing border dispute, international peacekeepers, including U.S. forces, are deployed in Operation SAFE BORDER to demilitarize the border area for four years.

U.S. troops airlift UN peacekeepers into Croatia for duties in the former Yugoslavia between 1995 and 1996 under Operation QUICK LIFT. During the same period, NATO conducts surveillance in Albania under Operation NOMAD VIGIL. The preparation for the Dayton multinational force is Operation DETERMINED EFFORT. NATO air strikes to prevent the Serbs from continuing ethnic cleansing are conducted in Operation

1995
(cont.)

DELIBERATE FORCE. The U.S. navy carries out Operation DECISIVE ENHANCEMENT, from 1995 through 1996, to enforce sanctions against the former Yugoslavia. Between 1996 and 1998, Operations DECISIVE GUARD and DELIBERATE GUARD enforce the no-fly zone in Bosnia and Herzegovina.

The Dayton Peace Accords are signed to end the violence in Bosnia-Herzegovina. The multinational peacekeeping operation to enforce these accords is JOINT ENDEAVOR/DECISIVE ENDEAVOR through 1996, followed by Operation JOINT GUARD from 1996 to 1998, which was a continued presence.

Under Operations VIGILANT SENTINEL/VIGILANT WARRIOR II, more U.S. troops are deployed to Kuwait to monitor Iraqi troop movements, continuing through 1997. Operation INTRINSIC ACTION, between 1995 and 1999, is joint exercises of U.S. and Kuwaiti forces.

In efforts to stop drug trafficking, the United States cooperates with Mexico in Operation ZORRO II through 1996.

Operation MARATHON PACIFIC/PROMPT RETURN 95 goes into effect near Wake Island in the southwest Pacific as an effort to catch Chinese boat people fleeing to a better life.

1996

Bill Clinton defeats Senator Robert Dole in the presidential election.

Operation DECISIVE EDGE enforces a no-fly zone over Bosnia-Herzegovina, and Operation NOMAD ENDEAVOR continues to the present to provide surveillance to the peacekeeping operations there. Operation DETERMINED GUARD, still ongoing, is U.S. navy enforcement of UN sanctions against Yugoslavia.

Operation ASSURED RESPONSE evacuates U.S. forces from Liberia during the civil war there.

Operation LASER STRIKE is a broad counter-drug operation in Venezuela, Colombia, Peru, Ecuador, Bolivia, and Brazil, and continues to the present.

Operation QUICK RESPONSE evacuates U.S. citizens from the Central African Republic.

Operation DESERT STRIKE is a cruise-missile response to Iraqi troop actions in the Kurdish area of the country. Some Kurds are evacuated to Guam under Operation PACIFIC HAVEN/QUICK TRANSIT after infighting in the Kurdish community of northern Iraq.

Operation GUARDIAN ASSISTANCE is U.S. navy air-monitoring of Rwandan refugees in Zaire and Rwanda.

1997   Operation NORTHERN WATCH, lasting through 2003, is enforcement of a no-fly zone by the United States, United Kingdom, and Turkey in northern Iraq.

Operation NEW HORIZONS is humanitarian building and training in the Caribbean Basin.

West African peacekeepers are airlifted into Liberia through Operation ASSURED LIFT.

The migrants held at Guantanamo Bay, Cuba, are monitored and security is enhanced in Operation PRESENT HAVEN.

U.S. citizens and others are evacuated from Albania in Operation SILVER WAKE.

U.S. citizens are evacuated from the Democratic Republic of Congo in Operation GUARDIAN RETRIEVAL.

Operation NOBLE OBELISK evacuates U.S. nationals and others from Sierra Leone.

Operation SILENT ASSURANCE takes place to ensure security during the North Africa–Middle East Economic Conference in Qatar.

1997
(cont.)

Operations PHOENIX SCORPION I to IV, between 1997 and 1998, are air and logistical support to operations in the Persian Gulf.

1998

Plan Colombia allows the United States to educate and arm Colombian forces in counter-drug operations. This is an ongoing activity.

After a natural disaster, Operation NOBLE RESPONSE assists Kenyans.

Operation SOLAR SUNRISE is a security answer to cyber attacks on U.S. Defense Department computer networks.

During UN discussions with Saddam Hussein's government over weapons of mass destruction, Operation DESERT THUNDER is designed to intimidate Iraq.

NATO conducts air operations over Bosnia-Herzegovina in support of security forces, continuing to the present, in Operation DELIBERATE FORGE.

Operation SHEPARD VENTURE is a deployment to assist in evacuating U.S. personnel from Guinea-Bissau.

The temporary embassy Marine detachment to Kenya after the Nairobi bombing is Operation RESOLUTE RESPONSE.

Operation INFINITE REACH targets Afghan and Sudanese terrorist bases after the Kenya and Tanzania embassy bombings.

Operation FUERTE APOYO assists forces from Honduras, Guatemala, El Salvador, and Nicaragua in the relief efforts after Hurricane Mitch.

Preparation for possible NATO activity in Kosovo is conducted through air operations called DETERMINED FORCE and COBALT FLASH, running through early 1999.

Air surveillance over Kosovo is conducted through Operation EAGLE EYE.

Operation PROVIDE HOPE V continues humanitarian assistance to the former Soviet republics.

Operation SHINING PRESENCE provides missiles and troops to aid Israel.

Operation DESERT FOX is cruise missile attacks on Iraq.

1999 NATO launches a coalition attack to save Kosovo from ethnic cleansing. ALLIED FORCE and NOBLE ANVIL are two of these operations.

The humanitarian operations to relocate Kosovar families and provide assistance are named SUSTAIN HOPE/ PROVIDE REFUGE/OPEN ARMS. Similarly, Operations ALLIED HARBOUR and SHINING HOPE are to assist in refugee events.

Operation AVID RESPONSE is a humanitarian relief effort after a massive earthquake in western Turkey.

Operation STABILIZE is a multinational effort to restore law and order after the independence referendum in East Timor.

An ongoing presence in Kuwait and education of the military is provided in Operation DESERT SPRING.

Operation FUNDAMENTAL RESPONSE assists Venezuelans affected by deadly flooding.

2000 Texas governor George W. Bush wins the closest presidential election in U.S. history over Vice President Al Gore.

Operations SILENT PROMISE and ATLAS RESPONSE provide humanitarian aid after flooding in Mozambique and South Africa.

2000 *(cont.)*	Operation DETERMINED RESPONSE is reprisals after the attack on the USS *Cole*.
2001	Operation NOBLE EAGLE, partial mobilization of reserves, and Operation BORDER SUPPORT, National Guard mobilization to secure borders, are both continuing operations.

Washington seeks to avenge Osama Bin Laden's attacks on the United States through overthrowing the Taliban government in Afghanistan in Operation ENDURING FREEDOM.

Operation FOCUS RELIEF trains West African peacekeepers for their work in Sierra Leone.

NATO naval operations in solidarity with the United States after the September 11 bombings is termed Operation ACTIVE ENDEAVOUR.

Hamid Karzai is installed as interim president of Afghanistan after a meeting of the Loya Jirga in December.

2002 President George W. Bush begins advocating an overthrow of the regime of Saddam Hussein, dictator in Iraq for more than twenty years.

The United States begins training and equipping the forces of Georgia for security and counterterrorism.

President George W. Bush gives the commencement speech at West Point, advocating preemption and prevention doctrine for the first time in U.S. history, causing alarm overseas and raising questions about U.S. intentions around the world.

The United Nations refuses to authorize the use of force by the U.S.-led coalition in Iraq to overthrow Saddam Hussein.

2003   A U.S.-led coalition launches an offensive against Iraq in March, Operation IRAQI FREEDOM, leading to the regime's ouster three weeks later. Massive nation-building efforts begin after public protests and major suspicions that the United States was interested in seizing Iraqi petroleum assets or colonizing the region as part of global domination.

The United States begins marine training exercises with Philippine forces.

In July, the United States grants Afghanistan more than a billion dollars in reconstruction assistance. This is intended to allow reconstruction in Afghanistan to proceed at a much more rapid pace.

In August, the military operations in Afghanistan transfer from U.S. military to NATO control.

In September, President Bush goes before the U.S. public to request $87 billion in additional resources for Iraqi and Afghan actions, most of which are military operations, but with some for reconstruction. The president also asks the United Nations for additional support, but the nations that had opposed U.S. actions in Iraq in March are still reluctant to support the president if he refuses to drop U.S. demands that it maintain control over the overall operations through the Coalition Provisional Authority under Paul Bremer. In December, Saddam Hussein becomes a prisoner of U.S. forces after he is discovered near his hometown. Contrary to coalition hopes, the car bombing attacks continue.

2004   In January, protests against indirect election of an Iraqi government for post-coalition authority escalate. The U.S. government finds itself in the odd position of defending a less pure democratic solution (caucus-chosen officials not selected by direct election) instead of the Shi'ite protestors' preferred solutions. Car bombings continue as well.

2004
(cont.)
Haitian President Jean-Bertrand Aristide is forced into exile in the Central African Republic by a popular uprising. This shows that even an elected civilian government cannot be guaranteed that it can meet the nation-building expectations of the Haitian people.

In early May, international furor broke out over photographs of vile, beastly treatment of Iraqi detainees in Iraq, primarily by U.S. and British troops. International humanitarian organizations acknowledged that they had raised alarms about prison treatment as early as August 2003, but this did not reach public attention. The question of how well prepared and trained the military police are arose as did inquiries of whether the military intelligence function had corrupted the police function in attempts to gather intelligence from detainees. As the condemnation spread across the world, the implications of the impact of this behavior on attempts to spread democracy in the Arab world became troublingly clear. While the majority of the concern related to U.S. soldiers, several of whom face courts-marshal for their activities, British soldiers were also accused of shooting Iraqis without provocation.

Note:
The chronology in this volume is exclusively the author's work but was researched heavily with a listing in the Kaplan reference listed below.

Further Reading

Dobbins, James, and Seth G. Jones. 2003. "America's Record on Nation Building: Are We Getting Better?" *New York Times* 13 June, A31.

Kaplan, Robert D. 2003. "Supremacy by Stealth." *Atlantic Monthly* July/August, 75, 77, 79, 81.

4

Biographical Sketches

Abizaid, John Philip (1951–)

The commander of U.S. Central Command in the post-conflict period in Iraq is this Arab American with significant operational, educational, and staff experience. General Abizaid is a graduate of the U.S. Military Academy at West Point and was also educated at the University of Jordan, the Hoover Institution at Stanford University, and Harvard. General Abizaid is an infantry officer who has commanded U.S. forces, largely in Europe, including Bosnia-Herzegovina and Kosovo. He was the sixty-sixth commandant of the Military Academy at West Point. General Abizaid also served with UN peacekeepers in Lebanon. Immediately before assuming the responsibilities of nation-building in Iraq, among other things, General Abizaid was the Director of Strategic Plans for the Joint Staff. Fluent in Arabic, General Abizaid brings a different flavor to this position than some of his predecessors.

Aideed, Mohammed (1934–1996)

This Somalian warlord became the target of U.S. troops seeking to bring peace and stability, the essence of nation-building, to Somalia in 1992–1993 after the population had suffered through tremendous deprivation, drought, and starvation. The longtime dictator of Somalia, Mohammed Siad Barre, was ousted in late 1991, plunging the country into chaos. After a year of turmoil, the United States decided to provide humanitarian food assistance

35

for the people, especially around Mogadishu. Aideed was probably the best known of the warlords, orchestrating gang activities against opposition as well as forces trying to bring stability and end lawlessness. For the initial months of the U.S. intervention, the United States did not come into direct conflict with Aideed. The difficulties began when the goal of the mission changed from humanitarian assistance, which the United States saw as a neutral act, to nation-building, which is a supremely political activity, and more UN forces were brought in. In October 1993, as UN forces sought to capture Aideed to stop his exploits, U.S. troops were caught in an ambush in downtown Mogadishu and several elite Rangers were killed. Soon after the ambush, President Clinton removed U.S. troops from Somalia, the United Nations proved incapable of acting without U.S. support, and Somalia was left in chaos. Aideed was subsequently killed in 1996, and his son, Hussein Mohammed, took his place as a warlord.

Albright, Madeleine Korbel (1937–)

Albright, secretary of state during the second Clinton administration, was the first woman to hold this position. Dr. Albright was a strong supporter of the concept that the United States had a responsibility as well as a right to help other states establish democratic, popularly elected governments along the lines of the United States. Extremely controversial, Albright had come to the United States from her native Czechoslovakia as a child, fleeing anti-Semitism. After teaching at Georgetown University, Albright served on Maine democratic senator Edmund Muskie's staff, on the National Security Council, and eventually as an adviser to candidate Bill Clinton. Upon his election, Albright became U.S. ambassador to the United Nations, where she argued forcefully for using the military in nation-building functions around the world, but particularly in southeastern Europe during the bloody civil wars of the 1990s. Albright came into conflict with military officers in the United States by having allegedly asked the chair of the Joint Chiefs of Staff General Colin Powell what good it was to have such a splendid military if the United States could not use it. During the second Clinton term, Albright replaced Secretary of State Warren Christopher. During her tenure at the State Department, the United States faced many important decisions about how far to push for the development of sovereign states from disintegrating former countries, such as Kosovo from the former republic of Yugoslavia. Albright's vision was that military and general U.S. intervention was vital to maintaining U.S. credibility as a defender of democracy.

Al-Hakim, Abdel-Aziz (N.D.)

This Shi'ite cleric was second to his brother Mohammed Bakr al-Hakim in the Supreme Council for the Islamic Revolution in Iraq prior to the latter's assassination in a Najaf bombing in late August 2003. Abdel-Aziz al-Hakim is also a member of Iraqi Governing Council. As a prominent cleric in a family that has sought to install an Islamic republic in Iraq, Al-Hakim has argued that the assassination manifested the power of remnants of Saddam Hussein's secular Ba'athist regime seeking to keep the Shi'ite majority under control in Iraq. He has taken a relatively pro-Iraqi Governing Council position throughout its governing period that has surprised many who found this incongruous with a desire to return to a Shari'a form of rule.

Ali Husaini Sistani, Grand Ayatollah (1930–)

This prominent Iranian-born Shi'ite cleric has made clear his intention to affect the nation-building efforts for post-Saddam Iraq, although he initially did not disagree with Saddam's overthrow or the initial U.S.-led occupation. With Shi'ites constituting 60 percent of Iraq's population, Sistani's position as spiritual leader for the fifteen million adherents is significant. Sistani did not object to the immediate aftermath of the invasion when the occupation began and the Coalition Provisional Authority was installed. The authority's reorganization of the governmental and constitutional processes cannot continue Saddam Hussein's discrimination based on religion in Sistani's view. A reclusive individual, he did not serve on the provisional Iraqi Governing Council, but as a revered religious figure his concerns cannot be ignored by the coalition. In late 2003, Sistani rejected the coalition's anticipated caucus-based government, scheduled for implementation in June 2004, calling instead for direct elections, which the Coalition said was too difficult in such a short time. At the same time, his goal of returning Iraq to a government having its base in *Shari'a*, Islamic law, is inconsistent with "one individual, one vote" and will continue the debate about the form of the new constitution. This has also allowed the UN to return to possible deployment in Iraq for the elections. In early February 2004, Sistani survived an assassination attempt, indicating how fractured politics and society in post-Saddam Iraq remain.

Annan, Kofi (1938–)

This diplomat, a native of Ghana, became the seventh Secretary General of the United Nations in 1997, continuing through a second term beginning in 2002. Mr. Annan is an economist by training who began his long UN career in 1962 as a budget officer in the World Health Organization. Annan has held several offices within the United Nations, working in refugee issues for much of the 1990s. He was the successor to Egyptian-born Secretary General Boutros Boutros-Ghali, who was accused of not doing enough for fiscal reform issues in his tenure in the early to mid-1990s. Mr. Annan took over at a time when the United States was in arrears in its dues to the organization. Congress made it clear it would not pay those dues without reform. During much of this period, Mr. Annan confronted serious international debate about intervention in the affairs of states that deemed themselves sovereign and not subject to UN intervention. In particular, Annan sought to bring the international community to an understanding of its ability to stop suffering and promote nation-building, but his mission was never an easy one. He confronted serious U.S. challenges on the issue of paying its dues and the need for the member states to adhere to the will of the United Nations. Annan has been secretary general during a period of massive and rapid upheaval in the international system. He identified and sought to address challenges in which the United Nations would be better equipped to cross boundaries than were soldiers. These included AIDS, SARS (severe acute respiratory syndrome), and the collapse of several dictators, including Saddam Hussein in Iraq and Slobodan Milosevic in Yugoslavia. The secretary general appeared to diverge dramatically from the Bush administration in the period leading up to the 2003 intervention to oust Saddam Hussein. In the aftermath of the August 2003 bombing of the UN headquarters in Baghdad when Annan's personal envoy to Iraq, Sergio Veiera de Mello, was killed, the secretary general made it clear that greater UN participation in nation-building efforts in Iraq would require greater participation by all member states, not merely the United States and Britain. The secretary general, as he was watching the development of greater tensions in Iraq, simultaneously saw the deterioration of conditions in Liberia and possibly again in Afghanistan. Kofi Annan, and the United Nations, received the Nobel Peace Prize in 2001.

Aristide, Jean-Bertrand (1953–)

This former Roman Catholic priest was ousted as the first elected president of Haiti in 1991, leading to the Organization of American States' altering its traditional opposition to violation of national sovereignty in favor of restoring a democratically elected government. Aristide was elected president based on his "common man" touch and commitment to social justice, so completely lacking in previous regimes in Haiti. The Haitian military did not support these sorts of revisions of the political system in the country and sought to silence him and his Levalas Party. Aristide was returned to office after the United States led an international coalition to oust the military in October 1994. He left the priesthood, married, and embarked on governing the country in what increasingly appeared to be a repressive manner. Many observers feel that nation-building in Haiti has consistently proven a tremendous failure as institutionalization of law and order has proven difficult.

In a surprise uprising that began in early February 2004 in the second largest city of Haiti, Aristide was ousted within a month of the original rumblings against him. He and his family went into exile in the Central African Republic but not without considerable controversy. In the days immediately following his ouster, Aristide charged that the United States had forced him to take this action. The United States responded that it only provided the physical ability for him to flee, and that the president made his own decision to leave office. In any case, Aristide's ouster is only the latest chapter in Haiti's tortured nation-building experience.

Barzani, Massoud (1946–)

This Sunni Kurd, representing two minorities in majority Shi'ite Arab Iraq, has been leader of the Kurdistan Democratic Party for a quarter of a century since inheriting it upon his father Mustafa's death. Because his father was important in the struggle for Kurdish independence, his childhood was spent moving between his birth country of Iran and the Soviet Union where the family fled after the collapse of the Kurdish Republic of Iran. In 1958, he went to Iraq. In the 1960s, Barzani was a *peshmerga*, an insurgent fighter, as the Kurds battled numerous governments in Baghdad. Barzani was in exile in the United States with his father upon the latter's death in 1979. Because he has shared power in the autonomous Kurdish area of northern Iraq with Jalal Talabani since the first Gulf War in 1991, Barzani is a prominent member of the Iraqi Governing Council. He is known as a reticent individual who speaks multiple languages but one continuing to push for the requirements of the Kurdish minority.

Bin Laden, Osama (1957–)

One of several sons of a wealthy Saudi businessman who specialized in international construction projects, Bin Laden is heir to a multimillion-dollar personal fortune. He first came to public attention in August 1998 when large bombs exploded on the same day in Dar-es-Salaam, Tanzania, and Nairobi, Kenya, at the U.S. embassies. The international intelligence and law enforcement communities were aware of Bin Laden, however, as early as the 1980s when he used a portion of his personal fortune to fund anti-Soviet *mujahadeen* forces in Afghanistan. Bin Laden wrote several diatribes about the "godless communist defilement" of Islamic Afghanistan and proved an able fighter, in conjunction with U.S. forces and CIA funding, against the Soviets. In the late 1980s and early 1990s, as Afghanistan became increasingly fragmented into its traditional warlord factions, Bin Laden's mission shifted from forcing the Soviets from Afghanistan to pushing the United States out as well, because of perceived similar defilements. Through the 1990s, Bin Laden became more strident in his hatred for the United States as he sought to impose Saudi Wahabbism throughout the Islamic world. Bin Laden, with his insistence on the preservation of Islam against the corruption by Western influence over the leadership of governments in the region as his mission, also appealed to disillusioned, often increasingly frustrated Islamic youth who saw their governments as partners with the United States in this evil. His hatred appeared to increase after the United States did not entirely leave Afghanistan to its own future when the Soviets withdrew in the late 1980s and later when King Fahd allowed U.S. ground forces—male and female—to prepare for Operation DESERT STORM, meaning that non-Muslims were violating sacred lands in the home of Islam. The basis to the House of Saud, the title of which is technically "the Conservators of the Two Holy Sites," conveys not a political but a religious responsibility. The Saudi government's failure to protect Islam from the Western infidels, along with the excessive behavior of royal family members, which offended so many in the kingdom as the general standard of living declined, drove Bin Laden to step up his campaign against U.S. targets. He was exiled from Saudi Arabia in the 1990s but took up residence in Afghanistan, with its pro-Islamic Taliban government. The United States began aggressively, but unsuccessfully, to target Bin Laden after the 1998 bombings, citing the terrorist group Al Qaeda, which Bin Laden had managed to network around the world. By 2000, Bin Laden became a frequently discussed concern of U.S. government counterterrorist officials. Almost immediately after the 11 September 2001 terrorist attacks in the United States, officials suspected Bin Laden in the attack. Within a month, President George W. Bush declared Bin Laden the world's most wanted man and launched a campaign to overthrow the Taliban government, which gave Al Qaeda and Bin Laden sanctuary in Afghanistan. The campaign ousted the Taliban, but Bin Laden managed to evade capture. In the months after September 2001, videotapes appeared via the Arab media outlet, Al Jazirah, which claimed to be messages from Bin Laden; but proof of his survival remains elusive. Two terrorist bombings in Indonesia, in October 2002 and August 2003, were linked to Al Qaeda, and many analysts believed these were all orchestrated by Bin Laden. A 1996 bombing in eastern Saudi Arabia and a May 2003 blast in Riyadh were all believed his work as well. He has been a major force in undermining nation-building efforts.

Blair, Anthony (1953–)

The charismatic son of a barrister and a lecturer, Tony Blair won control of the British Labour Party in 1994 just as the party contemplated its fifteenth year in opposition. Upon taking control, he brought the party's positions on crime, the economy, and other basic British problems into a much more centrist position, allowing him to gain election in 1997. Upon reelection in 2001, Blair worked to create the same close relationship with political opposite George W. Bush that he had had with Bush's predecessor, Bill Clinton. Blair's public discussion of his religion created a significant bond with President Bush, facilitating an even closer relationship after the September 11 attacks. Mr. Blair proved a determined, tireless ally of the Bush administration in the global war on terrorism, first sending assistance to the campaign in Afghanistan to oust the Taliban government and then to capture Osama Bin Laden. More importantly, Mr. Blair withstood tremendous popular opposition at home and from his European allies when he backed President Bush's intentions to use force to make Saddam Hussein's government relinquish its suspected weapons-of-mass-destruction program. Although Britain's tangible contributions to the coalition forces that actually moved into Iraq were relatively small, Blair's public rhetoric and willingness to stand in opposition to such strong pressure earned him much goodwill in the United States. Britain's leader also had some effect in moderating President Bush's actions, such as delaying the final assault in order to help Blair win public support at home. Blair's support of the decision also ensured Britain some role in the nation-building phase of the Afghan and Iraqi cases, but Britain will never return to the powerful position it had a century earlier as the main global colonial power. Subsequent press exposure, and the suicide of an arms specialist who was highly ranked in Blair's government, subjected Blair's support for Bush's war decision, as well as the veracity of the government's intelligence analysts, to even greater public scrutiny and led to questions as to whether the prime minister would survive this public doubt.

Boutros-Ghali, Boutros (1922–)

Boutros Boutros-Ghali, the Egyptian secretary general of the United Nations between 1992 and 1996, aggressively expanded nation-building and peacekeeping operations during his time at the United Nations. A former foreign minister, diplomat, and international lawyer, Boutros-Ghali had a strong record of advocating that international law and institutions be used for improvements in the equities of power around the world as well as for improving the life of people within states. Much of the international community staunchly defended sovereignty even if it meant that some brutalities occurred within states, but Boutros-Ghali's stance was that the United Nations, and therefore the global community, had a responsibility to protect the undefended within states. During his tenure as secretary general, the international community experienced genocide in Rwanda and portions of the former Yugoslavia, severe economic hardship and repression in Haiti, complete social, economic, and political collapse in Somalia, repression against attempted secession in Chechnya, and increased turmoil and political violence in Indonesia. Boutros-Ghali attempted to get the international community to respond to these incidents with peacekeepers. He also worked to increase the global commitment to sustainable development, introducing the Agenda for Peace, a vision of the international community working to prevent, not respond, to problems. Boutros-Ghali's tenure coincided with the first term of President Bill Clinton, and he often clashed with U.S. officials. Boutros-Ghali's advocacy of preventive actions in the international system was especially opposed by conservatives in the United States after they won control over the U.S. Congress in 1994, weakening President Clinton. Clashes also continued when the first secretary of state, Warren Christopher, was replaced by Madeleine Albright. The United States prevented Boutros-Ghali's reappointment for a second term in 1996.

Brahimi, Lakhdar (1934–)

This Algerian diplomat has become crucial to the nation-building efforts in Afghanistan where he became the UN mission head in 2001. Prior to this assignment, he served in his country as a representative to the Arab League as well as foreign minister. Brahimi also was Arab League Special Envoy to the turmoil-ridden nation of Lebanon in the 1980s. When he became involved in UN activities, Brahimi took positions as representative to troubled spots such as Angola and Zaire. With Sergio Veiera de Mello's August 2003 assassination in Baghdad, Brahimi became the UN's most visible on-the-ground spokesman for nation-building, although he resisted such characterization. In 2004, UN Secretary General Kofi Annan named Brahimi chief adviser on Iraqi transition to self-governance. As the United States approached the June 2004 deadline to turn governance over to the Iraqis, Brahimi became more important as a political power broker.

Bremer, Lewis Paul, III "Jerry" (1941–)

This retired career diplomat, with strong ties to a number of Bush administration figures, took over the nation-building

functions in Baghdad about a month after retired General Jay
Garner arrived in the Iraqi capital to head the same efforts. Bremer's position as head of the Coalition Provisional Authority
made him the top civilian authority in Iraq, even after an Iraqi
Interim Council was appointed in mid-2003. Bremer's appointment indicated not only that the State Department continued
having influence in post-conflict Iraq but also that Garner's
progress in getting the infrastructure back to a normal operating
level was unacceptable to Washington. Bremer's experience was
largely in Europe, having been ambassador to the Netherlands
and also serving in the Foreign Service in Malawi, Norway, and
Afghanistan; but he also has had a central role in the antiterror-
ism efforts in earlier administrations. Bremer also spent eleven
years with Kissinger and Associates, and served as co-chair, with
former Reagan administration attorney general Edward Meese,
of the Heritage Foundation Homeland Security Task Force. After
leaving government service, Bremer became the chairman and
chief executive officer for Marsh Crisis Consulting Company,
which works with private entities addressing terrorism, law-
suits, and natural disasters, clearly an outgrowth of his position
as ambassador at-large for counterterrorism in the mid-1980s. He
also chaired the National Commission on Terrorism. Prior to his
appointment in Iraq, Ambassador Bremer also served on President Bush's Homeland Security Advisory Council.

Bush, George Herbert Walker (1924–)

George H. W. Bush was president during the nation-building opportunities at the end of the cold war and the dismantling of the
Berlin Wall during the first year of his administration. With that
turn of events, the United States became the only superpower in
the world, and its economic and political system became the
model that had no peer. In August 2000, Saddam Hussein invaded neighboring Kuwait, attempting to incorporate it into his
vast petroleum reserves and to increase his bargaining power in
the international petroleum market. Bush placed hundreds of
thousands of troops in Saudi Arabia in the hope of forcing Hussein to quit Kuwait but finally launched an invasion in February
2001, after a six-week bombing campaign. The ninety-six-hour
ground campaign ended with Saddam not being overthrown, setting the stage for a decade of sanctions and subtle attempts to
overthrow Saddam—finally accomplished by a coalition organ-

ized by Bush's son, George W. Bush, in 2003. The elder Bush's administration took an ambivalent position on nation-building. It sought to alter the government in Iraq but was less than willing to stop the disintegration of Yugoslavia into Slovenia, Croatia, Serbia, and other parts. It watched the Soviet Union dissolve into fifteen republics but did little to provide assistance in nation-building efforts there. President Bush was in power as the Chinese Communist Party crushed demonstrators and democracy advocates in Tiananmen Square in June 1989 but then sought to return relations to the more cordial condition that had preceded the crackdown.

Bush, George Walker (1946–)

Texas governor George W. Bush came to office with virtually no foreign policy experience except the Texas relationship with Mexico. In the 2000 presidential campaign, the governor made clear his intense discomfort with nation-building as carried out by the Clinton administration. His chief foreign policy adviser, Condoleezza Rice, who went on to become his national security advisor, articulated in a famous article that the Bush administration would only take on vital U.S. interests and would not become bogged down in interminable efforts that eroded U.S. power and influence around the world. Eight months into his term, the terrorist attacks on the World Trade Center and Pentagon forced him to go beyond the rhetoric of the 2000 campaign. President Bush immediately launched a war on terrorism, followed within a month by a war on the Taliban government in Afghanistan with its close ties to avowed terrorist Osama Bin Laden. In ousting the Taliban, the administration gradually realized it would have to do significant nation-building to prevent the Taliban from returning. Critics charged, beginning in the summer of 2002 as the administration increasingly turned its attention to making the case for the ouster of Saddam Hussein in Iraq, that the job in Afghanistan still required close attention. Between the summer of 2002 and March 2003, President Bush repeatedly made the case that Saddam Hussein posed an international threat because of a series of massive weapons-of-mass-destruction programs. In mid-March 2003, with British assistance, the United States launched a campaign to remove Saddam Hussein from power. The international community still had serious reservations about the credibility of the evidence the president and administration cited but did not have the power to prevent U.S. actions. On 1 May 2003, President Bush declared that major hostilities were concluded, and the nation-building phase of Iraq took center stage. As the summer went on, the U.S.-led coalition proved slow at rebuilding the physical infrastructure of the country at the same time that attacks on U.S. forces increased. President Bush was also seriously questioned, as was Prime Minister Tony Blair in Britain, about the validity of intelligence estimates of the weapons programs that had been used as justification for the assault. Both Blair and Bush declared that they had not politicized intelligence but could not explain why the physical evidence of the alleged programs had not been found. President Bush was also forced to explain why the coalition forces to "liberate" Iraq were meeting such stiff resistance. The mid-August 2003 bombing of the UN headquarters, which killed the top UN envoy to Iraq, only added to the sense that coalition forces were under attack. The U.S. response was that these attacks were from sporadic Saddam-loyalists voicing their dying wish that the yet-to-be captured former leader return to power. In December 2003, U.S. troops discovered him hiding in a bunker and took him captive. He will face legal authorities but the precise format for his trial is under debate. But, some analysts rejected that argument on the grounds that this was simply Iraqis reacting to foreign governance. As 2004 wore on, President Bush remained convinced he had done the correct thing and described Iraq increasingly as a democracy, a nation-building challenge. At the same time this occurred, President Bush was pressured to send U.S. nation-builders into the west African country of Liberia to end a civil war of more than two decades' duration. After much resistance, President Bush sent in a small number of forces, pledging to remove them by later in 2003. Nation-building also takes place in this administration in Colombia, Georgia, and the Balkans, in spite of initial concerns.

Carter, James Earl, Jr. "Jimmy" (1925–)

Jimmy Carter has perhaps been as involved in nation-building in the years since he left the White House as he was during his one term in office between 1977 and 1981. Carter, a Democratic governor of Georgia, defeated President Gerald Ford in the first presidential election after the Watergate scandal rocked the United States. Taking perhaps the most avowedly religious background into office upon his inauguration, Carter altered the role of human rights in U.S. national security priorities. Carter pressured other states, such as the many authoritarian governments he saw in Latin America, to honor human rights for their own citizens. In doing so, he was accused by the leaders of those governments of interfering in domestic affairs instead of pushing basic human values. In the middle of his term, the U.S. economy stagnated, and the final year of his administration had the dual foreign-policy blows of forty-four U.S. citizens being held by Iranian "students" who seized the U.S. embassy in Tehran and the Soviet Union invading Afghanistan. Carter was defeated by California governor Ronald Reagan in 1980. Carter used his retirement to work at the Carter Center of Emory University, where he became a frequent international observer for free and fair elections, promoted better health care in destitute societies of the Third World, and pushed the United States to take responsible positions in international relations. Additionally, former president Carter conducted negotiations, sometimes on behalf of his successors in the White House, at other times to their discomfort, with particularly odious regimes such as those in Pyongyang, Haiti, and Cuba. Jimmy Carter received the 2002 Nobel Peace Prize.

Chalabi, Ahmad (1945–)

Thought to be a favorite of the Pentagon leadership in the early 2000s, Chalabi is from a wealthy Shi'ite family with ties to the Iraqi Hashemite dynasty. Both his father and grandfather held government positions but the family fled in the aftermath of the 1958 army coup against King Faisal II. Reared in Jordan, Lebanon, and Britain, Chalabi put his excellence in mathematics to use, gaining an undergraduate degree from the Massachusetts Institute of Technology and a doctorate from the University of Chicago. He spent several years teaching, then went into banking in Jordan until he had to flee from a somewhat unclear threat. By the early 1990s, Chalabi was in London where he created the Iraqi National Congress to work as a body to coordinate exile attempts to oust Saddam. As the decade continued, Chalabi increasingly lobbied in Washington for support to end Saddam's regime, arguing that popular support for such an enterprise would be strong and overwhelming within repressed Iraq. Congress appropriated $97 million under the Iraq Liberation Act for a campaign to overthrow the dictator, but little was accomplished until the war. Chalabi is a member of the Iraqi Governing Council but appears to have little support within Iraq because he was gone for four decades and is little known there. As nation-building efforts continued, he became increasingly a lightning rod for strong feelings.

Cheney, Richard Blaine (1941–)

A former congressman from Wyoming, Cheney served as secretary of defense under George H. W. Bush's administration and became George W. Bush's vice president in 2001. Cheney was a political science graduate student at the University of Wisconsin when he received an American Political Science Association fellowship in 1969 after attracting the attention of former congressman Donald Rumsfeld at the Office of Economic Opportunity. Cheney became Ford's White House chief of staff in 1975, the youngest individual to hold that position. When Ford left office in 1977, Cheney returned to Wyoming and was elected to Congress, where he served until 1989 when he became President George H. W. Bush's second nominee for secretary of defense. Cheney had earned a reputation in the House of Representatives as an expert on defense issues and also was seen by Republicans as reliable for his service on the Iran-Contra hearings investigating the Reagan policies in Iran and Central America in the summer of 1987. Secretary of Defense Cheney was in the Pentagon during a particularly eventful period—the Berlin Wall fell in November 1989, U.S. forces removed Panamanian dictator Manuel Noriega in early 1990, the Soviet Union itself dissolved on the last day of 1991, and Saddam Hussein invaded Kuwait in August 1990. Cheney proved an invaluable envoy for President George H. W. Bush when he convinced the Saudi royal family to allow the United States to station troops in the kingdom to oust Saddam from Kuwait. Upon Bush's defeat in 1992, Cheney returned to the private sector, where he contemplated a run for the presidency, but decided against it. Between 1995 and 2000, Cheney was chief executive officer for Halliburton Corporation, a major construction firm with global presence. Asked by Governor George W. Bush to help with the vetting process for vice presidential nominees, Cheney surfaced as Bush's vice presidential partner even after Cheney had suffered several heart attacks. He played an important role in waging the war on terrorism in the international community, lobbying for the overthrow of Saddam Hussein and making the argument that the weapons of mass destruction were an imminent threat to the United States. Subsequent to the hostilities in Iraq, critics charged that Vice President Cheney, along with President Bush, had overestimated both the positive reception the United States would receive upon arriving in Iraq and the weapons programs that Saddam had under way. Additionally, some criticized that Halliburton and other companies with ties to the administration would benefit from the post-conflict reconstruction efforts. Cheney brushed off these charges and kept a low profile but remained a crucial adviser, if not the most powerful vice president ever.

Clark, Wesley Kanne (1944–)

Former NATO Supreme Allied Commander General Wesley K. Clark retired from the army in 2000, having engaged in nationbuilding in the Balkans. General Clark grew up in Arkansas, graduated from the U.S. Military Academy in 1966, and then won a Rhodes Scholarship to study at Oxford. Clark served in Vietnam in the late 1960s, had a White House Fellowship to the Office of Management and Budget, taught social science at West Point, and studied at the National War College. In the mid-1990s, Clark took the position of J-5, Strategic Plans and Policy, for the Joint Staff, where he was serving during the Bosnia negotiations in Dayton. He earned a fourth star when he assumed the command of Southern Command for a year before taking his fourth star to the NATO job, where he was simultaneously U.S. Supreme Commander in Europe. In his three-year tenure in Brussels, General Clark was in a tough position in trying to engage in the nationbuilding efforts the Clinton administration supported in the former Yugoslavia but coming up against massive opposition from the army itself, other elements of the Pentagon, European allies, and the Serbs. During the campaign to protect Kosovo from Serbian ethnic cleansing, Clark found himself increasingly isolated. He was not reappointed for a second term by the Clinton administration and left his position in considerable distress, as shown by his book, *Waging Modern War.* Clark declared his candidacy for the presidency, running as a Democrat through the first dozen primaries, and later withdrew from the race. During the campaign against Saddam Hussein in March and April 2003, Clark was a visible analyst on Cable News Network, frequently questioning the Bush administration's strategy.

Clinton, William Jefferson (1946–)

President Clinton intimately involved the United States in nation-building activities in a number of places around the world. A former governor of Arkansas who arrived at the White House with extremely limited foreign policy experience, Clinton is considered by many as an interventionist president, considering the range of places into which U.S. forces were sent to address injustices against elements of the population. Clinton sent troops to Haiti in 1994, waged a brief campaign against Serbian aggressions to allow for the development of a state in Kosovo, and—perhaps most clearly—revised the role for U.S. troops in Somalia from that of his predecessor, George H. W. Bush. In the Somalia case, President Clinton's efforts led to a painful withdrawal for U.S. forces after eighteen U.S. military personnel were killed in a botched effort to find a Somali warlord, Mohammed Farrah Aideed. During his presidency, the United States greatly expanded its nation-building efforts through a series of initiations in many areas of the U.S. government.

Crocker, Ryan (1949–)

One of the most seasoned U.S. diplomats in the Middle East, Crocker played a central role in nation-building for Iraq in the immediate aftermath of Saddam's ouster by setting up the Iraqi Governing Council. Crocker has served as ambassador to Lebanon, Kuwait, and Syria while having prominent positions representing the U.S. government in Iran, Qatar, Iraq, and Egypt. A fluent Arabic speaker, Crocker also speaks Persian, having begun his diplomatic career in Iran in 1972. Extremely knowledgeable about the Middle East, Crocker agreed to be the interim envoy to post-Taliban Afghanistan as Hamid Karzai worked to put together a government for this fractured society. Crocker's creative solution to the ethnic and religious fractures that Saddam's decades in power created for Iraq gave the country breathing space to come to grips with what type of long-term governance it desires, a question still under discussion after the ambassador departed Baghdad for the National War College in 2003.

Dobbins, James (1942–)

Ambassador James Dobbins is one of the most experienced U.S. diplomats in nation-building, having served in Somalia, Haiti, and the Balkans in the 1990s, Afghanistan after the 2001 campaign to remove the Taliban, and in various other foreign service positions. In his work for nation-building, Dobbins managed reconstruction efforts worth more than one billion dollars. Upon retiring from the Foreign Service after seeing Hamid Karzai assume the leadership in Kabul, Dobbins coauthored a provocative book, *America's Role in Nation-Building: From Germany to Iraq*, from his position as director of the International Security and Defense Policy Center at the RAND Corporation. He also writes and speaks regularly on the perils this presents.

Eisenhower, Dwight David (1890–1969)

The retired Supreme Allied Commander–Europe in World War II, President Dwight D. Eisenhower handled some of the initial nation-building efforts that the United States conducted in Germany in the aftermath of World War II. A graduate of West Point, Eisenhower rapidly rose through the ranks during the initial months of World War II before General George C. Marshall chose him to lead the Normandy invasion in June 1944. Eisenhower proved an adept manager of not only the invasion but also the personalities in the European theater. After his successful lead of Allied forces that landed in Normandy and defeated the Third Reich in 1945, Eisenhower retained his position as supreme allied commander through 1946, organizing the initial moves to rebuild a devastated Europe. After his election to the presidency in 1952, Eisenhower oversaw some of the initial U.S. involvement in Vietnam after the French were ousted with the defeat at Dien Bien Phu in 1954 and also U.S. actions in other Third World areas as the cold war heated up. Eisenhower coined the term "domino theory" in a 1954 speech that raised the stakes for U.S. involvement in the Third World by arguing that it was easier to support nation-building against communism earlier rather than later. He warned that a military-industrial complex was developing in the United States, still a timely and growing concern more than forty years later.

Franks, Tommy (1945–)

The general in command of U.S. Central Command, Franks was the architect of the war that ousted Saddam Hussein in March and April of 2003, opening the door to nation-building efforts that are likely to last for a generation in Iraq. Franks is an artillery officer who rose through the ranks to orchestrate the campaign, known by the term "shock and awe" because of the magnitude of its power. In the initial days of the campaign, U.S. casualties and losses were higher than anticipated from the rhetoric about U.S. forces being welcomed by the open arms of Iraqi citizens wanting the United States and its coalition forces to liberate them from the repressive regime in Baghdad. Within three weeks, however, the United States had successfully ousted the Tikrit-based regime. Questions then began arising as to whether the United States had sufficient troop strength for nation-building and other requirements, but Franks's mission was the waging of war, not the winning of peace. Within weeks after the armed hostilities formally ended, Franks announced his retirement from the army after thirty-six years of active service.

Galbraith, Peter W. (1950–)

A former Senate Foreign Relations Committee senior staffer, Galbraith has been an important player in nation-building for newly independent Croatia and East Timor, as well as exercising great influence over U.S. policy for the Kurdish section of northern Iraq and South Asia. Galbraith is the son of the Harvard economist and John F. Kennedy's ambassador to India, John Kenneth Galbraith. The younger Galbraith spent fifteen years advising the Senate on foreign relations and gained a reputation as a hard-hitting, intense specialist on humanitarian issues, development of national institutions, and other vital aspects of nation-building. Galbraith was crucial to focusing international attention on Saddam Hussein's use of chemical agents against his Kurdish citizens in 1988, and he worked continually to keep a high level of awareness of the Kurdish plight in the aftermath of the first Gulf War (1991). During the Clinton administration, Galbraith assumed the ambassadorship in Croatia, where he also participated in the peace negotiations on Bosnia-Herzegovina. After taking a position at the National War College in the late 1990s, Galbraith was recruited by the United Nations to be the principal administrator of newly independent East Timor as it took the steps necessary to becoming a viable state.

Garner, Jay (1938–)

The head of the Office of Reconstruction and Humanitarian Assistance in the Pentagon with responsibility for reestablishing a civil society in Iraq after the conflict that ousted Saddam Hussein, Garner is a retired three-star army general. He became something of a lightning rod as he took the position because his former job as a lieutenant general led many critics to assume that the Pentagon was not in fact interested in a democratic government for the Iraqi people as much as a military government to exploit Iraq's vast petroleum resources. Garner attracted Secretary of Defense Donald Rumsfeld's support for this position because of the general's prior experience as the coordinator for Operation PROVIDE COMFORT, the program that rescued millions of Kurds who were threatened with starvation at the end of the first Gulf War in early 1991. Part of the criticism of Garner resulted from his affiliation with a pro-Israeli national security organization in Washington, leading to charges that General Garner was a tool of Israel cooperating with the United States in the Middle East. Other critics charged that Garner was too ideologically linked with Secretary of Defense Rumsfeld and certain geopolitical aspirations held by some staff at the Pentagon. Garner's job, however, proved much tougher than anticipated, resulting in his tenure lasting less than a month. Because he was unable to restore even rudimentary services to much of Baghdad, Garner was replaced in early May 2003 by the career diplomat and counterterrorism expert Ambassador L. Paul Bremer.

Ghani, Ashraf (N.D.)

This Afghan scholar has served as Adjunct Professor of Anthropology at the Johns Hopkins University and as senior anthropologist at the World Bank where he concentrated on state formation and religion through studying political economy. In the post-Taliban Afghanistan, President Hamid Karzai turned to Ghani to become finance minister. Ghani's experience with the World Bank made him a trusted figure upon which the international community could focus as they agreed to pour millions of dollars of reconstruction and nation-building funds into Afghanistan.

Holbrooke, Richard (1941–)

Ambassador Richard Holbrooke was one of the most visible advocates for nation-building in the U.S. government during the 1990s. Holbrooke served in the Foreign Service between 1962 and 1972 and was posted to Vietnam and Morocco as well as several important positions in Washington, D.C. Later in the 1970s, he worked for the Carter-Mondale campaign and then was appointed assistant secretary for East Asian affairs in the Carter administration. In the 1980s, Holbrooke served in investment banking but returned to government to serve as U.S. ambassador to Germany, as assistant secretary of state for European and Canadian affairs, as special envoy to the Balkans, as a negotiator at the Dayton peace negotiations, and finally as U.S. ambassador to the United Nations. In each instance, Ambassador Holbrooke supported efforts to bring peace, stability, and development—the essence of nation-building—to states in turmoil. He was especially aggressive in arguing that the United States and world communities could not stand by and allow the brutal activities of Slobodan Milosovic in the breakaway areas of the former Yugoslav republic.

Howe, Jonathan Trumball (1935–)

Admiral Jonathan T. Howe had a prestigious career in the U.S. navy, retired in the early 1990s, and was asked by UN secretary general Boutros Boutros-Ghali to serve as special envoy to Somalia, beginning in 1993 during the turmoil there. An extremely capable submariner, Admiral Howe also holds a doctorate and worked as military assistant to national security advisor Henry Kissinger. In response to the problems of delivering food in late 1992, President George H. W. Bush sent troops for humanitarian relief operations to Somalia. In the summer of 1993, the mission for those troops evolved into nation-building. Admiral Howe, by then retired, took the position of UN special envoy to Somalia and became involved in these nation-building aspects, including trying to capture prominent warlord Mohammed Farah Aideed. On 3 October 1993, as U.S. forces were the principal ones working to achieve this goal, a U.S. helicopter was shot down over Mogadishu and several armed personnel carriers were ambushed on the streets of the city. Eighteen U.S. troops were killed, and one U.S. serviceman was dragged through the streets on display, a horrible message for the United States, which believed it was taking a neutral position on behalf of the international community. Admiral Howe, by then seen as a major architect of this mission to capture Aideed, was unable to explain what had gone wrong. Subsequently, President Clinton withdrew U.S. forces from Somalia, and chaos continued.

Hussein, Saddam (1937–)

One of the harshest rulers ever, Saddam Hussein is also one of the most skilled of survivors of the twentieth and twenty-first centuries. Originally a member of the Ba'ath Revolutionary Party, a secular movement in the Middle East, Saddam seized power in 1979 after several years behind the throne. He launched an invasion of Iran in September 1980 that cost each side more than a million young men over an eight-year period and ended in a virtual standoff. During this conflict, Saddam became the first leader to use chemical gas during conflict since World War I. He also gassed his own Kurdish minority in the north of the country. In August 1990, facing mounting loan repayment and falling petroleum prices, Saddam resurrected an old Iraqi claim to Kuwait as a province of Iraq and seized the petroleum-rich state in a lightning strike. President George H. W. Bush spent six months preparing for an invasion, but Saddam took his chances and refused to budge. After a six-week air campaign softened targets in Iraq, a ninety-six-hour ground war ousted Iraqi troops but did not cause Saddam himself to fall. When this 1991 campaign ended, Saddam's surrender agreement specified that UN weapons inspectors would be allowed to check his country for illegal weapons, but he was uncooperative. After throwing out the weapons inspectors and proving uncooperative in the 1990s, the administration of George W. Bush began suggesting that Saddam was involved with the September 11 strikes and was an imminent threat to the international community. After nine months of this argument, President Bush, without UN sanction but with Prime Minister Tony Blair's support in Britain, launched an invasion of Iraq in March 2003. Saddam's government fell by mid-April but he was not caught for eight months. His two sons were killed in a raid against a safe house in the summer of 2003. No weapons of mass destruction were identified in Iraq but Saddam's government being gone is still considered by the Bush administration as more stabilizing to the region. The summer of 2003 saw continued attacks on the forces in Iraq, including massive car bombs at the Jordanian embassy, the UN headquarters, and even at a Shi'ite mosque in the holy city of Najaf. U.S. officials have claimed that these assaults are the remnants of Saddam loyalists. In December 2003, U.S. forces found Hussein cowering in a basement. He remains incarcerated awaiting trial, as violence continues in Iraq, in mid-2004.

Johnson, Lyndon Baines (1912–1973)

Johnson had been an exceptionally powerful Senate majority leader who, as vice president, assumed the presidency upon John F. Kennedy's assassination in 1963. President Johnson engaged in the massive U.S. nation-building effort in Vietnam, beginning with the Gulf of Tonkin incident in 1964 when Congress gave blanket approval for the United States to send forces to Vietnam for defense and nation-building. In the next four years of his administration, President Johnson ended up sending half a million U.S. ground troops and billions of dollars for nation-building efforts intended to prevent a communist takeover of South Vietnam. President Johnson was not concerned exclusively in Asia, sending 23,000 U.S. Marines in April 1965 into the Dominican Republic when a leftist government appeared to threaten U.S. citizens. Nation-building became a primary concern for the United States during President Johnson's administration but in the context of the cold war, seeing it as a way to checkmate Soviet expansionism rather than any sort of indigenous movement anywhere in the world. Johnson's intention in Southeast Asia was nation-building but his experience showed how tough this becomes.

Karzai, Hamid (1957–)

A fluent English-speaker, educated in India, and strongly supported by the United States, Karzai has held the position of chief of state in Afghanistan since 2001. As a Pashtun from Kandahar, he has connections to the important Pashtun population and its traditional ties to the last monarch of Afghanistan, Mohammed Zahr Shah, who was ousted in the 1970s. He also fought the Soviets during the 1980–1988 occupation, giving him credibility with those who had sought to return Afghanistan to domestic control. Initially, Karzai also supported the Taliban but found them too intolerant and withdrew his support by the mid-1990s. All in all, Karzai has shown a wily ability to court and sift through a wide range of ideological and religious groups. He proved wildly popular with the international community when he appeared at a donors' meeting in Tokyo to discuss Afghan nation-building commitments. In the years since the Loya Jirga elected him as interim president, he has survived several assassination attempts and has tried to maintain the pace of reconstruction of his nation. In this he has proven relatively unsuccessful, and Afghanistan has many difficulties ahead.

Kennedy, John Fitzgerald (1917–1963)

President Kennedy was crucial to the expansion of U.S. nation-building activities through the Peace Corps and the Agency for International Development. The United States was in the depths of the cold war struggle with the Soviet Union during his administration. As far back as the Eisenhower administration, the struggle was seen as a zero-sum game of states either for the U.S. approach to society, politics, and economics or supporting the enemy. The Kennedy administration sought to ameliorate the U.S. position by offering economic incentives in the form of foreign assistance, technological help through various programs, and basic education that would not only improve the lot of peoples around the world but also earn their allegiance. The Peace Corps was made up primarily of young, recently graduated volunteers who worked in the rural areas of lesser-developed states. Often providing language training or education in a particular skill like small-plot farming, the Peace Corps was a primary vehicle for winning the hearts of people in rural communities where the United States appeared to take an interest that native governments often ignored. The Agency for International Development (USAID), also initiated during the Kennedy administration, provided technical assistance and foreign aid at a much higher level than had been provided in the past. But the USAID program was seen by some around the world not as a benevolent program but as a cover for counterinsurgency operations that were intended to prevent the creation of anti–United States governments in Third World states. Because U.S. concerns about Soviet threats were paramount, nation-building took a secondary position to anti-Soviet activities. The greatest legacy of the Kennedy administration's nation-building was the escalation of U.S. involvement in Vietnam, Cambodia, and

Laos between 1961 and 1975, with the high-water mark in the late 1960s when more than 500,000 U.S. troops and thousands of civilian nation-builders were deployed there.

Khalilzad, Zalmay (1951–)

The first U.S. envoy to post-Taliban Afghanistan is an Afghan-born academic who spent many years in the Washington national security environment, both in the government and the think-tank communities. Khalilzad is one of a circle of University of Chicago–trained political scientists that has a vision of the post–cold war world that appears to involve a different role for nation-building than George W. Bush seemed to embrace during his 2000 election campaign. Khalilzad held a position in the Pentagon of the first President Bush, where he was involved with planning how to maintain U.S. dominance after the first Gulf War. During the Clinton period, he took a position at the RAND Corporation in wide-ranging national security analysis. After the U.S.-led invasion of Afghanistan in October 2001, the Bush administration sent Khalilzad to work with the government of Hamid Karzai as he began the process of creating a functioning, modern democratic system out of the ruins of the authoritarian, repressive religious regime.

Kim Jong-Il (1942–)

The son of the Great Leader who waged the Korean War and was the first president of North Korea, Kim Jong-Il is known as the Dear Leader and rules North Korea with autocratic brutality. He took over upon his father's death in 1994. He has proven a thoroughly insensitive leader to the needs of the twenty-three million North Koreans, which reveals a likely location for nation-building in the future. North Korea would be a challenge, however, as the reunification with a much-more-developed South Korea would be difficult to achieve without massive upheaval. But when that reunification will occur is far from clear, as North Korea persists in its nuclear weapon developments.

Kissinger, Henry Alfred (1923–)

Dr. Henry Kissinger, a German refugee who arrived in the United States in his teenage years, became one of the most influential secretaries of state and national security advisors in history. Dr. Kissinger was a Harvard graduate, and on the Harvard faculty with close ties to New York governor Nelson Rockefeller, when he attracted President-elect Richard M. Nixon's attention in late 1968. Convincing Nixon of his skill at negotiating the bureaucratic waters, Kissinger became national security advisor in January 1969, partly due to the new president's scheme to subjugate the State Department management of foreign affairs to White House control. Kissinger embarked on a career that included several forays into personal diplomacy on behalf of the president, such as arms talks with the Soviets, blazing the trail for an "opening" to Mao's China, and peace talks with the Vietnamese in Paris. In 1969 and 1970, Kissinger and Nixon widened the war in Southeast Asia beyond Vietnam and into Cambodia and Laos. Kissinger advocated *Realpolitik,* which recognized that politics means decisions based on power politics, not lesser domestic requirements. This frequently meant advocating nation-building, but in fact placed that activity into the larger context of the U.S.-Soviet competition of the cold war. Kissinger served as national security advisor and secretary of state as the United States withdrew from Vietnam; within three years, nation-building efforts within South Vietnam collapsed, and the North Vietnamese communist regime was victorious. Kissinger waged the cold war in several places on behalf of the United States and devised new approaches to dismantling regimes. These included Chile in the 1970s to overthrow minority socialist president Salvador Allende Gossens, Angola in the mid-1970s to prevent Soviet influence from growing, and various places in the Middle East. Subsequent to his government career, Kissinger became a prominent consultant.

Klein, Jacques Paul (1929–)

Klein is a career diplomat from the United States who has served as special representative of the secretary general of the United Nations to Liberia, special representative of the secretary general to Bosnia-Herzegovina, and principal deputy high representative with the office of the high representative in Bosnia-Herzegovina. Klein is also a retired U.S. air force major general and a graduate of the National War College, and he served in several positions in the Defense Department, where he offered an understanding of the need to coordinate the military and civilian arms of national security. His role in the most pressing nation-building efforts of the 1990s was very important. In the long struggle to bring some sort of stability and law to the former Yugoslav areas of Herzegovina and Bosnia, Klein was increasingly relied upon to coordinate the activities of the United Nations in conjunction with the United States and other NATO countries. His work in Liberia has been equally challenging, as that state underwent more than twenty years of upheaval, which strongly undercut the respect for law in the West African state.

Kristol, William (1952–)

William Kristol, a founder and editor of the *Weekly Standard*, is a major figure in the Republican Party seeking to rebuild the world in the image of the United States, beginning with ousting Saddam Hussein from Iraq. Kristol, son of two prominent neoconservatives, Irving Kristol and Gertrude Himmelfarb, was a Democrat through the mid-1970s when the neoconservative movement grew out of concerns that the Democratic Party was ignorant about the true nature of the Soviet threat against the United States. Kristol taught at Harvard and the University of Pennsylvania before joining the Reagan Department of Education under prominent conservative thinker William Bennett. With the election of George H. W. Bush, Kristol became the chief of staff for Vice President Dan Quayle. With the return of a Democrat to the White House in 1993, Kristol became involved with the founding of the *Weekly Standard*, an influential and avowedly conservative weekly. Kristol also received much public credit as a strategist in helping the Republicans retake the House of Representatives in 1994 and the White House in 2000. In 2000, Kristol argued forcefully that Saddam Hussein had to be removed because of the threats he posed to the Middle East, Israel, and international peace. Unlike George W. Bush's statements during the 2000 campaign, Kristol has not been philosophically opposed to nation-building. He believes that the United States can provide a philosophical and moral base for nation-building that can lead to better lives for the affected citizenry.

Lake, Anthony (1939–)

Tony Lake was a professor at Mount Holyoke College before becoming the first national security advisor to President Bill Clinton but had served in the State Department during the Kennedy, Johnson, and Carter administrations. Dr. Lake resigned from the Foreign Service in protest against the expansion of the conflict in the early 1970s under Henry Kissinger. Lake was on the State Department Policy Planning Staff during the late 1970s. During the Clinton administration, Lake was viewed as a primary mover in the expansion of nation-building efforts, first in Somalia, then in Haiti, and then in the Balkans. Trained as an African specialist, Lake was not able to push the administration to expand its efforts to stop the conflict in Rwanda and Burundi where more than a million people died in one hundred days of Hutu/Tutsi ethnic cleansing. Lake became the focus for critics who felt that the Clinton administration was too aggressive in its efforts to nation-build at the same time that the efforts stretched the U.S. military too thin. As the Clinton administration became increasingly enmeshed in the conflict in the former Yugoslavia, Lake became more frustrated. He left the administration after the first term.

MacArthur, Douglas (1880–1964)

General Douglas MacArthur might have been the most successful U.S. nation-builder, but he was in a radically different environment than contemporary nation-builders face. Born to a Civil War general and a southern belle, MacArthur graduated from the U.S. Military Academy at West Point and went on to become the most highly decorated officer of World War I and a brigadier general. After serving as commandant at West Point, the officer charged with dissolving the "bonus marchers" in 1932, and army chief of staff, General MacArthur went to the Philippines in the late 1930s to begin the process of granting independence. MacArthur fled the Philippines when the Japanese invaded in 1941, serving in various points across the Pacific throughout the war. Accepting the Japanese surrender on the USS *Missouri* in 1945, General MacArthur then went on to become head of occupied Japan from 1945 to 1950. General MacArthur not only supervised the physical rebuilding of Japan but also guided the development of the constitutional system still in place today. This occupation is often viewed as the model for how to go about changing a society from warlike to becoming a peaceful member of the international community. General MacArthur's last fifteen years of life were dissatisfying. He was removed from the command of U.S. forces in the Korean War in 1951 by President Truman for cause, withdrew from the scene, and died in 1964.

Mandela, Nelson Rolihlahla (1918–)

Nelson Rolihlahla Mandela, the first black president of the Republic of South Africa, has been a visible advocate for nation-building and social justice for forty years. A member of African royalty, Mandela was an attorney prohibited from practicing law under the apartheid laws of South Africa. In the 1950s, Mandela became a central figure in the African National Congress, the most visible organization trying to bring about black majority rule in South Africa. He was imprisoned in 1964 at Robben Island after a bombing and became probably the most famous political prisoner in the world. With the gradual dismantling of the apartheid laws in the late 1980s, the Afrikaner regime in Pretoria came under strong international pressure to release Mandela, which President de Klerk did in 1990. Mandela was elected president four years later. Mandela's tenure coincided with many sweeping changes in South Africa, which required it to adjust to majority rule while finding an appropriate role for Afrikaners. Upon leaving office in 1998, Mandela became an elder statesman for social justice and the need to continue building to form a true nation in South Africa.

Marshall, George Catlett (1880–1959)

The quintessential soldier-statesman, General George C. Marshall left his imprint not only on military affairs in the United States but on the postwar world. Born in Virginia not far removed from the Civil War environment, George Marshall attended the Virginia Military Institute rather than West Point but still managed to make his prowess as a military intellectual known. Serving in World War I, Marshall could see the deficiencies plaguing the U.S. military and, when it became obvious in the 1930s that rebuilding was necessary with all deliberate speed, set about to remedy them. He had a particular skill at recognizing talent and saw the skills of Colonel Dwight David Eisenhower being wasted as an assistant to General Douglas MacArthur in the Philippines as war began in Europe. By the end of the war, six years later, that same Eisenhower had become a four-star general alongside Marshall, who was chief of staff of the army. In the aftermath of World War II, General Marshall took off his uniform to serve President Truman as secretary of state. Marshall offered the speech at Harvard in June 1947 that outlined the Marshall Plan for reconstruction in Europe, perhaps the most audacious nation-building in the world. He subsequently served as secretary of defense as well. Known for his formality, grace, and manners, Marshall was a nonpartisan public servant, in uniform or in a suit. He recognized that nation-building was a blend of the military and civilian sides of any force.

McKinley, William (1843–1901)

William McKinley was the first president of the United States to engage in colonization that was supported on grounds that are today termed ones of nation-building, although the definition of nation-building was different at the time. A former congressman, Ohio governor McKinley won the presidency in 1896 during a severe economic depression. McKinley was president as U.S. relations with Spain deteriorated in 1897 and 1898, leading to the USS *Maine* being in Havana's harbor when it blew up in 1898. The U.S. government accused the Spanish government (history has left this question far less clear), proclaimed that U.S. forces were under siege, and launched the Spanish-American War, resulting in Spain's resounding defeat and Theodore Roosevelt getting the reputation of riding up San Juan Hill with the Rough Riders. Most importantly, the United States annexed former Spanish colonies in Guam, the Philippines, and Puerto Rico, whereas Cuba became nominally independent. The nation-building that President McKinley sought to conduct was to bring non-Catholic, democratic governance to the former Spanish colonies. This remaking of society has always been at the heart of nation-building for the United States. What differs from current efforts is that Spain was defeated in battle before the United States "took" these colonial areas. Reelected in 1900, McKinley died in Buffalo six months after his second inauguration after being shot by an assassin.

Myers, Richard B. (1942–)

The fifteenth chairman of the Joint Chiefs of Staff, General Richard Myers is an experienced pilot who entered the officer corps from the Reserve Officer Training Corps at Kansas State University. Before being nominated as chairman, General Myers had served as the vice chairman of the Joint Chiefs of Staff for a year and a half and as head of the U.S. Space Command and had extensive experience in air force jobs in Asia during his operational career. Myers had been nominated but not yet confirmed as chairman when the September 2001 attacks on the Pentagon and World Trade Center occurred. Almost immediately upon taking his new position, General Myers had to lead U.S. forces in the campaign to remove the Taliban from control over Afghanistan at the same time as the Bush administration sought to wage a global war on terrorism. General Myers also has played a prominent role in the argument to oust Saddam Hussein from Iraq, thus asking a significant portion of the U.S. military to conduct nation-building efforts in the Middle East.

Natsios, Andrew (1950–)

Andrew Natsios, as a veteran of the humanitarian assistance efforts of the first Bush administration and as head of the private voluntary organization World Vision, became the administrator of the U.S. Agency for International Development (USAID) in 2001. Natsios had served in the Humanitarian Relief portion of USAID between 1989 and 1991 before returning to the private sector. A specialist in famine-related relief, Natsios has been extremely busy with nation-building efforts in Afghanistan in the aftermath of the Taliban and in Iraq where the reconstruction efforts have been far more in the physical realm than anticipated. USAID is the focal point for nation-building efforts in the U.S. government and Natsios has been key to those efforts.

Nixon, Richard Milhous (1913–1994)

Richard Nixon, son of Quakers from southern California, was an enigmatic and polarizing figure for five decades of U.S. politics and the only president to resign from office. Elected to Congress in 1946 after a campaign in which he accused his opponent of being "pink," a term for Communist, Nixon emerged during the uproar over Alger Hiss and the spread of communism within the government. In the early 1950s, he left the House of Representatives for a California Senate seat and then managed to convince Eisenhower that he was useful as a vice presidential partner in the 1952 campaign. Eisenhower and Nixon, in the early years of the global struggle against the Soviet threat, engaged in nation-building in places like Iran (1953), Guatemala (1954), and the initial years of Vietnam's upheaval. Nixon lost the presidential race to John F. Kennedy in 1960, as well as the governorship of California two years later, but, to a great degree as a result of his perceived geostrategic skills, he outlasted Vice President Hubert H. Humphrey to win the presidency in 1968, claiming he had a "secret plan" to win the war in Vietnam in six months. Nixon, and his national security advisor and later secretary of state Henry Kissinger, saw nation-building as merely an extension of the global fight against communism rather than an inherently moral or useful objective for the United States. Their actions in Southeast Asia, including expanding the war from Vietnam into Laos and Cambodia, along with attempts to undermine the elected minority government in Chile between 1970 and 1973, illustrated this stance. Nixon did make a breathtaking change in U.S. strategy when he engaged Mao and Communist China with his February 1972 visit, and he signed the initial major arms-control agreements with the Soviet Union that same year. Nixon was forced to resign from the White House on 9 August 1974 when it became obvious that he knew about the Watergate break-in. By the late 1970s, Nixon was resurrecting his reputation as a geostrategist through strategically placed interviews and articles, as he attempted to spend his last years as a global senior statesman.

Oakley, Robert B. (1931–)

Ambassador Robert Oakley served as the presidential envoy to Pakistan, Somalia, and Zaire, as well as in several other capacities, during his thirty-four-year career in the Foreign Service, ending with his retirement in 1991. Oakley was involved in counterterrorism efforts long before September 11 alerted the nation to the potential for danger. He also advised several administrations on South Asia, the Middle East, and East Asian issues and served on the National Security Council staff and as assistant to the vice president and in other capacities. Oakley was special envoy to Somalia under George H. W. Bush and Bill Clinton, where he had the reputation with the Somalis of being an "honest broker." Beginning in the mid-1990s, Oakley became a prominent distinguished research fellow at the Institute for National Strategic

Studies at the National Defense University, where he was sought out for his expertise in nation-building in some of the toughest places around the world. During his stay at the institute, Oakley coedited a number of books on nation-building topics. He remains a crucial U.S. government consultant on nation-building.

Pachachi, Adnan (1923–)

This Sunni member of the Iraqi Governing Council, the twenty-five hand-picked individuals asked to serve as an ethnically and religiously representative interim government in Baghdad, served in the pre-Ba'athist governments of the 1960s. He entered the Iraqi Foreign Service in 1944, son of another Iraqi diplomat. He was a diplomat until the 1968 coup, which installed the Ba'athist government; during that period, one of Pachachi's jobs was foreign minister. Pachachi went into a thirty-two year exile from his homeland, actually taking Emiri citizenship. Prior to Saddam Hussein's overthrow in 2003, Pachachi formed the Independent Democratic Movement in hopes of returning to his country and establishing a secular, democratic government there. Pachachi's position as favored by the Bush administration was illustrated when he appeared in the gallery during President George W. Bush's 2003 State of the Union address.

Perle, Richard Norman (1941–)

A registered Democrat but closely associated with hawkish Republican administrations since 1980, Richard Perle is a hero to the hardliners in the United States and the bête noire to doves. Perle's rise to prominence came from being on the staff of Washington senator Henry "Scoop" Jackson with his attendant concerns about both the Soviet threat in the mid-1970s and the protection of Israel's security. Perle and Norman Podheretz, Midge Decter, Elliott Abrams, and Jeane J. Kirkpatrick formed the basis of the initial group of the neoconservative movement: traditionally Democratic-leaning strategists who feared that détente was pushing the United States into a dangerous position vis-à-vis the Soviet military. Perle attracted the attention of Ronald Reagan during the 1980 campaign and served as an assistant secretary of defense, best known for his hostility to arms-control agreements. His critics derided him in the 1980s as the "prince of darkness." Perle left the Reagan administration before it ended in 1989 and joined the private sector. During the early months of the second Bush administration, Perle returned to prominence as the head of the Defense Policy Board, an advisory device for political friends within the Pentagon. Perle is credited with the proposition that ousting Saddam from Baghdad would guarantee U.S. security at the same time that it would enhance Israeli security. In late 2002, Perle resigned as head of the Defense Policy Board after a minor scandal about conflict of interest but retained a seat on the board. Perle's view that Saddam posed a grave, immediate threat to the United States because of weapons of mass destruction was not proven, and he remains a controversial figure. Perle is, in many ways, the antithesis of a traditional nation-builder, but his views have influenced the U.S. government to take a minimalist approach.

Powell, Colin Luther (1937–)

The first African American national security advisor and chairman of the Joint Chiefs of Staff, General Colin L. Powell became George W. Bush's secretary of state in 2001. Powell grew up in New York City as the son of Jamaican immigrants and went through college on a Reserve Officer Training Corps scholarship. Powell served several tours in Vietnam, where he saw the effects and dangers of nation-building, as well gaining an understanding of how these efforts could affect the nation-builders, and became one of the leaders of the generation seeking to rebuild the U.S. army after the deterioration following the Vietnam War. In the 1970s and 1980s, Powell served in a number of non-army positions, as White House Fellow, as a student at the National War College, as military aide to administration figures, before President Reagan named him Special Assistant for National Security Affairs for the final two years of his administration (1987–1989). President George H. W. Bush made Powell chairman of the Joint Chiefs of Staff from 1989 to 1993, where he oversaw U.S. nation-building in several incidents: the invasion of Panama to capture General Manuel Noriega, the amassing of half a million troops to force Saddam Hussein out of Kuwait, and the use of U.S. marines and army troops to provide humanitarian assistance in Somalia. Powell's rule of thumb for use of U.S. forces related to his Vietnam experience: overwhelming force was essential if U.S. intervention was required. Powell's concerns about the use of the military tool of statecraft put him into conflict with the Clinton administration's expanded belief in nation-building. Powell retired in 1993 and rejected calls for a run for the presidency in both 1996 and 2000. He became involved in advising candidate George W. Bush and became secretary of state in 2001, giving the president much needed credibility in national security issues. As secretary of state, Powell found himself in a tough position: the diplomatic tool of statecraft required the use of military forces in situations in apparent violation of Powell's stated beliefs. The administration's reversal on the need for nation-building, coming after the September 11 attacks, made Powell's position even more difficult. The reliance on the military instead of diplomacy in Iraq led some to question whether the administration was being truthful about its intentions or the evidence of weapons of mass destruction, as well as what the U.S. goals really were. Powell led the State Department ably and oversaw the civilian side of nation-building in Afghanistan, Iraq, Colombia, Pakistan, Liberia, and other places where the Bush administration sought to alter conditions.

Reagan, Ronald Wilson (1911–)

Ronald Reagan, former actor and governor of California, stormed his way to the White House in 1980 as Jimmy Carter's administration failed in attempting to free forty-four hostages held in the U.S. embassy in Teheran, Iran. Reagan began as a Democrat, including as a screen actors' guild head, but switched to the Republican Party in the 1950s. By the 1960s, he was captivated by the Goldwater revolution, which advocated less government intervention in economic affairs and a much firmer stance against Soviet expansionism around the world. In 1976, Reagan waged an insurgency that came close to preventing President Gerald Ford, elevated to the presidency in August 1974 when Nixon resigned, from winning the Republican nomination. Reagan, with support from the antitax and social conservative wings of the party, also tapped into national security concerns about Soviet behavior and U.S. laxness resulting from détente and naiveté. Reagan saw nation-building much as Nixon and Kissinger did: as a means of preventing the Soviets from moving into places the United States was not occupying or controlling. Self-determination was subjugated to the global struggle between the United States and the Soviet Union. This was especially true in Central America, where the United States spent millions of dollars to support anticommunist, albeit often extremely brutal, governments (El Salvador, Honduras, and Guatemala) or trained and supported armed groups seeking to overthrow a pro-Soviet government (Nicaragua). This directly contradicted U.S. rhetoric about preserving national self-determination. Months after Reagan left office, Soviet control over Eastern Europe collapsed. Within three years, the Soviet Union itself was no more. Nation-building efforts around the world have increased as states in the past decade have been left to flounder without sufficient support or have been pushed to mirror U.S.-style economic and political systems. His second administration ended with scandal over arms sales to Iran in hopes of getting U.S. hostages released in the Middle East and to raise money for Nicaragua counter-revolutionaries.

Rice, Condoleezza (1954–)

The first woman to serve as national security advisor, Dr. Condoleezza Rice grew up in the segregated Alabama of Martin Luther King Jr. Her family was Republican and believed that she had the same opportunity to work as did anyone else of any other color in the United States. Rice, an accomplished pianist, attended the University of Notre Dame and the University of Denver, where she studied under Madeleine Albright's father, Josef Korbel, in international relations. A Russian area specialist, she accepted a position in the political science department at Stanford University and then served in the first Bush administration in the arms control negotiations with the failing Soviet state in the late 1980s. Returning to Stanford, she became university provost until her prominence in advising presidential candidate George W. Bush became widely known with an article she penned in *Foreign Affairs* magazine during the 2000 campaign. As national security advisor, Rice appeared to be in a difficult position between the two strong personalities of the secretaries of defense and state. She became a more visible presence after the events of September 11, becoming a more prominent spokesperson for the president and for his policies in pursuing terrorists. Most importantly, Rice assumed a much more aggressive posture in explaining the reasons the president seemed to reverse his campaign position on nation-building. She played an important part in the controversy that developed after the actions to remove Saddam Hussein because her statements about the quality and content of intelligence information on Iraq's weapons of mass destruction program were scrutinized. Rice retained President Bush's strong and unwavering support, which made her invaluable to his administration.

Critics, however, question her grasp of and control over nation-building efforts in Iraq.

Roosevelt, Franklin Delano (1882–1945)

The longest-serving president of the United States, FDR set the basic conditions for U.S. involvement in nation-building through his actions in the Caribbean Basin during the 1930s and those he set for decolonization of former European colonies after World War II. Roosevelt's father had been a businessman with significant ties in China during the nineteenth century, which gave him a sense of the conditions that developing states faced that were different from those in industrializing countries. Roosevelt, a former assistant secretary of the navy and governor of New York, took office as the United States faced one of the most severe economic and social crises of its history, which in fact included some of the same issues that nation-builders face around the world. Roosevelt promoted the Good Neighbor Policy in the Western Hemisphere but oversaw some of the most important U.S. interventions and support for nondemocratic, but stable, anticommunist regimes. During World War II, Roosevelt worked with British prime minister Winston Churchill to end Nazi and Fascist aggression around the world. At the same time, Roosevelt recognized that the post–World War II period would see the rising up of the colonized against the colonizers in Asia, Africa, and the Middle East. The United States had no formal colonies in its history except the Philippines, and Roosevelt sought to pressure the British and French to end their colonial relationships in favor of nascent democracies. Additionally, Roosevelt was the principal architect of the establishment of the new world order, which included multilateral institutions to address problems that had led to World War II: the United Nations, the World Bank (the International Bank of Reconstruction and Development), and the International Monetary Fund (the latter two are known as the Bretton Woods financial system).

Roosevelt, Theodore (1858–1919)

President Theodore Roosevelt was perhaps the first prominent nation-building U.S. president as he was president during the period when the first expansion into these efforts outside the country occurred. Roosevelt had a colorful career, which led him to the presidency upon William McKinley's assassination. Roosevelt had been involved in the effort to defeat the Spanish in Cuba in 1898. He was known as a Rough Rider who led men up San Juan Hill, but this had little true effect on the conflict, the outcome of which was never in any serious doubt because of the unequal powers of the United States and Spain. Roosevelt engaged directly in nation-building by undercutting Colombian governance in the province of Panama and supporting its desire for independence in 1902 and by initiating one of the great engineering marvels of the world with the building of the Panama Canal (1903–1912). Roosevelt left the imprint of U.S. imperialism in world affairs with his motto that the United States would "speak softly and carry a big stick" as it interacted with others. Roosevelt also sent marines into various places in the Caribbean Basin where debts to his citizens were not being paid. Roosevelt's aggressive style left a potent image of awakening U.S. power at the beginning of the century, which saw traditional empires replaced by U.S. hegemony.

Rostow, Walt Whitman (1916–2003)

Walt Whitman Rostow was President Lyndon B. Johnson's special assistant for national security affairs after McGeorge Bundy returned to Harvard in late 1965. Rostow, along with his brother Eugene, became prominent academics-turned-policymakers in the 1960s. Rostow's academic training was as an economic historian. He wrote *Stages of Economic Growth*, a 1960 publication that advocated linear growth in stages, which would inevitably lead to an "economic takeoff" and development. Rostow served not only President Johnson but also his two immediate predecessors. It was the arguments about the stages and inevitability of economic growth that convinced President Johnson and Secretary of Defense McNamara to rely on Rostow's arguments in developing strategy for Vietnam. Rostow was national security advisor during some of the greatest buildups of U.S. troops during the war, but he never doubted that the strategy would give Vietnam time to go through its stages of development. Rostow left government service to return to teaching and ended his career with thirty-one years at the University of Texas in Austin where he was Professor Emeritus of Economic History when he died.

Rumsfeld, Donald Harold (1932–)

Donald Rumsfeld is the only man to have served as defense secretary in two different administrations. Rumsfeld, a native of the north shore of Chicago, was also a congressman, White House chief of staff in the Ford administration, ambassador to NATO, chief executive of a corporation, and head of an influential commission advocating nuclear weapons in space. Rumsfeld went into the navy after attending Princeton on a Reserve Officer Training Corps scholarship, served on active duty from 1954 to 1957, and was then in the reserves for another eighteen years. He arrived in the nation's capital in 1957 as a House staffer and was elected to that body in 1962. After four terms in the House, Rumsfeld headed Nixon's Office of Economic Opportunity and then served as director of the Economic Stabilization Program. He was the U.S. ambassador to NATO from 1973 to 1974. President Gerald Ford brought Rumsfeld back to Washington to head the presidential transition team in the wake of President Nixon's resignation in 1974. Rumsfeld then served as chief of staff through 1975. Richard B. Cheney replaced him when Rumsfeld became the youngest secretary of defense in 1975. With the end of the Ford administration in 1977, Rumsfeld returned to Chicago to run G.D. Searle, a global pharmaceutical company. Serving subsequently in other private ventures, Rumsfeld then chaired the U.S. Ballistic Missile Threat Commission in 1998, which advocated a ballistic missile defense for the United States. When President George W. Bush and Vice President Cheney were seeking a credible defense secretary in 2001, they turned to Rumsfeld. Many people felt he was frustrated in the first months of the administration, but September 11 turned Mr. Rumsfeld into a media sensation with his daily briefings about the war in Afghanistan. Rumsfeld and his deputy Paul Wolfowitz argued forcefully that Saddam Hussein had weapons of mass destruction and that force was needed to remove him. After the 2003 conflict revealed no such weapons, Rumsfeld still defended the action as important for U.S. and global security and maintained that, regardless of the appearance, the U.S. venture in Iraq would not be a quagmire or involve guerrilla warfare. Rumsfeld's tenure as secretary in the Bush administration included a major expansion of U.S. nation-building efforts by the armed forces while also seeing the growth of private corporations to involve themselves in these activities around the world.

Talabani, Jalal (1933–)

One of two prominent Sunni Kurds in the Iraqi Governing Council established with Saddam's ouster in April 2003, Talabani has been the head of the Patriotic Union of Kurdistan (PUK) for many years. Known to many as "Mam" Jalal (Uncle Jalal), Talabani graduated from Baghdad University law school and was a founder of the Kurdistan Students Union, which was part of the now-rival Kurdistan Democratic Party. Talabani participated in the 1961 Kurdish insurgency against the Baghdad government. Talabani was a principal in founding the PUK in 1975, complicating the Kurdish attempts at independence from Iraq since the PUK-KDP split fractured the population. With the Gulf War of 1991, Kurdish hopes for independence rose when a no-fly zone was established in northern Iraq and the political split between the two groups appeared to ameliorate. Tensions escalated in 1994 but a peace accord between the two organizations was signed four years later in Washington and further eased in 2002 in the lead up to the 2003 invasion. Talabani's PUK, based in Sulaymaniyah, has its strength in the southeastern portion of the Kurdish region and has 20,000 men in its militia.

Taylor, Charles McArthur (1948–)

The longtime dictator in Liberia who became the focus of the late-1990s civil war to remove him from power, Charles Taylor finally departed Monrovia on 11 August 2003, at the same time that President George W. Bush sent a small group of U.S. troops into the country to help restore democracy and engage in nation-building. Liberia, with its modern founding by freed U.S. slaves, began to disintegrate in the 1980s after Sargeant Samuel Doe seized power. Taylor, a warlord from outside of Monrovia, fought along with his supporters, beginning in the 1980s, to oust Doe. Taylor was able to exert power over the country, but other warlords almost immediately began to assert themselves, and civil war ensued. Taylor's reign in Liberia led to brutal conditions, with Westerners being evacuated in the late 1990s. In the 1990s, Western African countries under the auspices of ECOWAS (the Economic Community of West African States) began trying to place peacekeepers but were forced to withdraw. U.S. involvement in Liberia appears to be a prime example of the Bush administration's genuine commitment to spread U.S. democratic values to states when vital interests are not evident.

Truman, Harry S. (1884 –1972)

Truman was a haberdasher from Missouri who engaged in some of the most successful of U.S. nation-building: the Marshall Plan for European reconstruction and the rebuilding of Japan. Vice President Truman succeeded to the presidency upon Roosevelt's death in mid-April 1945 after being on the scene for only a couple of months. Not a particularly good businessman, Truman was tied to the Kansas City Pendergast political machine, which is how he was elected as a Democrat to the Senate in the 1930s. Truman had seen how violence could destroy a community when he served with U.S. expeditionary forces in World War I in Europe but had little other foreign affairs experience. In August 1945, he authorized dropping two atomic weapons on Japan, bringing the war in the Pacific to a close. He sent General Douglas MacArthur to serve as the administrator in Japan to lead all of the reconstruction efforts: rewriting the constitution, the physical reconstruction of the country, health assistance, and much more. In Europe, Truman recognized that Communist sympathizers appeared on the verge of electoral victories in Italy, France, and possibly Greece, just when British economic troubles made it impossible for the Crown to continue providing assistance there. In a ten-week period of 1947, President Truman enunciated the Truman Doctrine about defending democratic governments (arguably still in force today), oversaw the support for the Marshall Plan, and watched the "Mr. X" article from *Foreign Affairs* warn of Soviet expansionism in the future, which accelerated the deterioration of Soviet-U.S. relations. Truman got Congress to approve massive aid as a stopgap against communism. In the later 1940s, he orchestrated the Berlin airlift and, two years later, waged the Korean War. Truman did not run again in 1952, but by then Europe was getting back on its feet financially, democratic systems appeared to be in place, and the U.S. nuclear arsenal was growing in case of a Soviet attack.

Vieira de Mello, Sergio (1948–2003)

The Brazilian diplomat who had UN responsibility for working to create a new nation in East Timor after its independence in 1999,

Vieira de Mello received a similar call from the secretary general to represent the UN in Iraq in the aftermath of the 2003 conflict. A suave, multilingual career diplomat, he had important jobs as a high commissioner for refugees, as well as having worked in Cambodia, Kosovo, Bosnia, and Rwanda. His role in Iraq in 2003 was that of Special Representative, for the purpose of holding the broadest portfolio for the international body. Less than ten days before he was scheduled to leave Baghdad to return to his position as High Commissioner for Human Rights, Vieira de Mello was assassinated on 19 August 2003 in a massive truck bombing outside the UN headquarters.

Wolfowitz, Paul Dundes (1943–)

A major intellectual figure in the Republican administrations of the last quarter of the twentieth and the early twenty-first centuries, Wolfowitz was a product of Cornell University and the University of Chicago, where he studied with the famous political scientist Leo Strauss. Wolfowitz became known as the driving force behind many of the nation-building efforts, as well as the overall national security orientation, of President George W. Bush's administration. Wolfowitz began his government career, after having taught at Yale, in the Arms Control and Disarmament Agency in the mid-1970s. He then served as deputy assistant secretary of defense for regional programs in the Carter administration. He also served in the State Department on the Policy Planning Staff and as ambassador to Indonesia for President Ronald Reagan and as undersecretary of defense for policy during the first Bush administration. During the Clinton administration, Wolfowitz was dean and professor of international relations at the Paul Nitze School of Advanced International Studies at Johns Hopkins University. In March 2001, Wolfowitz was sworn in as deputy secretary of defense and became an active supporter of the proposition that the United States could remake the world in its own image through dealing with states not only hostile to its national interests but also those that were "failing" around the world. Wolfowitz's positions became even more influential after the September 11 incidents, and he became the architect of U.S. actions in Afghanistan and then in Iraq.

5

Documents

An Agenda for Peace

The Agenda for Peace was one of the cornerstones of the global movement to broaden UN activities beyond the traditional interstate conflict resolution to a much more invasive approach. Secretary General Boutros Boutros-Ghali was held accountable for this change, but he was illustrating other changes under way. The idea of a global responsibility for peacemaking went beyond the views of traditional Westphalian international relations practiced by the United States and much of Western Europe. The Agenda represented a concerted UN move toward peacekeeping, in particular, at a time when the United States and its military opposed this mission. This document shows the vastness of the task.

Introduction

1. In its statement of 31 January 1992, adopted at the conclusion of the first meeting held by the Security Council at the level of Heads of State and Government, I was invited to prepare, for circulation to the Members of the United Nations by 1 July 1992, an "analysis and recommendations on ways of strengthening and making more efficient within the framework and provisions of the Charter the capacity of the United Nations for preventive diplomacy, for peacemaking and for peace-keeping."[1]

2. The United Nations is a gathering of sovereign States and what it can do depends on the common ground that they create between them. The adversarial decades of the cold war made the original promise of the Organization impossible to fulfill. The January 1992

Summit therefore represented an unprecedented recommitment, at the highest political level, to the Purposes and Principles of the Charter.

3. In these past months a conviction has grown, among nations large and small, that an opportunity has been regained to achieve the great objectives of the Charter—a United Nations capable of maintaining international peace and security, of securing justice and human rights and of promoting, in the words of the Charter, "social progress and better standards of life in larger freedom." This opportunity must not be squandered. The Organization must never again be crippled as it was in the era that has now passed . . .

5. The sources of conflict and war are pervasive and deep. To reach them will require our utmost effort to enhance respect for human rights and fundamental freedoms, to promote sustainable economic and social development for wider prosperity, to alleviate distress and to curtail the existence and use of massively destructive weapons. The United Nations Conference on Environment and Development, the largest summit ever held, has just met at Rio de Janeiro. Next year will see the second World Conference on Human Rights. In 1994 Population and Development will be addressed. In 1995 the World Conference on Women will take place, and a World Summit for Social Development has been proposed. Throughout my term as Secretary-General I shall be addressing all these great issues. I bear them all in mind as, in the present report, I turn to the problems that the Council has specifically requested I consider: preventive diplomacy, peacemaking and peace-keeping—to which I have added a closely related concept, post-conflict peace-building.

I. The Changing Context

8. In the course of the past few years the immense ideological barrier that for decades gave rise to distrust and hostility—and the terrible tools of destruction that were their inseparable companions—has collapsed. Even as the issues between States north and south grow more acute, and call for attention at the highest levels of government, the improvement in relations between States east and west affords new possibilities, some already realized, to meet successfully threats to common security.

9. Authoritarian regimes have given way to more democratic forces and responsive Governments. The form, scope and intensity of these processes differ from Latin America to Africa to Europe to Asia, but they are sufficiently similar to indicate a global phenomenon. Parallel to these political changes, many States are seeking more open forms of economic policy, creating a world wide sense of dynamism and movement.

10. To the hundreds of millions who gained their independence in the surge of decolonization following the creation of the United

Nations, have been added millions more who have recently gained freedom. Once again new States are taking their seats in the General Assembly. Their arrival reconfirms the importance and indispensability of the sovereign State as the fundamental entity of the international community.

11. We have entered a time of global transition marked by uniquely contradictory trends. Regional and continental associations of States are evolving ways to deepen cooperation and ease some of the contentious characteristics of sovereign and nationalistic rivalries. National boundaries are blurred by advanced communications and global commerce, and by the decisions of States to yield some sovereign prerogatives to larger, common political associations. At the same time, however, fierce new assertions of nationalism and sovereignty spring up, and the cohesion of States is threatened by brutal ethnic, religious, social, cultural or linguistic strife. Social peace is challenged on the one hand by new assertions of discrimination and exclusion and, on the other, by acts of terrorism seeking to undermine evolution and change through democratic means.

12. The concept of peace is easy to grasp; that of international security is more complex, for a pattern of contradictions has arisen here as well. As major nuclear Powers have begun to negotiate arms reduction agreements, the proliferation of weapons of mass destruction threatens to increase and conventional arms continue to be amassed in many parts of the world. As racism becomes recognized for the destructive force it is and as apartheid is being dismantled, new racial tensions are rising and finding expression in violence. Technological advances are altering the nature and the expectation of life all over the globe. The revolution in communications has united the world in awareness, in aspiration and in greater solidarity against injustice. But progress also brings new risks for stability: ecological damage, disruption of family and community life, greater intrusion into the lives and rights of individuals.

13. This new dimension of insecurity must not be allowed to obscure the continuing and devastating problems of unchecked population growth, crushing debt burdens, barriers to trade, drugs and the growing disparity between rich and poor. Poverty, disease, famine, oppression and despair abound, joining to produce 17 million refugees, 20 million displaced persons and massive migrations of peoples within and beyond national borders. These are both sources and consequences of conflict that require the ceaseless attention and the highest priority in the efforts of the United Nations. A porous ozone shield could pose a greater threat to an exposed population than a hostile army. Drought and disease can decimate no less mercilessly than the weapons of war. So at this moment of renewed opportunity, the efforts of the Organization to build peace, stability and security must encompass matters beyond military threats in order to break the fetters of strife

and warfare that have characterized the past. But armed conflicts today, as they have throughout history, continue to bring fear and horror to humanity, requiring our urgent involvement to try to prevent, contain and bring them to an end.

14. Since the creation of the United Nations in 1945, over 100 major conflicts around the world have left some 20 million dead. The United Nations was rendered powerless to deal with many of these crises because of the vetoes—279 of them—cast in the Security Council, which were a vivid expression of the divisions of that period.

15. With the end of the cold war there have been no such vetoes since 31 May 1990, and demands on the United Nations have surged. Its security arm, once disabled by circumstances it was not created or equipped to control, has emerged as a central instrument for the prevention and resolution of conflicts and for the preservation of peace. Our aims must be:

To seek to identify at the earliest possible stage situations that could produce conflict, and to try through diplomacy to remove the sources of danger before violence results;

Where conflict erupts, to engage in peacemaking aimed at resolving the issues that have led to conflict;

Through peace-keeping, to work to preserve peace, however fragile, where fighting has been halted and to assist in implementing agreements achieved by the peacemakers;

To stand ready to assist in peace-building in its differing contexts: rebuilding the institutions and infrastructures of nations torn by civil war and strife; and building bonds of peaceful mutual benefit among nations formerly at war;

And in the largest sense, to address the deepest causes of conflict: economic despair, social injustice and political oppression. It is possible to discern an increasingly common moral perception that spans the world's nations and peoples, and which is finding expression in international laws, many owing their genesis to the work of this Organization.

16. This wider mission for the world Organization will demand the concerted attention and effort of individual States, of regional and non-governmental organizations and of all of the United Nations system, with each of the principal organs functioning in the balance and harmony that the Charter requires. The Security Council has been assigned by all Member States the primary responsibility for the maintenance of international peace and security under the Charter. In its broadest sense this responsibility must be shared by the General Assembly and by all the functional elements of the world Organization. Each has a special and indispensable role to play in an integrated approach to human security. The Secretary-General's contribution rests on the pattern of trust and cooperation established between him and the deliberative organs of the United Nations.

17. The foundation-stone of this work is and must remain the State. Respect for its fundamental sovereignty and integrity are crucial to any common international progress. The time of absolute and exclusive sovereignty, however, has passed; its theory was never matched by reality. It is the task of leaders of States today to understand this and to find a balance between the needs of good internal governance and the requirements of an ever more interdependent world. Commerce, communications and environmental matters transcend administrative borders; but inside those borders is where individuals carry out the first order of their economic, political and social lives. The United Nations has not closed its door. Yet if every ethnic, religious or linguistic group claimed statehood, there would be no limit to fragmentation, and peace, security and economic well-being for all would become ever more difficult to achieve.

18. One requirement for solutions to these problems lies in commitment to human rights with a special sensitivity to those of minorities, whether ethnic, religious, social or linguistic. The League of Nations provided a machinery for the international protection of minorities. The General Assembly soon will have before it a declaration on the rights of minorities. That instrument, together with the increasingly effective machinery of the United Nations dealing with human rights, should enhance the situation of minorities as well as the stability of States.

19. Globalism and nationalism need not be viewed as opposing trends, doomed to spur each other on to extremes of reaction. The healthy globalization of contemporary life requires in the first instance solid identities and fundamental freedoms. The sovereignty, territorial integrity and independence of States within the established international system, and the principle of self-determination for peoples, both of great value and importance, must not be permitted to work against each other in the period ahead. Respect for democratic principles at all levels of social existence is crucial: in communities, within States and within the community of States. Our constant duty should be to maintain the integrity of each while finding a balanced design for all.

II. Definitions

20. The terms preventive diplomacy, peacemaking and peace-keeping are integrally related and as used in this report are defined as follows:

Preventive diplomacy is action to prevent disputes from arising between parties, to prevent existing disputes from escalating into conflicts and to limit the spread of the latter when they occur.

Peacemaking is action to bring hostile parties to agreement, essentially through such peaceful means as those foreseen in Chapter VI of the Charter of the United Nations.

Peace-keeping is the deployment of a United Nations presence in the field, hitherto with the consent of all the parties concerned, normally involving United Nations military and/or police personnel and frequently civilians as well. Peace-keeping is a technique that expands the possibilities for both the prevention of conflict and the making of peace.

21. The present report in addition will address the critically related concept of post-conflict peace-building—action to identify and support structures which will tend to strengthen and solidify peace in order to avoid a relapse into conflict. Preventive diplomacy seeks to resolve disputes before violence breaks out; peacemaking and peace-keeping are required to halt conflicts and preserve peace once it is attained. If successful, they strengthen the opportunity for post-conflict peace-building, which can prevent the recurrence of violence among nations and peoples.

22. These four areas for action, taken together, and carried out with the backing of all Members, offer a coherent contribution towards securing peace in the spirit of the Charter. The United Nations has extensive experience not only in these fields, but in the wider realm of work for peace in which these four fields are set. Initiatives on decolonization, on the environment and sustainable development, on population, on the eradication of disease, on disarmament and on the growth of international law—these and many others have contributed immeasurably to the foundations for a peaceful world. The world has often been rent by conflict and plagued by massive human suffering and deprivation. Yet it would have been far more so without the continuing efforts of the United Nations. This wide experience must be taken into account in assessing the potential of the United Nations in maintaining international security not only in its traditional sense, but in the new dimensions presented by the era ahead.

III. Preventive Diplomacy

23. The most desirable and efficient employment of diplomacy is to ease tensions before they result in conflict—or, if conflict breaks out, to act swiftly to contain it and resolve its underlying causes. Preventive diplomacy may be performed by the Secretary-General personally or through senior staff or specialized agencies and programmes, by the Security Council or the General Assembly, and by regional organizations in cooperation with the United Nations. Preventive diplomacy requires measures to create confidence; it needs early warning based on information gathering and informal or formal fact-finding; it may also involve preventive deployment and, in some situations, demilitarized zones.

Measures to Build Confidence

24. Mutual confidence and good faith are essential to reducing the likelihood of conflict between States. Many such measures are available to Governments that have the will to employ them. Systematic exchange of military missions, formation of regional or subregional risk reduction centres, arrangements for the free flow of information, including the monitoring of regional arms agreements, are examples. I ask all regional organizations to consider what further confidence-building measures might be applied in their areas and to inform the United Nations of the results. I will undertake periodic consultations on confidence-building measures with parties to potential, current or past disputes and with regional organizations, offering such advisory assistance as the Secretariat can provide.

Fact-Finding

25. Preventive steps must be based upon timely and accurate knowledge of the facts. Beyond this, an understanding of developments and global trends, based on sound analysis, is required. And the willingness to take appropriate preventive action is essential. Given the economic and social roots of many potential conflicts, the information needed by the United Nations now must encompass economic and social trends as well as political developments that may lead to dangerous tensions . . .

   In addition to collecting information on which a decision for further action can be taken, such a mission can in some instances help to defuse a dispute by its presence, indicating to the parties that the Organization, and in particular the Security Council, is actively seized of the matter as a present or potential threat to international security . . .

Early Warning

26. In recent years the United Nations system has been developing a valuable network of early warning systems concerning environmental threats, the risk of nuclear accident, natural disasters, mass movements of populations, the threat of famine and the spread of disease. There is a need, however, to strengthen arrangements in such a manner that information from these sources can be synthesized with political indicators to assess whether a threat to peace exists and to analyse what action might be taken by the United Nations to alleviate it. This is a process that will continue to require the close cooperation of the various specialized agencies and functional offices of the United Nations. The analyses and recommendations for preventive action that emerge will be made available by me, as appropriate, to the Security Council and other United Nations organs. I recommend in addition that the Security Council invite a reinvigorated and restructured

Economic and Social Council to provide reports, in accordance with
Article 65 of the Charter, on those economic and social developments
that may, unless mitigated, threaten international peace and
security . . .

Preventive Deployment

28. United Nations operations in areas of crisis have generally been
established after conflict has occurred. The time has come to plan for
circumstances warranting preventive deployment, which could take
place in a variety of instances and ways. For example, in conditions of
national crisis there could be preventive deployment at the request of
the Government or all parties concerned, or with their consent; in inter-
State disputes such deployment could take place when two countries
feel that a United Nations presence on both sides of their border can
discourage hostilities; furthermore, preventive deployment could take
place when a country feels threatened and requests the deployment of
an appropriate United Nations presence along its side of the border
alone. In each situation, the mandate and composition of the United
Nations presence would need to be carefully devised and be clear to all.

29. In conditions of crisis within a country, when the Government
requests or all parties consent, preventive deployment could help in a
number of ways to alleviate suffering and to limit or control violence.
Humanitarian assistance, impartially provided, could be of critical
importance; assistance in maintaining security, whether through
military, police or civilian personnel, could save lives and develop
conditions of safety in which negotiations can be held; the United
Nations could also help in conciliation efforts if this should be the wish
of the parties. In certain circumstances, the United Nations may well
need to draw upon the specialized skills and resources of various parts
of the United Nations system; such operations may also on occasion
require the participation of non-governmental organizations.

30. In these situations of internal crisis the United Nations will
need to respect the sovereignty of the State; to do otherwise would not
be in accordance with the understanding of Member States in accepting
the principles of the Charter. The Organization must remain mindful of
the carefully negotiated balance of the guiding principles annexed to
General Assembly resolution 46/182 of 19 December 1991. Those
guidelines stressed, inter alia, that humanitarian assistance must be
provided in accordance with the principles of humanity, neutrality and
impartiality; that the sovereignty, territorial integrity and national unity
of States must be fully respected in accordance with the Charter of the
United Nations; and that, in this context, humanitarian assistance
should be provided with the consent of the affected country and, in
principle, on the basis of an appeal by that country. The guidelines also
stressed the responsibility of States to take care of the victims of
emergencies occurring on their territory and the need for access to

those requiring humanitarian assistance. In the light of these guidelines, a Government's request for United Nations involvement, or consent to it, would not be an infringement of that State's sovereignty . . .

31. In inter-State disputes, when both parties agree, I recommend that if the Security Council concludes that the likelihood of hostilities between neighbouring countries could be removed by the preventive deployment of a United Nations presence on the territory of each State, such action should be taken. The nature of the tasks to be performed would determine the composition of the United Nations presence.

32. In cases where one nation fears a cross-border attack, if the Security Council concludes that a United Nations presence on one side of the border, with the consent only of the requesting country, would serve to deter conflict, I recommend that preventive deployment take place. Here again, the specific nature of the situation would determine the mandate and the personnel required to fulfil it.

Demilitarized Zones

33. In the past, demilitarized zones have been established by agreement of the parties at the conclusion of a conflict. In addition to the deployment of United Nations personnel in such zones as part of peace-keeping operations, consideration should now be given to the usefulness of such zones as a form of preventive deployment, on both sides of a border, with the agreement of the two parties, as a means of separating potential belligerents, or on one side of the line, at the request of one party, for the purpose of removing any pretext for attack. Demilitarized zones would serve as symbols of the international community's concern that conflict be prevented.

IV. Peacemaking

34. Between the tasks of seeking to prevent conflict and keeping the peace lies the responsibility to try to bring hostile parties to agreement by peaceful means. Chapter VI of the Charter sets forth a comprehensive list of such means for the resolution of conflict. These have been amplified in various declarations adopted by the General Assembly, including the Manila Declaration of 1982 on the Peaceful Settlement of International Disputes[2] and the 1988 Declaration on the Prevention and Removal of Disputes and Situations Which May Threaten International Peace and Security and on the Role of the United Nations in this Field.[3] They have also been the subject of various resolutions of the General Assembly, including resolution 44/21 of 15 November 1989 on enhancing international peace, security and international cooperation in all its aspects in accordance with the Charter of the United Nations. The United Nations has had wide

experience in the application of these peaceful means. If conflicts have gone unresolved, it is not because techniques for peaceful settlement were unknown or inadequate. The fault lies first in the lack of political will of parties to seek a solution to their differences through such means as are suggested in Chapter VI of the Charter, and second, in the lack of leverage at the disposal of a third party if this is the procedure chosen. The indifference of the international community to a problem, or the marginalization of it, can also thwart the possibilities of solution. We must look primarily to these areas if we hope to enhance the capacity of the Organization for achieving peaceful settlements.

35. The present determination in the Security Council to resolve international disputes in the manner foreseen in the Charter has opened the way for a more active Council role. With greater unity has come leverage and persuasive power to lead hostile parties towards negotiations. I urge the Council to take full advantage of the provisions of the Charter under which it may recommend appropriate procedures or methods for dispute settlement and, if all the parties to a dispute so request, make recommendations to the parties for a pacific settlement of the dispute.

36. The General Assembly, like the Security Council and the Secretary-General, also has an important role assigned to it under the Charter for the maintenance of international peace and security. As a universal forum, its capacity to consider and recommend appropriate action must be recognized. To that end it is essential to promote its utilization by all Member States so as to bring greater influence to bear in pre-empting or containing situations which are likely to threaten international peace and security.

37. Mediation and negotiation can be undertaken by an individual designated by the Security Council, by the General Assembly or by the Secretary-General. There is a long history of the utilization by the United Nations of distinguished statesmen to facilitate the processes of peace. They can bring a personal prestige that, in addition to their experience, can encourage the parties to enter serious negotiations. There is a wide willingness to serve in this capacity, from which I shall continue to benefit as the need arises. Frequently it is the Secretary-General himself who undertakes the task. While the mediator's effectiveness is enhanced by strong and evident support from the Council, the General Assembly and the relevant Member States acting in their national capacity, the good offices of the Secretary-General may at times be employed most effectively when conducted independently of the deliberative bodies. Close and continuous consultation between the Secretary-General and the Security Council is, however, essential to ensure full awareness of how the Council's influence can best be applied and to develop a common strategy for the peaceful settlement of specific disputes.

The World Court

38. The docket of the International Court of Justice has grown fuller but it remains an under-used resource for the peaceful adjudication of disputes. Greater reliance on the Court would be an important contribution to United Nations peacemaking . . .

Amelioration through Assistance

40. Peacemaking is at times facilitated by international action to ameliorate circumstances that have contributed to the dispute or conflict. If, for instance, assistance to displaced persons within a society is essential to a solution, then the United Nations should be able to draw upon the resources of all agencies and programmes concerned. At present, there is no adequate mechanism in the United Nations through which the Security Council, the General Assembly or the Secretary-General can mobilize the resources needed for such positive leverage and engage the collective efforts of the United Nations system for the peaceful resolution of a conflict. I have raised this concept in the Administrative Committee on Coordination, which brings together the executive heads of United Nations agencies and programmes; we are exploring methods by which the inter-agency system can improve its contribution to the peaceful resolution of disputes.

Sanctions and Special Economic Problems

41. In circumstances when peacemaking requires the imposition of sanctions under Article 41 of the Charter, it is important that States confronted with special economic problems not only have the right to consult the Security Council regarding such problems, as Article 50 provides, but also have a realistic possibility of having their difficulties addressed. I recommend that the Security Council devise a set of measures involving the financial institutions and other components of the United Nations system that can be put in place to insulate States from such difficulties. Such measures would be a matter of equity and a means of encouraging States to cooperate with decisions of the Council.

Use of Military Force

42. It is the essence of the concept of collective security as contained in the Charter that if peaceful means fail, the measures provided in Chapter VII should be used, on the decision of the Security Council, to maintain or restore international peace and security in the face of a "threat to the peace, breach of the peace, or act of aggression." The Security Council has not so far made use of the most coercive of these measures—the action by military force foreseen in Article 42. In the situation between Iraq and Kuwait, the Council chose to authorize Member States to take measures on its behalf. The Charter, however,

provides a detailed approach which now merits the attention of all Member States.

43. Under Article 42 of the Charter, the Security Council has the authority to take military action to maintain or restore international peace and security. While such action should only be taken when all peaceful means have failed, the option of taking it is essential to the credibility of the United Nations as a guarantor of international security. This will require bringing into being, through negotiations, the special agreements foreseen in Article 43 of the Charter, whereby Member States undertake to make armed forces, assistance and facilities available to the Security Council for the purposes stated in Article 42, not only on an ad hoc basis but on a permanent basis. Under the political circumstances that now exist for the first time since the Charter was adopted, the long-standing obstacles to the conclusion of such special agreements should no longer prevail. The ready availability of armed forces on call could serve, in itself, as a means of deterring breaches of the peace since a potential aggressor would know that the Council had at its disposal a means of response. Forces under Article 43 may perhaps never be sufficiently large or well enough equipped to deal with a threat from a major army equipped with sophisticated weapons. They would be useful, however, in meeting any threat posed by a military force of a lesser order. I recommend that the Security Council initiate negotiations in accordance with Article 43, supported by the Military Staff Committee, which may be augmented if necessary by others in accordance with Article 47, paragraph 2, of the Charter. It is my view that the role of the Military Staff Committee should be seen in the context of Chapter VII, and not that of the planning or conduct of peace-keeping operations.

Peace-Enforcement Units

44. The mission of forces under Article 43 would be to respond to outright aggression, imminent or actual. Such forces are not likely to be available for some time to come. Cease-fires have often been agreed to but not complied with, and the United Nations has sometimes been called upon to send forces to restore and maintain the cease-fire. This task can on occasion exceed the mission of peace-keeping forces and the expectations of peace-keeping force contributors. I recommend that the Council consider the utilization of peace-enforcement units in clearly defined circumstances and with their terms of reference specified in advance. Such units from Member States would be available on call and would consist of troops that have volunteered for such service. They would have to be more heavily armed than peace-keeping forces and would need to undergo extensive preparatory training within their national forces. Deployment and operation of such forces would be under the authorization of the Security Council and would, as in the case of peace-keeping forces, be under the command of

the Secretary-General. I consider such peace-enforcement units to be warranted as a provisional measure under Article 40 of the Charter. Such peace-enforcement units should not be confused with the forces that may eventually be constituted under Article 43 to deal with acts of aggression or with the military personnel which Governments may agree to keep on stand-by for possible contribution to peace-keeping operations.

45. Just as diplomacy will continue across the span of all the activities dealt with in the present report, so there may not be a dividing line between peacemaking and peace-keeping. Peacemaking is often a prelude to peace-keeping—just as the deployment of a United Nations presence in the field may expand possibilities for the prevention of conflict, facilitate the work of peacemaking and in many cases serve as a prerequisite for peace-building.

V. Peace-Keeping

46. Peace-keeping can rightly be called the invention of the United Nations. It has brought a degree of stability to numerous areas of tension around the world.

Increasing Demands

47. Thirteen peace-keeping operations were established between the years 1945 and 1987; 13 others since then. An estimated 528,000 military, police and civilian personnel had served under the flag of the United Nations until January 1992. Over 800 of them from 43 countries have died in the service of the Organization. The costs of these operations have aggregated some $8.3 billion till 1992. The unpaid arrears towards them stand at over $800 million, which represents a debt owed by the Organization to the troop-contributing countries. Peace-keeping operations approved at present are estimated to cost close to $3 billion in the current 12-month period, while patterns of payment are unacceptably slow. Against this, global defence expenditures at the end of the last decade had approached $1 trillion a year, or $2 million per minute.

48. The contrast between the costs of United Nations peace-keeping and the costs of the alternative, war—between the demands of the Organization and the means provided to meet them—would be farcical were the consequences not so damaging to global stability and to the credibility of the Organization. At a time when nations and peoples increasingly are looking to the United Nations for assistance in keeping the peace—and holding it responsible when this cannot be so—fundamental decisions must be taken to enhance the capacity of the Organization in this innovative and productive exercise of its function. I am conscious that the present volume and unpredictability

of peace-keeping assessments poses real problems for some Member States. For this reason, I strongly support proposals in some Member States for their peace-keeping contributions to be financed from defence, rather than foreign affairs, budgets and I recommend such action to others. I urge the General Assembly to encourage this approach.

49. The demands on the United Nations for peace-keeping, and peace-building, operations will in the coming years continue to challenge the capacity, the political and financial will and the creativity of the Secretariat and Member States. Like the Security Council, I welcome the increase and broadening of the tasks of peace-keeping operations.

New Departures in Peace-Keeping

50. The nature of peace-keeping operations has evolved rapidly in recent years. The established principles and practices of peace-keeping have responded flexibly to new demands of recent years, and the basic conditions for success remain unchanged: a clear and practicable mandate; the cooperation of the parties in implementing that mandate; the continuing support of the Security Council; the readiness of Member States to contribute the military, police and civilian personnel, including specialists, required; effective United Nations command at Headquarters and in the field; and adequate financial and logistic support. As the international climate has changed and peace-keeping operations are increasingly fielded to help implement settlements that have been negotiated by peacemakers, a new array of demands and problems has emerged regarding logistics, equipment, personnel and finance, all of which could be corrected if Member States so wished and were ready to make the necessary resources available.

Personnel

51. Member States are keen to participate in peace-keeping operations. Military observers and infantry are invariably available in the required numbers, but logistic units present a greater problem, as few armies can afford to spare such units for an extended period. Member States were requested in 1990 to state what military personnel they were in principle prepared to make available; few replied. I reiterate the request to all Member States to reply frankly and promptly. Stand-by arrangements should be confirmed, as appropriate, through exchanges of letters between the Secretariat and Member States concerning the kind and number of skilled personnel they will be prepared to offer the United Nations as the needs of new operations arise.

52. Increasingly, peace-keeping requires that civilian political officers, human rights monitors, electoral officials, refugee and humanitarian aid specialists and police play as central a role as the

military. Police personnel have proved increasingly difficult to obtain in the numbers required. I recommend that arrangements be reviewed and improved for training peace-keeping personnel—civilian, police, or military—using the varied capabilities of Member State Governments, of non-governmental organizations and the facilities of the Secretariat. As efforts go forward to include additional States as contributors, some States with considerable potential should focus on language training for police contingents which may serve with the Organization. As for the United Nations itself, special personnel procedures, including incentives, should be instituted to permit the rapid transfer of Secretariat staff members to service with peace-keeping operations. The strength and capability of military staff serving in the Secretariat should be augmented to meet new and heavier requirements.

Logistics

53. Not all Governments can provide their battalions with the equipment they need for service abroad. While some equipment is provided by troop-contributing countries, a great deal has to come from the United Nations, including equipment to fill gaps in under-equipped national units. The United Nations has no standing stock of such equipment. Orders must be placed with manufacturers, which creates a number of difficulties. A pre-positioned stock of basic peace-keeping equipment should be established, so that at least some vehicles, communications equipment, generators, etc., would be immediately available at the start of an operation. Alternatively, Governments should commit themselves to keeping certain equipment, specified by the Secretary-General, on stand-by for immediate sale, loan or donation to the United Nations when required.

54. Member States in a position to do so should make air- and sea-lift capacity available to the United Nations free of cost or at lower than commercial rates, as was the practice until recently.

VI. Post-Conflict Peace-Building

55. Peacemaking and peace-keeping operations, to be truly successful, must come to include comprehensive efforts to identify and support structures which will tend to consolidate peace and advance a sense of confidence and well-being among people. Through agreements ending civil strife, these may include disarming the previously warring parties and the restoration of order, the custody and possible destruction of weapons, repatriating refugees, advisory and training support for security personnel, monitoring elections, advancing efforts to protect human rights, reforming or strengthening governmental institutions and promoting formal and informal processes of political participation.

56. In the aftermath of international war, post-conflict peace-building may take the form of concrete cooperative projects which link two or more countries in a mutually beneficial undertaking that can not only contribute to economic and social development but also enhance the confidence that is so fundamental to peace. I have in mind, for example, projects that bring States together to develop agriculture, improve transportation or utilize resources such as water or electricity that they need to share, or joint programmes through which barriers between nations are brought down by means of freer travel, cultural exchanges and mutually beneficial youth and educational projects. Reducing hostile perceptions through educational exchanges and curriculum reform may be essential to forestall a re-emergence of cultural and national tensions which could spark renewed hostilities.

57. In surveying the range of efforts for peace, the concept of peace-building as the construction of a new environment should be viewed as the counterpart of preventive diplomacy, which seeks to avoid the breakdown of peaceful conditions. When conflict breaks out, mutually reinforcing efforts at peacemaking and peace-keeping come into play. Once these have achieved their objectives, only sustained, cooperative work to deal with underlying economic, social, cultural and humanitarian problems can place an achieved peace on a durable foundation. Preventive diplomacy is to avoid a crisis; post-conflict peace-building is to prevent a recurrence.

58. Increasingly it is evident that peace-building after civil or international strife must address the serious problem of land mines, many tens of millions of which remain scattered in present or former combat zones. De-mining should be emphasized in the terms of reference of peace-keeping operations and is crucially important in the restoration of activity when peace-building is under way: agriculture cannot be revived without de-mining and the restoration of transport may require the laying of hard surface roads to prevent re-mining. In such instances, the link becomes evident between peace-keeping and peace-building. Just as demilitarized zones may serve the cause of preventive diplomacy and preventive deployment to avoid conflict, so may demilitarization assist in keeping the peace or in post-conflict peace-building, as a measure for heightening the sense of security and encouraging the parties to turn their energies to the work of peaceful restoration of their societies.

59. There is a new requirement for technical assistance which the United Nations has an obligation to develop and provide when requested: support for the transformation of deficient national structures and capabilities, and for the strengthening of new democratic institutions. The authority of the United Nations system to act in this field would rest on the consensus that social peace is as important as strategic or political peace. There is an obvious connection between

democratic practices—such as the rule of law and transparency in decision-making—and the achievement of true peace and security in any new and stable political order. These elements of good governance need to be promoted at all levels of international and national political communities.

VII. Cooperation with Regional Arrangements and Organizations

60. The Covenant of the League of Nations, in its Article 21, noted the validity of regional understandings for securing the maintenance of peace. The Charter devotes Chapter VIII to regional arrangements or agencies for dealing with such matters relating to the maintenance of international peace and security as are appropriate for regional action and consistent with the Purposes and Principles of the United Nations. The cold war impaired the proper use of Chapter VIII and indeed, in that era, regional arrangements worked on occasion against resolving disputes in the manner foreseen in the Charter.

61. The Charter deliberately provides no precise definition of regional arrangements and agencies, thus allowing useful flexibility for undertakings by a group of States to deal with a matter appropriate for regional action which also could contribute to the maintenance of international peace and security. Such associations or entities could include treaty-based organizations, whether created before or after the founding of the United Nations, regional organizations for mutual security and defence, organizations for general regional development or for cooperation on a particular economic topic or function, and groups created to deal with a specific political, economic or social issue of current concern.

62. In this regard, the United Nations has recently encouraged a rich variety of complementary efforts. Just as no two regions or situations are the same, so the design of cooperative work and its division of labour must adapt to the realities of each case with flexibility and creativity. In Africa, three different regional groups—the Organization of African Unity, the League of Arab States and the Organization of the Islamic Conference—joined efforts with the United Nations regarding Somalia. In the Asian context, the Association of South-East Asian Nations and individual States from several regions were brought together with the parties to the Cambodian conflict at an international conference in Paris, to work with the United Nations. For El Salvador, a unique arrangement—"The Friends of the Secretary-General"—contributed to agreements reached through the mediation of the Secretary-General. The end of the war in Nicaragua involved a highly complex effort which was initiated by leaders of the region and conducted by individual States, groups of States and the Organization

of American States. Efforts undertaken by the European Community and its member States, with the support of States participating in the Conference on Security and Cooperation in Europe, have been of central importance in dealing with the crisis in the Balkans and neighbouring areas.

63. In the past, regional arrangements often were created because of the absence of a universal system for collective security; thus their activities could on occasion work at cross-purposes with the sense of solidarity required for the effectiveness of the world Organization. But in this new era of opportunity, regional arrangements or agencies can render great service if their activities are undertaken in a manner consistent with the Purposes and Principles of the Charter, and if their relationship with the United Nations, and particularly the Security Council, is governed by Chapter VIII.

64. It is not the purpose of the present report to set forth any formal pattern of relationship between regional organizations and the United Nations, or to call for any specific division of labour. What is clear, however, is that regional arrangements or agencies in many cases possess a potential that should be utilized in serving the functions covered in this report: preventive diplomacy, peace-keeping, peacemaking and post-conflict peace-building. Under the Charter, the Security Council has and will continue to have primary responsibility for maintaining international peace and security, but regional action as a matter of decentralization, delegation and cooperation with United Nations efforts could not only lighten the burden of the Council but also contribute to a deeper sense of participation, consensus and democratization in international affairs.

65. Regional arrangements and agencies have not in recent decades been considered in this light, even when originally designed in part for a role in maintaining or restoring peace within their regions of the world. Today a new sense exists that they have contributions to make. Consultations between the United Nations and regional arrangements or agencies could do much to build international consensus on the nature of a problem and the measures required to address it. Regional organizations participating in complementary efforts with the United Nations in joint undertakings would encourage States outside the region to act supportively. And should the Security Council choose specifically to authorize a regional arrangement or organization to take the lead in addressing a crisis within its region, it could serve to lend the weight of the United Nations to the validity of the regional effort. Carried forward in the spirit of the Charter, and as envisioned in Chapter VIII, the approach outlined here could strengthen a general sense that democratization is being encouraged at all levels in the task of maintaining international peace and security, it being essential to continue to recognize that the primary responsibility will continue to reside in the Security Council.

VIII. Safety of Personnel

66. When United Nations personnel are deployed in conditions of strife, whether for preventive diplomacy, peacemaking, peace-keeping, peace-building or humanitarian purposes, the need arises to ensure their safety. There has been an unconscionable increase in the number of fatalities. Following the conclusion of a cease-fire and in order to prevent further outbreaks of violence, United Nations guards were called upon to assist in volatile conditions in Iraq. Their presence afforded a measure of security to United Nations personnel and supplies and, in addition, introduced an element of reassurance and stability that helped to prevent renewed conflict. Depending upon the nature of the situation, different configurations and compositions of security deployments will need to be considered. As the variety and scale of threat widens, innovative measures will be required to deal with the dangers facing United Nations personnel.

67. Experience has demonstrated that the presence of a United Nations operation has not always been sufficient to deter hostile action. Duty in areas of danger can never be risk-free; United Nations personnel must expect to go in harm's way at times. The courage, commitment and idealism shown by United Nations personnel should be respected by the entire international community. These men and women deserve to be properly recognized and rewarded for the perilous tasks they undertake. Their interests and those of their families must be given due regard and protected.

68. Given the pressing need to afford adequate protection to United Nations personnel engaged in life-endangering circumstances, I recommend that the Security Council, unless it elects immediately to withdraw the United Nations presence in order to preserve the credibility of the Organization, gravely consider what action should be taken towards those who put United Nations personnel in danger. Before deployment takes place, the Council should keep open the option of considering in advance collective measures, possibly including those under Chapter VII when a threat to international peace and security is also involved, to come into effect should the purpose of the United Nations operation systematically be frustrated and hostilities occur.

IX. Financing

69. A chasm has developed between the tasks entrusted to this Organization and the financial means provided to it. The truth of the matter is that our vision cannot really extend to the prospect opening before us as long as our financing remains myopic. There are two main areas of concern: the ability of the Organization to function over the longer term; and immediate requirements to respond to a crisis.

70. To remedy the financial situation of the United Nations in all its aspects, my distinguished predecessor repeatedly drew the attention of Member States to the increasingly impossible situation that has arisen and, during the forty-sixth session of the General Assembly, made a number of proposals. Those proposals which remain before the Assembly, and with which I am in broad agreement, are the following:

Proposal one: This suggested the adoption of a set of measures to deal with the cash flow problems caused by the exceptionally high level of unpaid contributions as well as with the problem of inadequate working capital reserves: (a) Charging interest on the amounts of assessed contributions that are not paid on time; (b) Suspending certain financial regulations of the United Nations to permit the retention of budgetary surpluses; (c) Increasing the Working Capital Fund to a level of $250 million and endorsing the principle that the level of the Fund should be approximately 25 per cent of the annual assessment under the regular budget; (d) Establishment of a temporary Peace-keeping Reserve Fund, at a level of $50 million, to meet initial expenses of peace-keeping operations pending receipt of assessed contributions; (e) Authorization to the Secretary-General to borrow commercially, should other sources of cash be inadequate.

Proposal two: This suggested the creation of a Humanitarian Revolving Fund in the order of $50 million, to be used in emergency humanitarian situations. The proposal has since been implemented.

Proposal three: This suggested the establishment of a United Nations Peace Endowment Fund, with an initial target of $1 billion. The Fund would be created by a combination of assessed and voluntary contributions, with the latter being sought from Governments, the private sector as well as individuals. Once the Fund reached its target level, the proceeds from the investment of its principal would be used to finance the initial costs of authorized peace-keeping operations, other conflict resolution measures and related activities.

71. In addition to these proposals, others have been added in recent months in the course of public discussion. These ideas include: a levy on arms sales that could be related to maintaining an Arms Register by the United Nations; a levy on international air travel, which is dependent on the maintenance of peace; authorization for the United Nations to borrow from the World Bank and the International Monetary Fund—for peace and development are interdependent; general tax exemption for contributions made to the United Nations by foundations, businesses and individuals; and changes in the formula for calculating the scale of assessments for peace-keeping operations.

72. As such ideas are debated, a stark fact remains: the financial foundations of the Organization daily grow weaker, debilitating its political will and practical capacity to undertake new and essential activities. This state of affairs must not continue. Whatever decisions

are taken on financing the Organization, there is one inescapable necessity: Member States must pay their assessed contributions in full and on time. Failure to do so puts them in breach of their obligations under the Charter.

73. In these circumstances and on the assumption that Member States will be ready to finance operations for peace in a manner commensurate with their present, and welcome, readiness to establish them, I recommend the following:

(a) Immediate establishment of a revolving peace-keeping reserve fund of $50 million; (b) Agreement that one third of the estimated cost of each new peace-keeping operation be appropriated by the General Assembly as soon as the Security Council decides to establish the operation; this would give the Secretary-General the necessary commitment authority and assure an adequate cash flow; the balance of the costs would be appropriated after the General Assembly approved the operation's budget; (c) Acknowledgement by Member States that, under exceptional circumstances, political and operational considerations may make it necessary for the Secretary-General to employ his authority to place contracts without competitive bidding.

74. Member States wish the Organization to be managed with the utmost efficiency and care. I am in full accord. I have taken important steps to streamline the Secretariat in order to avoid duplication and overlap while increasing its productivity. Additional changes and improvements will take place. As regards the United Nations system more widely, I continue to review the situation in consultation with my colleagues in the Administrative Committee on Coordination. The question of assuring financial security to the Organization over the long term is of such importance and complexity that public awareness and support must be heightened. I have therefore asked a select group of qualified persons of high international repute to examine this entire subject and to report to me. I intend to present their advice, together with my comments, for the consideration of the General Assembly, in full recognition of the special responsibility that the Assembly has, under the Charter, for financial and budgetary matters.

X. An Agenda for Peace

75. The nations and peoples of the United Nations are fortunate in a way that those of the League of Nations were not. We have been given a second chance to create the world of our Charter that they were denied. With the cold war ended we have drawn back from the brink of a confrontation that threatened the world and, too often, paralysed our Organization.

76. Even as we celebrate our restored possibilities, there is a need to ensure that the lessons of the past four decades are learned and that

the errors, or variations of them, are not repeated. For there may not be a third opportunity for our planet which, now for different reasons, remains endangered.

77. The tasks ahead must engage the energy and attention of all components of the United Nations system—the General Assembly and other principal organs, the agencies and programmes. Each has, in a balanced scheme of things, a role and a responsibility.

78. Never again must the Security Council lose the collegiality that is essential to its proper functioning, an attribute that it has gained after such trial. A genuine sense of consensus deriving from shared interests must govern its work, not the threat of the veto or the power of any group of nations. And it follows that agreement among the permanent members must have the deeper support of the other members of the Council, and the membership more widely, if the Council's decisions are to be effective and endure.

79. The Summit Meeting of the Security Council of 31 January 1992 provided a unique forum for exchanging views and strengthening cooperation. I recommend that the Heads of State and Government of the members of the Council meet in alternate years, just before the general debate commences in the General Assembly. Such sessions would permit exchanges on the challenges and dangers of the moment and stimulate ideas on how the United Nations may best serve to steer change into peaceful courses. I propose in addition that the Security Council continue to meet at the Foreign Minister level, as it has effectively done in recent years, whenever the situation warrants such meetings.

80. Power brings special responsibilities, and temptations. The powerful must resist the dual but opposite calls of unilateralism and isolationism if the United Nations is to succeed. For just as unilateralism at the global or regional level can shake the confidence of others, so can isolationism, whether it results from political choice or constitutional circumstance, enfeeble the global undertaking. Peace at home and the urgency of rebuilding and strengthening our individual societies necessitates peace abroad and cooperation among nations. The endeavours of the United Nations will require the fullest engagement of all of its Members, large and small, if the present renewed opportunity is to be seized.

81. Democracy within nations requires respect for human rights and fundamental freedoms, as set forth in the Charter. It requires as well a deeper understanding and respect for the rights of minorities and respect for the needs of the more vulnerable groups of society, especially women and children. This is not only a political matter. The social stability needed for productive growth is nurtured by conditions in which people can readily express their will. For this, strong domestic institutions of participation are essential. Promoting such institutions means promoting the empowerment of the unorganized, the poor, the

marginalized. To this end, the focus of the United Nations should be on the "field," the locations where economic, social and political decisions take effect. In furtherance of this I am taking steps to rationalize and in certain cases integrate the various programmes and agencies of the United Nations within specific countries. The senior United Nations official in each country should be prepared to serve, when needed, and with the consent of the host authorities, as my Representative on matters of particular concern.

82. Democracy within the family of nations means the application of its principles within the world Organization itself. This requires the fullest consultation, participation and engagement of all States, large and small, in the work of the Organization. All organs of the United Nations must be accorded, and play, their full and proper role so that the trust of all nations and peoples will be retained and deserved. The principles of the Charter must be applied consistently, not selectively, for if the perception should be of the latter, trust will wane and with it the moral authority which is the greatest and most unique quality of that instrument. Democracy at all levels is essential to attain peace for a new era of prosperity and justice.

83. Trust also requires a sense of confidence that the world Organization will react swiftly, surely and impartially and that it will not be debilitated by political opportunism or by administrative or financial inadequacy. This presupposes a strong, efficient and independent international civil service whose integrity is beyond question and an assured financial basis that lifts the Organization, once and for all, out of its present mendicancy.

84. Just as it is vital that each of the organs of the United Nations employ its capabilities in the balanced and harmonious fashion envisioned in the Charter, peace in the largest sense cannot be accomplished by the United Nations system or by Governments alone. Non-governmental organizations, academic institutions, parliamentarians, business and professional communities, the media and the public at large must all be involved. This will strengthen the world Organization's ability to reflect the concerns and interests of its widest constituency, and those who become more involved can carry the word of United Nations initiatives and build a deeper understanding of its work.

85. Reform is a continuing process, and improvement can have no limit. Yet there is an expectation, which I wish to see fulfilled, that the present phase in the renewal of this Organization should be complete by 1995, its Fiftieth Anniversary. The pace set must therefore be increased if the United Nations is to keep ahead of the acceleration of history that characterizes this age. We must be guided not by precedents alone, however wise these may be, but by the needs of the future and by the shape and content that we wish to give it.

86. I am committed to broad dialogue between the Member States

and the Secretary-General. And I am committed to fostering a full and open interplay between all institutions and elements of the Organization so that the Charter's objectives may not only be better served, but that this Organization may emerge as greater than the sum of its parts. The United Nations was created with a great and courageous vision. Now is the time, for its nations and peoples, and the men and women who serve it, to seize the moment for the sake of the future.

Notes:

1. See S/23500, statement by the President of the Council, section entitled "Peacemaking and peace-keeping."
2. General Assembly resolution 37/10, annex.
3. General Assembly resolution 43/51, annex.

Reference:

An Agenda for Peace, Preventive Diplomacy, Peacemaking and Peace-keeping. Report of the Secretary-General, pursuant to the statement adopted by the Summit Meeting of the Security Council on 31 January 1992 (17 June 1992). Available at http://www.un.org/Docs/SG/agpeace (accessed 20 May 2004).

William J. Clinton, "Address to the Nation" (24 March 1999)

President Clinton's decision to intervene to prevent further ethnic cleansing in Kosovo marked the end of a long debate within the U.S. government. Many, as evidenced by candidate George W. Bush during the 2000 presidential campaign, believed the United States had no role in such nation-building activities, while a substantial portion of the Clinton administration, probably most vocally shown by Secretary of State Madeleine K. Albright, argued that this is a key role for the country as it seeks to promote its democratic values overseas, hence reinforcing U.S. global leadership.

The Saga of Kosovo

My fellow Americans, today our Armed Forces joined our NATO allies in air strikes against Serbian forces responsible for the brutality in Kosovo. We have acted with resolve for several reasons.

We act to protect thousands of innocent people in Kosovo from a mounting military offensive. We act to prevent a wider war; to diffuse a powder keg at the heart of Europe that has exploded twice before in this century with catastrophic results. And we act to stand united with our allies for peace. By acting now we are upholding our values, protecting our interests and advancing the cause of peace.

Tonight I want to speak to you about the tragedy in Kosovo and why it matters to America that we work with our allies to end it. First, let me explain what it is we are responding to. Kosovo is a province of Serbia, in the middle of southeastern Europe, about 160 miles east of Italy. That's less than the distance between Washington and New York, and only about 70 miles north of Greece. Its people are mostly ethnic Albanian and mostly Muslim.

In 1989, Serbia's leader, Slobodan Milosevic, the same leader who started the wars in Bosnia and Croatia, and moved against Slovenia in the last decade, stripped Kosovo of the constitutional autonomy its people enjoyed; thus denying them their right to speak their language, run their schools, shape their daily lives. For years, Kosovars struggled peacefully to get their rights back. When President Milosevic sent his troops and police to crush them, the struggle grew violent.

Last fall our diplomacy, backed by the threat of force from our NATO Alliance, stopped the fighting for a while, and rescued tens of thousands of people from freezing and starvation in the hills where they had fled to save their lives. And last month, with out allies and Russia, we proposed a peace agreement to end the fighting for good. The Kosovar leaders signed that agreement last week. Even though it does not give them all they want, even though their people were still being savaged, they saw that a just peace is better than a long and unwinnable war.

The Serbian leaders, on the other hand, refused even to discuss key elements of the peace agreement. As the Kosovars were saying "yes" to peace, Serbia stationed 40,000 troops in and around Kosovo in preparation for a major offensive—and in clear violation of the commitments they had made.

Now, they've started moving from village to village, shelling civilians and torching their houses. We've seen innocent people taken from their homes, forced to kneel in the dirt and sprayed with bullets; Kosovar men dragged from their families, fathers and sons together, lined up and shot in cold blood. This is not war in the traditional sense. It is an attack by tanks and artillery on a largely defenseless people, whose leaders already have agreed to peace.

Ending this tragedy is a moral imperative. It is also important to America's national interest. Take a look at this map. Kosovo is a small place, but it sits on a major fault line between Europe, Asia and the Middle East, at the meeting place of Islam and both the Western and Orthodox branches of Christianity. To the south are our allies, Greece and Turkey; to the north, our new democratic allies in Central Europe. And all around Kosovo there are other small countries, struggling with their own economic and political challenges—countries that could be overwhelmed by a large, new wave of refugees from Kosovo. All the ingredients for a major war are there: ancient grievances, struggling democracies, and in the center of it all a dictator in Serbia who has done nothing since the Cold War ended but start new wars and pour gasoline on the flames of ethnic and religious division.

Sarajevo, the capital of neighboring Bosnia, is where World War I began. World War II and the Holocaust engulfed this region. In both wars Europe was slow to recognize the dangers, and the United States waited even longer to enter the conflicts. Just imagine if leaders back then had acted wisely and early enough, how many lives could have been saved, how many Americans would not have had to die.

We learned some of the same lessons in Bosnia just a few years ago. The world did not act early enough to stop that war, either. And let's not forget what happened—innocent people herded into concentration camps, children gunned down by snipers on their way to school, soccer fields and parks turned into cemeteries; a quarter of a million people killed, not because of anything they have done, but because of who they were. Two million Bosnians became refugees. This was genocide in the heart of Europe—not in 1945, but in 1995. Not in some grainy newsreel from our parents' and grandparents' time, but in our own time, testing our humanity and our resolve.

At the time, many people believed nothing could be done to end the bloodshed in Bosnia. They said, well, that's just the way those people in the Balkans are. But when we and our allies joined with courageous Bosnians to stand up to the aggressors, we helped to end the war. We learned that in the Balkans, inaction in the face of brutality simply invites more brutality. But firmness can stop armies and save lives. We must apply that lesson in Kosovo before what happened in Bosnia happens there, too.

Over the last few months we have done everything we possibly could to solve this problem peacefully. Secretary Albright has worked tirelessly for a negotiated agreement. Mr. Milosevic has refused.

On Sunday I sent Ambassador Dick Holbrooke to Serbia to make clear to him again, on behalf of the United States and our NATO allies, that he must honor his own commitments and stop his repression, or face military action. Again, he refused.

Today, we and our 18 NATO allies agreed to do what we said we would do, what we must do to restore the peace. Our mission is clear: to demonstrate the seriousness of NATO's purpose so that the Serbian leaders understand the imperative of reversing course. To deter an even bloodier offensive against innocent civilians in Kosovo and, if necessary, to seriously damage the Serbian military's capacity to harm the people of Kosovo. In short, if President Milosevic will not make peace, we will limit his ability to make war.

Now, I want to be clear with you, there are risks in this military action—risks to our pilots and the people on the ground. Serbia's air defenses are strong. It could decide to intensify its assault on Kosovo, or to seek to harm us or our allies elsewhere. If it does, we will deliver a forceful response.

Hopefully, Mr. Milosevic will realize his present course is self-destructive and unsustainable. If he decides to accept the peace agreement and demilitarize Kosovo, NATO has agreed to help to implement it with a peace-keeping force. If NATO is invited to do so, our troops should take part in that mission to keep the peace. But I do not intend to put our troops in Kosovo to fight a war.

Do our interests in Kosovo justify the dangers to our Armed Forces? I've thought long and hard about that question. I am convinced that the dangers of acting are far outweighed by the dangers of not acting—dangers to defenseless people and to our national interests. If we and our allies were to allow this war to continue with no response, President Milosevic would read our hesitation as a license to kill. There would be many more massacres, tens of thousands more refugees, more victims crying out for revenge.

Right now our firmness is the only hope the people of Kosovo have to be able to live in their own country without having to fear for their own lives. Remember: We asked them to accept peace, and they did. We asked them to promise to lay down their arms, and they agreed. We pledged that we, the United States and the other 18 nations of NATO, would stick by them if they did the right thing. We cannot let them down now.

Imagine what would happen if we and our allies instead decided just to look the other way, as these people were massacred on NATO's doorstep. That would discredit NATO, the cornerstone on which our security has rested for 50 years now.

We must also remember that this is a conflict with no natural national boundaries. Let me ask you to look again at a map. The red dots are towns the Serbs have attacked. The arrows show the movement of refugees—north, east and south. Already, this movement is threatening the young democracy in Macedonia, which has its own Albanian minority and a Turkish minority. Already, Serbian forces have made forays into Albania from which Kosovars have drawn support. Albania is a Greek minority. Let a fire burn here in this area and the flames will spread. Eventually, key U.S. allies could be drawn into a wider conflict, a war we would be forced to confront later—only at far greater risk and greater cost.

I have a responsibility as President to deal with problems such as this before they do permanent harm to our national interests. America has a responsibility to stand with our allies when they are trying to save innocent lives and preserve peace, freedom and stability in Europe. That is what we are doing in Kosovo.

If we've learned anything from the century drawing to a close, it is that if America is going to be prosperous and secure, we need a Europe that is prosperous, secure, undivided and free. We need a Europe that is coming together, not falling apart; a Europe that shares our values and shares the burdens of leadership. That is the foundation on which the security of our children will depend.

That is why I have supported the political and economic unification of Europe. That is why we brought Poland, Hungary and the Czech Republic into NATO, and redefined its missions, and reached out to Russia and Ukraine for new partnerships.

Now, what are the challenges to that vision of a peaceful, secure, united, stable Europe? The challenge of strengthening a partnership with a democratic Russia, that, despite our disagreements, is a constructive partner in the work of building peace. The challenge of resolving the tension between Greece and Turkey and building bridges with the Islamic world. And, finally, the challenge of ending instability in the Balkans so that these bitter ethnic problems in Europe are resolved by the force of argument, not the force of arms; so that future generations of Americans do not have to cross the Atlantic to fight another terrible war.

It is this challenge that we and our allies are facing in Kosovo. That is why we have acted now—because we care about saving innocent lives; because we have an interest in avoiding an even crueler and costlier war; and because our children need and deserve a peaceful, stable, free Europe.

Our thoughts and prayers tonight must be with the men and women of our Armed Forces who are undertaking this mission for the sake of our values and our children's future. May God bless them and may God bless America.

Reference:

Clinton, William. 1999. "President Clinton's March 24, 1999 Address to the Nation." Available at http://homepages.uc.edu/thro/Kosovo/ClintonMrch24.html (accessed 16 March 2004).

Campaign 2000: Vice President Gore and Governor Bush Participate in Second Presidential Debate (11 October 2000)

Prior to beginning the war in Iraq in mid-March 2003, George W. Bush's campaign debate remarks on nation-building, excerpted below, were most often cited as the crux of his views opposed to sending U.S. forces to engage in nation-building. After taking office, the administration embraced nation-building as an obligation to prevent further terrorism as occurred on September 11.

Jim Lehrer, Moderator
Lehrer: Welcome to this second election 2000 debate between the Republican candidate for president, Governor George W. Bush of Texas, and the Democratic candidate, Vice President Al Gore.
Lehrer: One of you is about to be elected the leader of the single-most powerful nation in the world economically, financially, militarily, diplomatically, you name it. Have you formed any guiding principles for exercising this enormous power?
Bush: I have. I have. The first question is what's in the best interests of the United States? What's in the best interests of our people?
When it comes to foreign policy, that'll be my guiding question: Is it in our nation's interests? Peace in the Middle East is in our nation's interests. Having a hemisphere that is free for trade and peaceful is in our nation's interests. Strong relations in Europe is in our nation's interests. I've thought a lot about what it means to be the president. I also understand that an administration is not one person, but an administration is dedicated citizens who are called by the president to serve the country, to serve a cause greater than self.
One of the things I've done in Texas is, I've been able to put together a good team of people. I've been able to set clear goals. The goals are to be an education system that leaves no child behind, Medicare for our seniors, a Social Security system that's safe and secure, foreign policy that's in our nation's interests, and a strong military. And then, bring people together to achieve those goals.
Lehrer: Vice President Gore?
Gore: Yes, Jim, I thought a lot about that particular question. And I see our greatest natural—national strength coming from what we stand for in the world. I see it as a question of values . . .It's really true, even the ones that sometimes shake their fist at us, as soon as they have a change that allows the people to speak freely, they're wanting to

develop some kind of blueprint that will help them be like us more—freedom, free markets, political freedom.

So I think first and foremost, our power ought to be wielded to—in ways that form a more perfect union. The power of example is America's greatest power in the world. And that means, for example, standing up for human rights . . .

But our real power comes, I think, from our values.

Lehrer: Should the people of the world look at the United States, Governor, and say—should they fear us? Should they welcome our involvement? Should they see us as a friend to everybody in the world? How do you—how would you project us around the world, as president?

Bush: Well, I think they ought to look at us as a country that understands freedom, where it doesn't matter who you are or how you're raised or where you're from, that you can succeed. I don't think they ought to look at us with envy. It really depends upon how our nation conducts itself in foreign policy. If we're an arrogant nation, they'll resent us. If we're a humble nation but strong, they'll welcome us. And our nation stands alone right now in the world in terms of power. And that's why we've got to be humble and yet project strength in a way that promotes freedom. So I don't think they ought to look at us in any other than what we are. We're a freedom loving nation. And if we're an arrogant nation, they'll view us that way. But if we're a humble nation, they'll respect us as an honorable nation.

Gore: I agree with that. I agree with that. I think that one of the problems that we have faced in the world is that we are so much more powerful than any single nation has been in relationship to the rest of the world than at any time in history—that I know about anyway—that there is some resentment of U.S. power. So I think that the idea of humility is an important one. But I think that we also have to have a sense of mission in the world. We have to protect our capacity to push forward what America's all about. That means not only military strength and our values, it also means keeping our economy strong.

You know, in the last—two decades ago, it was routine for leaders of foreign countries to come over here and say, "You guys have got to do something about these horrendous deficits because it's causing tremendous problems for the rest of the world," and we were lectured to all the time. The fact that we have the strongest economy in history today—it's not good enough, we need to do more—but the fact that it is so strong enables us to project the power for good that America can represent.

Lehrer: Does that give us—does our wealth, our good economy, our power, bring with it special obligations to the rest of the world?

Bush: Yes, it does. Take, for example, Third World debt. I think—I think we ought to be forgiving Third World debt under certain conditions. I think, for example, if we're convinced that a Third World country that's got a lot of debt would reform itself, that the money wouldn't go into the hands of a few, but would go to help people, then I think it makes sense for us to use our wealth in that way. Or do you trade debt for valuable rain forest lands? Makes some sense. Yes, we do have an obligation in the world, but we can't be all things to all people. We can help build coalitions, but we can't put our troops all around the world. We can lend money, but we've got to do it wisely. We shouldn't be lending money to corrupt officials. So we've got to be guarded in our generosity.

Lehrer: Well, let's go through some of the specifics now. New question, Vice President Gore, the governor mentioned the Middle East. Here we're talking at this stage of the game about diplomatic power that we have. What do you think the United States should do right now to resolve that conflict over there?

Gore: The first priority has to be on ending the violence, dampening down the tensions that have risen there. We need to call upon Syria to release the three Israeli soldiers who have been captured. We need to insist that Arafat send out instructions to halt some of the provocative acts of violence that have been going on. I think that we also have to keep a weather eye toward Saddam Hussein, because he's taking advantage of this situation to once again make threats. And he needs to understand that he's not only dealing with Israel, he's dealing with us if he is making the kind of threats that he's talking about there.

The use of diplomacy in this situation has already—well, it goes hour by hour and day by day now; it's a very tense situation there. But in the last 24 hours, there has been some subsiding of the violence there. It's too much to hope that this is going to continue, but I do hope that it will continue. Our country has been very active with regular conversations with the leaders there. And we just have to take it day to day right now. But one thing I would say where diplomacy is concerned, Israel should—should feel absolutely secure about one thing: Our bonds with Israel are larger than agreements or disagreements on some details of diplomatic initiatives. They are historic, they are strong, and they are enduring. And our ability to serve as an honest broker is something that we need to shepherd.

Lehrer: Governor?

Bush: Well, I think during the campaign, particularly now during this difficult period, we ought to be speaking with one voice. And I appreciate the way the administration has worked hard to calm the tensions. Like the vice president, I call on Chairman Arafat to have his people pull back to make the peace. I think credibility is going to be very important in the future in the Middle East. I want everybody to know, should I be the president, Israel's going to be our friend. I'm going to stand by Israel. Secondly, that I think it's important to reach out to moderate Arab nations like Jordan and Egypt, Saudi Arabia and Kuwait. It's important to be friends with people when you don't need each other so that when you do, there's a strong bond of friendship. And that's going to be particularly important in dealing not only with situations such as now occurring in Israel, but with Saddam Hussein. The coalition against Saddam has fallen apart or it's unraveling, let's put it that way. The sanctions are being violated. We don't know whether he's developing weapons of mass destruction. He'd better not be or there's going to be a consequence, should I be the president. But it's important to have credibility and credibility is formed by being strong with your friends and resoluting your determination. It's one of the reasons why I think it's important for this nation to develop an anti-ballistic missile system that we can share with our allies in the Middle East, if need be, to keep the peace; to be able to say to the Saddam Husseins of the world or the Iranians, "Don't dare threaten our friends." It's also important to keep strong ties in the Middle East, credible ties, because of the energy crisis we're now in. After all, a lot of the energy is produced from the Middle East. And so I appreciate what the administration is doing. I hope you can get a sense of, should I be fortunate enough to be the president, how my administration will react in the Middle East.

Lehrer: So you don't believe, Vice President Gore, that we should take sides and resolve this right now? There a lot of people pushing, "Hey, the United States should declare itself and not be so neutral in this particular situation."

Gore: Well, we stand with Israel, but we have maintained the ability to serve as an honest broker. And one of the reasons that's important is that Israel cannot have direct dialogue with some of the people on the other side of conflicts, especially during times of tension, unless that dialogue comes through us. And if we throw away that ability to serve as an honest broker, then we have thrown—we will have thrown away a strategic asset that's important not only to us but also to Israel.

Lehrer: Do you agree with that, Governor?

Bush: I do. I do think this, though. I think that when it comes to timetables, it can't be the United States timetable as to how discussions take place. It's got to be a timetable that all parties can agree to, other than—like the Palestinians and the Israelis. Secondly, any lasting peace is going to have to be a peace that's good for both sides, and, therefore, the term honest broker makes sense. Whether it—this current administration's worked hard to keep the parties at the table. I will try to do the same thing. But it won't be on my timetable; it'll be on a timetable that people are comfortable with in the Middle East.

Lehrer: People watching here tonight are very interested in Middle East policy. And they're so interested that they want to make a—they want to base their vote on differences between the two of you as president, how you would handle Middle East policy. Is there any difference?

Gore: I haven't heard a big difference right—in the last few exchanges.

Bush: Well, I think—it's hard to tell. I think that, you know, I would hope to be able to convince people I could handle the Iraqi situation better. I mean, we don't . . .

Lehrer: Saddam Hussein, you mean?

Bush: Yes.

Lehrer: You could get him out of there?

Bush: I'd like to, of course. And I presume this administration would as well. But we don't know. There's no inspectors now in Iraq. The coalition that was in place isn't as strong as it used to be. He is a danger. We don't want him fishing in troubled waters in the Middle East. And it's going to be hard to—it's going to be important to rebuild that coalition to keep the pressure on him.

Lehrer: Do you feel that is a failure of the Clinton administration?

Bush: I do.

Lehrer: Mr. Vice President?

Gore: Well, when I got to be a part of the current administration, it was right after I was one of the few members of my political party to support former President Bush in the Persian Gulf War resolution. And at the end of that war, for whatever reasons, it was not finished in a way that removed Saddam Hussein from power. I know there are all kinds of circumstances and explanations. But the fact is that that's the situation that was left when I got there. And we have maintained the sanctions. Now, I want to go further. I want to give robust support to the groups that are trying to overthrow Saddam Hussein. And I know there are allegations that they're too weak to do it, but that's what they said about the forces that were opposing Milosevic in Serbia.

And, you know, the policy of enforcing sanctions against Serbia has just resulted in a spectacular victory for democracy just in the past week. And it seems to me that, having taken so long to see the sanctions work there, building upon the policy of containment that was successful over a much longer period of time against the former Soviet Union and the Communist Bloc, it seems a little early to declare that we should give up on the sanctions. I know the governor's not necessarily saying that. But, you know, all of these flights that have come in? All of them have been in accordance with the sanctions regime, I'm told, except for three where they notified. And they're trying to break out of the box, there's no question about it. I don't think they should be allowed to.

Lehrer: Are you—did he correct you—did he state your position correctly? You're not calling for eliminating the sanctions, are you?

Bush: No, of course not. Absolutely not. I want them to be tougher.

Lehrer: Let's go—move to Milosevic and Yugoslavia. And it falls into the area of our military power. Governor, new question, should the fall of Milosevic be seen as a triumph for U.S. military intervention?

Bush: I think it's a triumph; I thought the president made the right decision in joining NATO in bombing Serbia. I supported them when they did so. I called upon the Congress not to hamstring the administration and—in terms of forcing troop withdrawals on a timetable that wasn't in necessarily our best interests or fit our nation's strategy. And so I think it's good public policy. I think it worked. And I'm pleased I took the—made the decision I made. I'm pleased the president made the decision he made, because freedom took hold in that part of the world. And there's a lot of work left to be done, however.

Lehrer: But you think it would not have happened—do you believe—do you think that Milosevic would not have fallen if the United States and NATO had not intervened militarily? Is this a legitimate use of our military power?

Bush: Yes, I think it is, absolutely. I don't think he would had fallen had we not used force. And I know there's some in my party that disagreed with that sentiment, but I supported the president. I thought he made the right decision to do so. I didn't think he necessarily made the right decision to take land troops off the table right before we committed ourselves offensively, but nevertheless, it worked. The administration deserves credit for having made it work. It's as important for NATO to have it work. It's important for NATO to be strong and confident to help keep the peace in Europe. And one of the reasons I felt so strongly that the United States needed to participate was because of our relations with NATO. And NATO is going to be an important part of keeping the peace in the future. Now, there's more work to do. It remains to be seen how or whether or not there's going to be a political settlement to Kosovo. And I certainly hope there is one. I'm also on record as saying, at some point in time, I hope our European friends become the peacekeepers in Bosnia and in the Balkans. I hope that they put the troops on the ground so that we can withdraw our troops and focus our military on fighting and winning war.

Lehrer: Mr. Vice President?

Gore: Well, I've been kind of a hard-liner on this issue for more than eight years. When I was in the Senate before I became vice president, I was pushing for stronger action against Milosevic. He caused the deaths of so many people. He was the last Communist Party boss there. And then he became a dictator by some other label, he was still essentially a Communist dictator. And unfortunately now, he is trying to reassert himself in Serbian politics already. Just today the members of his political party said that they were going to ignore the orders of the new president of Serbia, and that they question his legitimacy. And he's still going to try to be actively involved. He is an indicted war criminal. He should be held accountable. Now, I did want to pick up on one of the statements earlier. And maybe I have heard—maybe I've heard the previous statements wrong, Governor. In some of the discussions we've had about when it's appropriate for the U.S. to use force around the world, at times the standards that you've laid down have given me the impression that if it's—if it's something like a genocide taking place or what they called ethnic cleansing in Bosnia, that that alone would not be—that that wouldn't be the kind of situation that would cause you to think that the U.S. ought to get involved with troops. Now, have to be other factors involved for me to want to be involved. But by itself, that, to me, can bring into play a fundamental American strategic interest because I think it's based on our values. Now, have I got that wrong?

Lehrer: Governor?

Bush: OK, yes. I'm trying to figure out who the questioner was. If I think it's in our nation's strategic interests, I'll commit troops. I thought it was in our strategic interests to keep Milosevic in check because of our relations in NATO, and that's why I took the positions I took. I think it's important for NATO to be strong and confident. I felt like an unchecked-Milosevic would harm NATO. And so it depends on the situation, Mr. Vice President.

Lehrer: Well, let's keep—let's stay on the subject for a moment. New question, related to this. There have been—I figured this out—in the last 20 years, there have been eight major actions involving the introduction of U.S. ground, air or naval forces. Let me name them: Lebanon, Granada, Panama, the Persian Gulf, Somalia, Bosnia, Haiti, Kosovo. If you had been president, are any of those interventions—would any of those interventions not have happened?

Gore: Can you run through the list again?

Lehrer: Sure. Lebanon.

Gore: I thought that was a mistake.

Lehrer: Granada.

Gore: I supported that.

Lehrer: Panama.

Gore: I supported that one.

Lehrer: Persian Gulf.

Gore: Yes, I voted for it, supported it.

Lehrer: Somalia.

Gore: Well, of course, and that, again—no, I think that that was ill-considered. I did support it at the time. It was in the previous administration, in the Bush-Quayle administration, and I think in retrospect the lessons there are ones that we—that we should take very, very seriously.

Lehrer: Bosnia.

Gore: Oh, yes.

Lehrer: Haiti.

Gore: Yes.

Lehrer: And then Kosovo.

Gore: Yes.

Lehrer: We talked about that. Want me to do it with you? Go through each one?

Bush: No.

Lehrer: Lebanon.

Bush: No, I'm fine. I'll make a couple of comments.

Lehrer: Sure. Absolutely. Sure.

Bush: Somalia. Started off as a humanitarian mission then changed into a nation-building mission, and that's where the mission went wrong. The mission was changed. And as a result, our nation paid a price. And so I don't think our troops ought to be used for what's called nation-building. I think our troops ought to be used to fight and win war. I think our troops ought to be used to help overthrow a dictator that's in our—and it's in our—when it's in our best interests. But in this case, it was a nation-building exercise. And same with Haiti, I wouldn't have supported either.

Lehrer: What about Lebanon?

Bush: Yes.

Lehrer: Granada?

Bush: Yes.

Lehrer: Panama?

Bush: Yes.

Lehrer: Obviously, the . . .

Bush: Well, some of them I've got a conflict of interest on, if you know what I mean.

Lehrer: I do. I do. The Persian Gulf, obviously.

Bush: Yes.

Lehrer: And Bosnia. And you've already talked about Kosovo.

Bush: Yes.

Lehrer: But the reverse side of the question, Governor, that Vice President Gore mentioned—for instance, 600,000 people died in Rwanda in 1994. There was no U.S. intervention. There was no intervention from the outside world. Was that a mistake not to intervene?

Bush: I think the administration did the right thing in that case, I do. It was a horrible situation. No one liked to see it on our—you know, on our TV screens. But it's a case where we need to make sure we've got a, you know, kind of an early warning system in place in places where there could be ethnic cleansing and genocide the way we saw it there in Rwanda. And that's a case where we need to, you know, use our influence to have countries in Africa come together and help deal with the situation. The administration—it seems like we're having a great love fest now—but the administration made the right decision on training Nigerian troops for situations just such as this in Rwanda. And so I thought they made the right decision not to send U.S. troops into Rwanda.

Lehrer: Do you have any second thoughts on that based on what you said a moment ago about genocide and . . .

Gore: I'd like to come back to the question of nation-building. But let me address this question directly first.

Lehrer: We'll do that later.

Gore: Fine. We did actually send troops into Rwanda to help with the humanitarian relief measures. My wife, Tipper, who's here, actually went on a military plane with General Shalikashvili on one of those flights. But I think in retrospect we were too late getting in there. We would have saved more lives if we had acted earlier. But I do not think that it was an example of a conflict where we should have put our troops in to try to separate the parties for this reason, Jim: One of my— one of the criteria that I think is important in deciding when and if we should ever get involved around the world is whether or not our national security interest is involved, if we can really make the difference with military force, if we've tried everything else, if we have allies.

In the Balkans, we had allies, NATO, ready, willing and able to go and carry a big part of the burden. In Africa, we did not. Now we have tried—our country's tried to create an Africa crisis response team there, and we've met some resistance. We have had some luck with Nigeria, but in Sierra Leone. And that, now that Nigeria's become a democracy—and we hope it stays that way—then maybe we can build on that. But because we had no allies and because it was very unclear that we could actually accomplish what we would want to accomplish by putting military forces there, I think it was the right thing not to jump in, as heartbreaking as it was, but I think we should have come in much quicker with the humanitarian mission.

Lehrer: So what would you say, Governor, to somebody who would say, "Hey, wait a minute. Why not Africa? I mean, why the Middle East? Why the Balkans, but not Africa when 600,000 people's lives are at risk?"

Bush: Well, I understand. And Africa's important, and we've got to do a lot of work in Africa to promote democracy and trade. And there's some—the vice president mentioned Nigeria. It's a fledgling democracy. We've got to work with Nigeria. That's an important continent. But there's got to be priorities. And the Middle East is a priority for a lot of reasons, as is Europe and the Far East and our own hemisphere. And those are my four top priorities should I be the president. It's not to say we won't be engaged nor trying—nor should we—you know, work hard to get other nations to come together to prevent atrocity. I thought the best example of a way to handle the situation is East Timor when we provided logistical support to the Australians, support that only we can provide. I thought that was a good model. But we can't be all things to all people in the world, Jim. And I think that's where maybe the vice president and I begin to have some differences. I am worried about over-committing our military around the world. I want to be judicious in its use. You mentioned Haiti. I wouldn't have sent troops to Haiti. I didn't think it was a mission worthwhile. It was a nation-building mission. And it was not very successful. It cost us billions, a couple of billions of dollars, and I'm not so sure democracy is any better off in Haiti than it was before.

Lehrer: Vice President Gore, do you agree with the governor's views on nation-building, the use of military, our military to—for nation-building, as he described it and defined it?

Gore: I don't think we agree on that. I would certainly also be judicious in evaluating any potential use of American troops overseas. I think we have to be very reticent about that. But, look, Jim, the world is changing so rapidly. The way I see it, the world's getting much closer together. Like it or not, we are now the—the United States is now the natural leader of the world. All these other countries are looking to us. Now, just because we cannot be involved everywhere, and shouldn't be, doesn't mean that we should shy away from going in anywhere. Now, both of us are, kind of, I guess stating the other's position in a maximalist, extreme way, but I think there is a difference here.

This idea of nation-building is a kind of pejorative phrase. But think about the great conflict of the past century, World War II. During the years between World War I and World War II, a great lesson was learned by our military leaders and the people of the United States. The lesson was that in the aftermath of World War I we kind of turned our backs and left them to their own devices, and they brewed up a lot of trouble that quickly became World War II. And acting upon that lesson in the aftermath of our great victory in World War II, we laid down the Marshall Plan, President Truman did.

We got eminently involved in building NATO and other structures there. We still have lots of troops in Europe. And what did we do in the late '40s and '50s and '60s? We were nation-building. And it was economic, but it was also military. And the confidence that those countries recovering from the wounds of war had by having troops there—we had civil administrators come in to set up their ways of building their towns back.

Lehrer: You said in the Boston debate, Governor, on this issue of nation-building, that the United States military is overextended now. Where is it overextended? Where are there U.S. military that you would bring home if you become president?

Bush: Well, first, let me just say one comment about what the vice president said. I think one of the lessons in between World War I and World War II is we let our military atrophy, and we can't do that. We've got to rebuild our military. But one of the problems we have in the military is we're in a lot of places around the world. And I mentioned one, and that's the Balkans. I'd very much like to get our troops out of there. I recognize we can't do it now, nor do I advocate an immediate withdrawal. That would be an abrogation of our agreement with NATO; no one's suggesting that. But I think it ought to be one of our priorities, to work with our European friends to convince them to put troops on the ground. And there is an example. Haiti is another example.

Now, there are some places where, I think, you know, I supported the administration in Colombia; I think it's important for us to be training Colombians in that part of the world. Our hemisphere is in our interest, to have a peaceful Colombia.

But . . .

Lehrer: If you're just going to—you know, the use of the military, there's—some people are now suggesting that if you don't want to use the military to maintain the peace, to do the civil thing, is it time to consider a civil force of some kind that comes in after the military that builds nations or all of that? Is that on your radar screen?

Bush: I don't think so. I think—I think what we need to do is convince people who live in the lands they live in to build the nations. Maybe I'm missing something here. I mean, we're going to have kind of a nation-building corps from America? Absolutely not. Our military's meant to fight and win war. That's what it's meant to do. And when it gets over extended, morale drops. And I'm not—I strongly believe we need to have a military presence in the Korea Peninsula, not only to keep the peace in peninsula, but to keep regional stability. And I strongly believe we need to keep a presence in NATO. But I'm going to be judicious as to how to use the military. It needs to be in our vital interest, the mission needs to be clear, and the exit strategy obvious.

Gore: Well, I don't disagree with that. I certainly don't disagree that we ought to get our troops home from places like the Balkans as soon as we can, as soon as the mission is complete. That's what we did in Haiti. There are—there are no more than a handful of American military personnel in Haiti now. And the Haitians have their problems, but we gave them a chance to restore democracy. And that's really about all we can do. But if you have a situation like that right in our backyard with chaos about to break out and flotillas forming to come across the water and all kinds of violence there, right in one of our neighboring countries there, then I think that we did the right thing there.

And as for this idea of nation-building. The phrase sounds grandiose. And, you know, we can't be—we can't allow ourselves to get overextended. I certainly agree with that. And that's why I've supported building—building up our capacity. I've devoted in the budget I've proposed, as I said last week, more than twice as much as the governor has proposed. I think that it's in better shape now than he generally does. We've had some disagreements about that. He said that two divisions would have to report not ready for duty, and that's not what the Joint Chiefs say. But there's no doubt that we have to continue building up readiness and military strength, and we have to also be very cautious in the way we use our military.

Lehrer: In the nonmilitary area of influencing events around the world, in the financial and economic area, World Bank President Wolfensohn said recently, Governor, that U.S. contributions to overseas development assistance is lower now almost than it has ever been. Is that a problem for you? Do you think—what is your—what is your idea about what the United States' obligations are? We're talking about financial assistance and that sort of thing to other countries, the poorer countries?

Bush: Well, I mentioned Third World debt.

Lehrer: Sure.

Bush: That's a place where we can use our generosity to influence, in a positive way, influence nations. I believe we ought to have foreign aid, but I don't think we ought to just have foreign aid for the sake of foreign aid. I think foreign aid needs to be used to encourage markets and reform. I think a lot of times we just spend aid and say we feel better about it, and it ends up being spent the wrong way. And there's some pretty egregious examples recently, one being Russia where we had IMF loans that ended up in the pockets of a lot of powerful people and didn't help the nation. I think the IMF has got a role in the world, but I don't want to see the IMF out there as a way to say to world bankers, "If you make a bad loan, we'll bail you out." It needs to be available for emergency situations. I thought the president did the right thing with Mexico and was very strongly supportive of the administration in Mexico. But I don't think IMF and our—ought to be a stop-loss for people who ought to be able to evaluate risks themselves. And so, I look at every place where we're investing money; I just want to make sure the return is good.

Lehrer: You think we're meeting our obligations properly?

Gore: No, I would make some changes. I think there need to be reforms in the IMF. I've generally supported it, but I've seen them make some calls that I thought were highly questionable. And I think that there's a general agreement in many parts of the world now that there ought to be changes in the IMF. The World Bank I think is generally doing a better job. But I think one of the big issues here that doesn't get nearly enough attention is the issue of corruption. The governor mentioned it earlier. I've worked on this issue. It's an enormous problem. And corruption in official agencies, like militaries and police departments around the world, customs official—that's one of the worst forms of it. And we have got to, again, lead by example and help these other countries that are trying to straighten out their situations find the tools in order to do it.

I just think, Jim, that this is an absolutely unique period in world history. The world's coming together, as I said, they're looking to us. And we have a fundamental choice to make: Are we going to step up to the plate as a nation, the way we did after World War II, the way that generation of heroes said, "OK, the United States is going to be the leader"? And the world benefited tremendously from the courage that they showed in those post-war years.

I think that in the aftermath of the Cold War, it's time for us to do something very similar, to step up to the plate, to provide the leadership: leadership on the environment, leadership to make sure the world economy keeps moving in the right direction. Again, that means not running big deficits here and not squandering our surplus; it means having intelligent decisions that keep our prosperity going and shepherds that economic strength so that we can provide that leadership role.

Bush: Let me comment on that.

Lehrer: Sure.

Bush: Yes, I'm not so sure the role of the United States is to go around the world and say, "This is the way it's got to be. We can help." And maybe it's just our difference in government, the way we view government. I mean, I want to empower people, I don't—you know, I want to help people help themselves, not have government tell people what to do. I just don't think it's the role of the United States to walk into a country, say, "We do it this way, so should you." Now, I think we can help, and I know we've got to encourage democracy and the marketplaces. But take Russia, for example. We went into Russia, we said, "Here's some IMF money," and it ended up in Viktor Chernomyrdin's pocket and others. And yet we played like there was reform. The only people that are going to reform Russia are Russia. They're going to have to make the decision themselves. Mr. Putin is going to have to make the decision as to whether or not he wants to adhere to rule of law and normal accounting practices so that if countries and or entities invest capital, there's a reasonable rate of return, a way to get the money out of the economy. But Russia has to make the decision. We can work with them on security matters for example, but it's their call to make. So I'm not exactly sure where the vice president is coming from. But I think one way for us to end up being viewed as the ugly American is for us to go around the world saying, "We do it this way, so should you." Now, we trust freedom. We know freedom is a powerful, powerful—a powerful force much bigger than the United States of America, as we saw recently in the Balkans. But maybe I misunderstand where you're coming from, Mr. Vice President, but I think the United States must be humble and must be proud and confident of our values, but humble in how we treat nations that are figuring out how to chart their own course . . .

I want to make sure we rebuild our military to keep the peace. I worry about morale in today's military. The warning signs are clear. It's time to have a new commander in chief who will rebuild the military, to pay our men and women more, and make sure they're housed better, and have a focused mission for our military.

And we're going to say to our seniors: Our promises we've made to you will be promises kept.

Reference:

CNN/AllPolitics, Presidential Debates Transcript, 11 October 2000. Available at http://www.cnn.com/ELECTION/2000/debates/transcripts/u221011.html (accessed 16 January 2004).

Presidential News Conference (11 October 2001)

No event is likely ever again to have the same effect on the United States and the global community as did the terrorism of 11 September 2001. This is not because terrorism does not occur outside of the United States; it surely does with great frequency. But, the view that much of the U.S. population had of the international environment changed tremendously overnight. For the administration, the idea of setting up democratic, free market regimes in places where potentially threatening regimes existed took on a national urgency, which had seemed impossible only a year before. The president's views in this portion of the news conference illustrate the point.

Question: Mr. President, you've said on repeated occasions that you're not into nation-building. Yet, it appears in this case, given the politics of the region, it may play a crucial role in resolving this crisis. Prime Minister Blair of Britain has said that the coalition, if the Taliban falls, will work to create a broadly based government. I'm wondering, sir, has that become a priority of your administration now, to devise a plan for a new government in Afghanistan? And what part might King Zaher Shah play in that?

The President: Well, I think it's—John, it's a—first let me reiterate, my focus is bringing Al Qaeda to justice and saying to the host government, you had your chance to deliver. Actually, I will say it again—if you cough him up, and his people, today, that we'll reconsider what we're doing to your country. You still have a second chance. Bring him in. And bring his leaders and lieutenants and other thugs and criminals with him. I think we did learn a lesson, however, from—and should learn a lesson—from the previous engagement in the

Afghan area, that we should not just simply leave after a military objective has been achieved. That's why—and I sent that signal by announcing that we're going to spend $320 million of aid to the Afghan people. That's up from roughly $170 million this year. I personally think that a—and I appreciate Tony Blair's—and I've discussed this with him—his vision about Afghan after we're successful—Afghanistan after we're successful. One of the things we've got to make sure of is that all parties, all interested parties have an opportunity to be a part of a new government; that we shouldn't play favorites between one group or another within Afghanistan. Secondly, we've got to work for a stable Afghanistan so that her neighbors don't fear terrorist activity again coming out of that country. Third, it would be helpful, of course, to eradicate narco-trafficking out of Afghanistan, as well. I believe that the United Nations would—could provide the framework necessary to help meet those conditions. It would be a useful function for the United Nations to take over the so-called "nation-building,"—I would call it the stabilization of a future government—after our military mission is complete. We'll participate; other countries will participate. I've talked to many countries will participate. I've talked to many countries that are interested in making sure that the post-operations Afghanistan is one that is stable, and one that doesn't become yet again a haven for terrorist criminals.

Reference:

"President Holds Prime Time News Conference." Available at http://www.whitehouse.gov/news/releases/2001/10/20011011–7.htm l (accessed 16 March 2004).

Force, Forces, and Forecasting: Preparing U.S. Armed Forces for an Uncertain Future

While politicians argued about the desirability of nation-building prior to the events of September 11, the U.S. military and those of many states around the world had already reached the conclusion that force restructuring to meet the needs of increasing calls to engage in nation-building (whether it was peacemaking, peacekeeping, or postconflict stabilization) would increasingly be needed. The chairman of the Joint Chiefs of Staff in the United States offered these remarks on the needs of the force in the early weeks of 2001.

Today, I think most of you know that the defense budget is about $300 billion. And to many $300 billion is viewed as an excessive amount to spend on defense. "Defense from what?" they ask. "Why so much? . . . The Cold War is over." *"Where's the peace dividend?"* Well, in 1985, we were spending 6.5% of our Gross Domestic Product on defense. And today, as you know, we spend just over 3% of GDP. At the 1985 rate, our budget this year in DoD would be double what it is today. That, Ladies and Gentlemen, is quite a *peace dividend!*

Maybe we need to look at what we spend on defense in a different light. Although we are the Department of Defense, what we're really about is national security—not just defense. Our national security—in a broader context than defense—provides for our economic prosperity, our role as a world leader, and also the assistance programs we provide for friends, partners, and allies around the globe. Our national security is enhanced by a strong defense industry making world-class equipment that becomes the envy of all and ultimately it contributes to strong overseas sales which also enhances our security, increases our military interoperability, binds us closer to friends and partners, and promotes our Nation's economic prosperity. So, the peace dividend has been significant, and the contributions defense dollars make to our national security allow our great citizens to enjoy freedom, economic prosperity, and the opportunity to live in the greatest Nation on the face of the earth . . .

When I spoke to the graduating class at Annapolis last May, it struck me that these young men and women and their peers across America would be among our senior leaders of the force of 2020. In the meantime, we will be counting on them to be the junior leaders of today's force. For them to do what we ask of them—to be the best force in the world—we must give them the best tools! This means ensuring that they have the resources necessary to remain trained and ready today, it means recapitalizing our weapons systems that we place in their hands as well as the infrastructure that we ask them to work and live in, and it means properly compensating them throughout.

We simply cannot afford to support near-term readiness at the expense of future readiness and modernization. It's not an "either-or" proposition. We must do both. The essential question, of course, is *HOW?* Let me explore that just a bit. We should take the National Security and National Military Strategies, figure out what is necessary to support the objectives of those strategies, and then develop the force structure to support them. In other words, we should figure out *what* to do before we decide *how* we are going to do it. The resourcing piece then comes after these two steps. This, ladies and gentlemen, is the critical part! We have to get this right and we must do it in the right order! Strategy first then force structure. We should not establish a budget ceiling absent strategy and then build a force structure that's constrained by the top line. Force structure cannot be "reverse-engineered." To do this would cost us more in the long term—in terms of dollars, in terms of readiness, and, potentially, in lives.

That means, of course, that we need a "feed-back" mechanism to revisit force structure when the strategic environment changes or the strategy itself changes. We must, therefore, understand the changing nature of the international security environment. Because it holds the key to what our strategic imperatives will be, and thus what our military capabilities MUST be. Let me spend a few minutes or so on how I see the security environment changing over the next few years.

For starters, events over the past decade in such places as Southwest Asia, the Balkans, Haiti, Africa, Indonesia, the Kashmir, and elsewhere provide a window into the future strategic landscape. It's murky, it's frustrating, and it's increasingly dangerous. And while, today, North Korea and Iraq may pose the most serious challenges to America's interests, I do not believe these near-term threats will determine the shape of the world through the first decades of this new century. It's clear to me that the future of Asia will *not* be decided in Pyongyang, but rather on the high frontiers of the Kashmir, on the floor of the Tokyo stock exchange, and in the special economic zones of Shanghai and Hong Kong . . .

Ladies and gentlemen, although we have reason to be somewhat encouraged by the recent signs of at least "rhetorical" moderation in Tehran, in Pyongyang, and, to a lesser degree, in Beijing it would be premature to let our guard down. In order to shape *tomorrow* we must deal effectively with the Bosnias, the Koreas, the Kosovos, and the East Timors *today*. However, we cannot allow them to distract us from the truly vital issues that loom before us. Developments in Asia, the Middle East, and Russia have the potential to dramatically affect America's economic, political, and security interests. This demands our greatest investment in time, in energy, and in diplomacy.

The United States' global leadership role with our inherent worldwide interests continues to demand a broad range of military activities from engagement to warfighting. It's clear that the military has and will continue to become involved in areas other than just those that affect our vital national interests. The strategic environment will undoubtedly cause us to deploy forces to achieve limited military objectives. However, we must be mindful that long-term commitments to achieve nation building, and the like, place our readiness at risk.

Obviously, the decision to use force is *the* most important decision that our Nation's leaders make. In arriving at decisions of such consequence, we would all do well to remember that there's no cookie cutter solution that can be applied to the complex array of contingencies—both great and small—which confront America in this new Century. There are at least, however, at least four clear parameters that should inform decisions about employing force:

First, any intervention, unless linked to a discernible national interest, is, in all probability, not sustainable.

Second, the further removed from our vital national interests that an intervention is, the more challenging it becomes to sustain support over time.

Third, sustaining our involvement in military operations abroad requires the support of the American people as reflected by the Congress.

And, finally, we must be willing to ask ourselves two very tough questions: the first, "Do we dare to use force when force is needed?" And, second, just as important for the world's sole superpower, "Do we dare admit that force cannot solve every problem?"

As I look to the future and consider the possible scenarios that could result in a decision to use force, there are some general trends that become apparent, such as:

- The strategic "Flash to Bang" time is getting shorter. I don't need to tell this audience about instantaneous communications that compresses the time between finding out about events and the demand to "do something."
- As the diversity of threats and non-state actors increase, so, too, will the complexity of military tasks. Future adversaries may try to stay below the threshold of clear aggression, further complicating appropriate response options.
- We can expect more failed states, as people struggle for independence, for political legitimacy, and economic and resource advantage in climates of violence, repression, and deprivation.
- The range and types of conflict will expand. We can expect non-state actors, asymmetric attacks, anti-access strategies, retreat to the lower ends of the spectrum of conflict, and information warfare. When you combine these with the very real potential for high-intensity regional conflict or even threats to our homeland, you can see the enormous challenges that our future Joint Force Commanders will face.

The world remains a dangerous place, indeed, and America's superiority generates envy in many and outright hatred in others. As I've said before, I'm not in the business of playing "Chicken Little." I fully recognize that, today, America has no peer competitor. However, we must remain alert to the possibility of peer competition in the future. And there is also the potential for the emergence of a single conventional power or a combination of forces that could mount a focused campaign against US interests. In our business, we need to keep in mind that this environment could develop a lot sooner than any of us might think.

Well, we've been discussing the *"what"* and the *"how"* of our national security challenges, the next question is *"How much?"* The last QDR set a goal for procurement, for example, at $60 billion, which we were able to achieve in the fiscal year '01 budget. Based on the best projections available at the time, we thought this would be adequate to maintain an acceptable level of modernization. Reality has dictated otherwise! In the last three years alone, the demanding pace of operations demonstrated how inadequate that level was. $60 billion might have been adequate to sustain modernization had not the increased operational tempo and unknown aging factors driven us to consume it at increasing rates.

Many have worked hard at figuring out what procurement figure would be appropriate. Deputy Secretary of Defense John Hamre left office arguing for $100 billion. The Congressional Budget Office pegged it at about $90 billion. While those figures are probably closer to the mark, I cannot today give you a precise dollar amount. One of the challenges of the QDR will be to determine what is an acceptable, sustainable rate. But I think we need to keep a larger perspective in mind. That calls for understanding what, in the larger sense, we're here for. I've mentioned it fairly frequently throughout my tenure as Chairman. It must be the fundamental focus of our efforts in the QDR and in the larger military planning system. Despite the changing security environment in which we find ourselves, the Armed Forces exist to *fight . . . and win . . . America's wars.* The global interests, responsibilities, and the obligations we have as a Nation will endure. And there is no indication that the threats to those interests, and responsibilities, or obligations to our allies will disappear. This is the one place where there is clarity about the future and that is undeniable. Given this emerging security environment—and our broad interests— the force must have the capability to dominate across the full spectrum of military operations *all at once.* Not only able to dominate in one place, at one moment in time, but be flexible and responsive enough to undertake multiple tasks in multiple locations simultaneously. That's what our friends, allies, and our partners expect of a global power. That's what is required for a Nation with worldwide interests.,

Second, we continue to demand greater jointness among the Services. While there is great value in preserving the individual Service cultures, when it comes to warfighting, the Joint Task Force must become our new core competency. To this end, we have established Joint Forces Command out of what was previously US Atlantic Command (USACOM) in Norfolk. Its charter is nothing less than developing operational concepts to advance the tenets of joint warfighting.

Ladies and Gentlemen, America is a very prosperous Nation and America can afford whatever defense it wants. But without a strong defense, the prosperity that makes America the envy of the world is threatened. And let's remember—what we spend on our "Defense" budget must be viewed in the context of what America spends for our National Security—something that affects every American.

Let me close with one final thought. Just as it is your sacred trust to keep the American people informed, it is our sacred trust to defend America and American interests. As I testified a few months ago, your military is ready today to meet any threat. But part of our great military are showing strain and are starting to fray and so we must take clear, concrete, and bold steps to keep it well prepared in this new century. As President-Elect Bush said in his address last night—"A military that is equal to any challenge and superior to any adversary."

Thank you.

Reference:

Shelton, Henry H. 2001. "Forces, Forces, and Forecasting: Preparing U.S. Armed Forces for an Uncertain Future." *Vital Speeches of the Day* 67, no. 7 (15 January): 194–198. Available at http://www.dtlc.mil/jcs/chairman NationalPressClub.htm (accessed 20 May 2004).

President Discusses Humanitarian Aid to Afghanistan with UN Secretary General (28 November 2001)

The secretary general of the United Nations and the president of the United States often come into conflict in their approaches to various problems, because the former has responsibility to the more than two hundred member states of the United Nations and the president has to answer to more than 270 million citizens of the United States. As would happen again with Iraq, President Bush and Secretary General Annan had different concerns about nation-building and Afghanistan, as well as the basic question of who had responsibility for what role.

The President: It's my honor to welcome back to the White House our friend, Secretary General Kofi Annan. Today we've had a valuable discussion about how to make sure that the good intentions of America and others around the world are met. And those intentions have to do with feeding people who starve in Afghanistan. Prior to September the 11th there was a lot of hunger in that country, primarily because it was run by a government that didn't really care about the human condition. After September the 11th, obviously the war has aggravated the situation, and as I declared to the American people, our good government and our great nation is going to do something about it.

And around the table today are people who are responsible to making sure, as best as they possibly can, food is delivered, and medicine is delivered, and clothing is delivered to innocent, hurting people of Afghanistan. And the Secretary General has been so great on this issue, and he's assembled a wonderful team who are here to brief the Secretary of State and myself about the efforts. The degree of difficulty is high. There's no question we've got a large task ahead of ourselves. We've got ample money, and the United States government has been a major contributor of that money. We've got the food. The fundamental question is, in an environment that is not very secure, how do we get the food to the people. And that's what we're working on. And I'm convinced that we can do a very good job of meeting that objective.

So, Mr. General, thanks for coming. It's an honor to have you back. I appreciate you bringing your team with you.

Secretary General Annan: Thank you very much, Mr. President, for the discussions this morning with my team. The Afghan people have suffered for quite a long time through a series of wars, and recently, drought. And we've been trying to get food to them. And as the President said, it's not always been easy. Even sometimes when we have the food in the country, we cannot always get it to the needy. We are now, with the help of the U.S. and other donors, able to get in as much food as we think we will need. But because of the insecurity, we have difficulties reaching the needy and the people, and we are working on that. And I hope the situation will clarify in the not-too-distant future to allow us to reach all those in need. I think it is important for the public to know the numbers we are dealing with, and here I'm talking about refugees—Afghan refugees in the neighboring countries, particularly Pakistan and Iran, and the internally displaced people. We are talking about 6 million needy people—between 6 million to 7.5 million. We are going to do our best, with the support that we are getting. And I think, on the political front, if I may say a word, we are meeting the Afghan parties in Bonn. Mr. Brahimi is discussing with them as we sit here. And so far, they're off to a good start. The parties seem to want a broad-based government, and I hope they will be able to settle this—the establishment of the government before they leave Bonn.

The willingness of the U.S. and other donor countries and the international community is clear, to work with them in rebuilding their society. But we need a partner, and the partner has to be an effective Afghan government that is cohesive, that is stable, that will work with the donor community to ensure that the resources that are being applied to rehabilitation and reconstruction is used effectively. The challenge is theirs. They have an historic opportunity to put the past behind them and form a broad-based government that will be loyal to the Afghan people, and respect its international obligations. And if they do that, from all the commitments that I have heard from the President and other leaders, the resources will be there over the period in a sustained manner to help rebuild Afghanistan. So I urge them to seize the moment for the sake of their people and for the sake of their country.

The President: Thank you, Mr. General.

Reference:

"President Discusses Humanitarian Aid to Afghanistan with UN Secretary General." Available at http://www.whitehouse.gov/news/releases/2001/11/20011128–7.html (accessed 15 March 2004).

President Delivers State of the Union Address (29 January 2002)

President Bush's first State of the Union Address after September 11 had numerous references to U.S. goals and responsibilities clearly lacking a year earlier. The questions of whether the United States would meet the goals in Afghanistan set forth in these remarks remains an open one but it establishes certain responsibilities for the United States, which have traditionally been those that many in this country feared or opposed.

The President: Thank you very much. Mr. Speaker, Vice President Cheney, members of Congress, distinguished guests, fellow citizens: As we gather tonight, our nation is at war, our economy is in recession, and the civilized world faces unprecedented dangers. Yet the state of our Union has never been stronger. We last met in an hour of shock and suffering. In four short months, our nation has comforted the victims, begun to rebuild New York and the Pentagon, rallied a great coalition, captured, arrested, and rid the world of thousands of terrorists, destroyed Afghanistan's terrorist training camps, saved a people from starvation, and freed a country from brutal oppression. The American flag flies again over our embassy in Kabul. Terrorists who once occupied Afghanistan now occupy cells at Guantanamo Bay. And terrorist leaders who urged followers to sacrifice their lives are running for their own.

America and Afghanistan are now allies against terror. We'll be partners in rebuilding that country. And this evening we welcome the distinguished interim leader of a liberated Afghanistan: Chairman Hamid Karzai. The last time we met in this chamber, the mothers and daughters of Afghanistan were captives in their own homes, forbidden from working or going to school. Today women are free, and are part of Afghanistan's new government. And we welcome the new Minister of

Women's Affairs, Doctor Sima Samar. Our progress is a tribute to the spirit of the Afghan people, to the resolve of our coalition, and to the might of the United States military. When I called our troops into action, I did so with complete confidence in their courage and skill. And tonight, thanks to them, we are winning the war on terror. The men and women of our Armed Forces have delivered a message now clear to every enemy of the United States: Even 7,000 miles away, across oceans and continents, on mountaintops and in caves—you will not escape the justice of this nation. For many Americans, these four months have brought sorrow, and pain that will never completely go away. Every day a retired firefighter returns to Ground Zero, to feel closer to his two sons who died there. At a memorial in New York, a little boy left his football with a note for his lost father: Dear Daddy, please take this to heaven. I don't want to play football until I can play with you again some day. Last month, at the grave of her husband, Michael, a CIA officer and Marine who died in Mazur-e-Sharif, Shannon Spann said these words of farewell: "Semper Fi, my love." Shannon is with us tonight. Shannon, I assure you and all who have lost a loved one that our cause is just, and our country will never forget the debt we owe Michael and all who gave their lives for freedom. Our cause is just, and it continues. Our discoveries in Afghanistan confirmed our worst fears, and showed us the true scope of the task ahead. We have seen the depth of our enemies' hatred in videos, where they laugh about the loss of innocent life. And the depth of their hatred is equaled by the madness of the destruction they design. We have found diagrams of American nuclear power plants and public water facilities, detailed instructions for making chemical weapons, surveillance maps of American cities, and thorough descriptions of landmarks in America and throughout the world. What we have found in Afghanistan confirms that, far from ending there, our war against terror is only beginning. Most of the 19 men who hijacked planes on September the 11th were trained in Afghanistan's camps, and so were tens of thousands of others. Thousands of dangerous killers, schooled in the methods of murder, often supported by outlaw regimes, are now spread throughout the world like ticking time bombs, set to go off without warning. Thanks to the work of our law enforcement officials and coalition partners, hundreds of terrorists have been arrested. Yet, tens of thousands of trained terrorists are still at large. These enemies view the entire world as a battlefield, and we must pursue them wherever they are. So long as training camps operate, so long as nations harbor terrorists, freedom is at risk. And America and our allies must not, and will not, allow it. Our nation will continue to be steadfast and patient and persistent in the pursuit of two great objectives. First, we will shut down terrorist camps, disrupt terrorist plans, and bring terrorists to justice. And, second, we must prevent the terrorists and regimes who seek chemical, biological or nuclear weapons from threatening the United States and the world. Our military has put the terror training camps of Afghanistan out of business, yet camps still exist in at least a dozen countries. A terrorist underworld—including groups like Hamas, Hezbollah, Islamic Jihad, Jaish-i-Mohammed— operates in remote jungles and deserts, and hides in the centers of large cities. While the most visible military action is in Afghanistan, America is acting elsewhere. We now have troops in the Philippines, helping to train that country's armed forces to go after terrorist cells that have executed an American, and still hold hostages. Our soldiers, working with the Bosnian government, seized terrorists who were plotting to bomb our embassy. Our Navy is patrolling the coast of Africa to block the shipment of weapons and the establishment of terrorist camps in Somalia. My hope is that all nations will heed our call, and eliminate the terrorist parasites who threaten their countries and our own. Many nations are acting forcefully. Pakistan is now cracking down on terror, and I admire the strong leadership of President Musharraf. But some governments will be timid in the face of terror. And make no mistake about it: If they do not act, America will. Our second goal is to prevent regimes that sponsor terror from threatening America or our friends and allies with weapons of mass destruction. Some of these regimes have been pretty quiet since September the 11th. But we know their true nature. North Korea is a regime arming with missiles and weapons of mass destruction, while starving its citizens. Iran aggressively pursues these weapons and exports terror, while an unelected few repress the Iranian people's hope for freedom.

Iraq continues to flaunt its hostility toward America and to support terror. The Iraqi regime has plotted to develop anthrax, and nerve gas, and nuclear weapons for over a decade. This is a regime that has already used poison gas to murder thousands of its own citizens— leaving the bodies of mothers huddled over their dead children. This is a regime that agreed to international inspections—then kicked out the inspectors. This is a regime that has something to hide from the civilized world. States like these, and their terrorist allies, constitute an axis of evil, arming to threaten the peace of the world. By seeking weapons of mass destruction, these regimes pose a grave and growing danger. They could provide these arms to terrorists, giving them the means to match their hatred. They could attack our allies or attempt to blackmail the United States. In any of these cases, the price of indifference would be catastrophic. We will work closely with our coalition to deny terrorists and their state sponsors the materials, technology, and expertise to make and deliver weapons of mass destruction. We will develop and deploy effective missile defenses to protect America and our allies from sudden attack. And all nations should know: America will do what is necessary to ensure our nation's security. We'll be deliberate, yet time is not on our side. I will not wait on events, while dangers gather. I will not stand by, as peril draws closer and closer. The United States of America will not permit the world's most dangerous regimes to threaten us with the world's most destructive weapons. Our war on terror is well begun, but it is only begun. This campaign may not be finished on our watch—yet it must be and it will be waged on our watch. We can't stop short. If we stop now—leaving terror camps intact and terror states unchecked—our sense of security would be false and temporary. History has called America and our allies to action, and it is both our responsibility and our privilege to fight freedom's fight. Our first priority must always be the security of our nation, and that will be reflected in the budget I send to Congress. My budget supports three great goals for America: We will win this war; we'll protect our homeland; and we will revive our economy. September the 11th brought out the best in America, and the best in this Congress. And I join the American people in applauding your unity and resolve. Now Americans deserve to have this same spirit directed toward addressing problems here at home. I'm a proud member of my party—yet as we act to win the war, protect our people, and create jobs in America, we must act, first and foremost, not as Republicans, not as Democrats, but as Americans. It costs a lot to fight this war. We have spent more than a billion dollars a month—over $30 million a day—and we must be prepared for future operations. Afghanistan proved that expensive precision weapons defeat the enemy and spare innocent lives, and we need more of them. We need to replace aging aircraft and make our military more agile, to put our troops anywhere in the world quickly and safely. Our men and women in uniform deserve the best weapons, the best equipment, the best training—and they also deserve another pay raise. My budget includes the largest increase in defense spending in two decades—because while the price of freedom and security is high, it is never too high. Whatever it costs to defend our country, we will pay. The next priority of my budget is to do everything possible to protect our citizens and strengthen our nation against the ongoing threat of another attack. Time and distance from the events of September the 11th will not make us safer unless we act on its lessons. America is no longer protected by vast oceans. We are protected from attack only by vigorous action abroad, and increased vigilance at home. My budget nearly doubles funding for a sustained strategy of homeland security, focused on four key areas: bioterrorism, emergency response, airport and border security, and improved intelligence. We will develop vaccines to fight anthrax and other deadly diseases. We'll increase funding to help states and communities train and equip our heroic police and firefighters. We will improve intelligence collection and sharing, expand patrols at our borders, strengthen the security of air travel, and use technology to track the arrivals and departures of visitors to the United States. Homeland security will make America not only stronger, but, in many ways, better. Knowledge gained from bioterrorism research will improve public health. Stronger police and fire departments will mean safer neighborhoods. Stricter border enforcement will help combat illegal drugs. And as government works to better secure our homeland, America will continue to depend on the eyes and ears of alert citizens. A few days before Christmas, an airline flight attendant spotted a passenger lighting a match. The crew and passengers quickly subdued the man, who had been trained by Al Qaeda and was armed with explosives. The people on that plane were alert and, as a result, likely saved nearly 200 lives. And tonight we welcome and thank flight attendants Hermis Moutardier and Christina Jones . . . If anyone doubts this, let them look to Afghanistan, where the Islamic "street" greeted the fall of tyranny with song and celebration. Let the skeptics look to Islam's own rich history, with its centuries of learning, and tolerance and progress. America will lead by defending liberty and justice because they are right and true and unchanging for all people everywhere. No nation owns these aspirations, and no nation is exempt from them. We have no intention of imposing our culture. But America will always stand firm for the non-negotiable demands of human dignity: the rule of law; limits on the power of the state; respect for women; private property; free speech; equal justice; and religious tolerance. America will take the side of brave men and women who advocate these values around the world, including the Islamic world, because we have a greater objective than eliminating threats and containing resentment. We seek a just and peaceful world beyond the war on terror. In this moment of opportunity, a common danger is erasing old rivalries. America is working with Russia and China and India, in ways we have never before, to achieve peace and prosperity. In every region, free markets and free trade and free societies are proving their power to lift lives. Together with friends and allies from Europe to Asia, and Africa to Latin America, we will demonstrate that the forces of terror cannot stop the momentum of freedom. The last time I spoke here, I expressed the hope that life would return to normal. In some ways, it has. In others, it never will. Those of us who have lived through these challenging times have been changed by them. We've come to know truths that we will never question: evil is real, and it must be opposed. Beyond all differences of race or creed, we are one country, mourning together and facing danger together. Deep in the American character, there is honor, and it is stronger than cynicism. And many have discovered again that even in tragedy— especially in tragedy—God is near. In a single instant, we realized that this will be a decisive decade in the history of liberty, that we've been called to a unique role in human events. Rarely has the world faced a choice more clear or consequential. Our enemies send other people's children on missions of suicide and murder. They embrace tyranny and death as a cause and a creed. We stand for a different choice, made long ago, on the day of our founding. We affirm it again today. We choose freedom and the dignity of every life. Steadfast in our purpose, we now press on. We have known freedom's price. We have shown freedom's power. And in this great conflict, my fellow Americans, we will see freedom's victory. Thank you all. May God bless.

Reference:

"President Delivers State of the Union Address." Available at http://www.whitehouse.gov/news/releases/2002/01/20020129–11.ht ml (accessed 16 March 2004).

Colin L. Powell, Remarks at Asia Society Annual Dinner, New York (10 June 2002)

Secretary Powell's remarks at the annual Asia Society address a part of the world where nation-building remains a crucial activity. This speech is an indication of U.S. recognition that the job in Asia, while it has been in progress for generations, remains unfinished and has many hurdles to overcome to complete it. The speech illuminates the varied areas that nation-building must consider in all societies.

It's just as President Bush put it in his recent commencement speech at West Point: "Today," he said, "the great powers are . . . increasingly united by common values, instead of divided by conflicting ideologies. The United States, Japan and our Pacific friends, and now all of Europe, share a deep commitment to human freedom . . . Even in China," he said, "leaders are discovering that economic reform is the only lasting source of national wealth. In time, they will find that social and political freedom is the only true source of national greatness." Slowly, inexorably, nations one after another all over the world are learning freedom works like nothing else. Some nations are still afraid of it. Others are determined to control its progress. Some backslide. But the trend is real and it is in our interest to nurture it at every turn and in every region.

Therefore, our first goal and highest priority for Asia must be to help create the secure conditions under which freedom can flourish— economic freedom and political freedom. And security, first and foremost, is essential to economic growth and political freedom. For fifty years, over 50 years, the United States has been the balance wheel of security in Asia. To this day, Asia's stability depends on our forward-deployed presence and our key alliances with Japan, South Korea, the Philippines, Thailand and Australia.

Our alliances convey strength, purpose, and confidence but not aggression, not hostility. Our allies have thrived on our stabilizing presence. Others in the region have also benefited, though they are sometimes reluctant to admit it.

For five decades, our presence on the Korean peninsula has provided the security that South Korea needed to grow its economy and democracy. Our 37,000 military men and women in Korea today have exactly the same mission I had when I commanded an infantry battalion 30 years ago facing the DMZ: stop an attack from North Korea at all costs. Our alliance with the Republic of Korea is strong and resilient and has withstood many difficult challenges. So strong and so resilient that it can even withstand the strain from the heart-stopping World Cup tie earlier this morning. There can also be no doubt, my friends, that postwar Japan was able to recover and prosper by relying, by seeing, American military power. For that same past half century, our strength has made it possible for Japan to limit its defense expenditures and concentrate its enormous energy on economic growth, on democracy-building. And in recent years, our alliance with Japan has provided a framework within which Japan can contribute more to its own defense as well as to peace and security worldwide. Last September, I participated in a moving ceremony marking the 50th anniversary of the United States–Japan alliance. It was held at the Presidio in San Francisco, overlooking a Pacific that was truly at peace. We hailed our living alliance and declared it capable of adapting to the 21st century environment. Little did we know that three days later on September 11 our words would be put to the test. We could not have asked for a more resolute response from Japan. Japan went out of its way to help, by first passing legislation that for the first time ever permits its Maritime Self Defense ships to participate far from Japan's shores in anti-terrorism efforts. Today, as part of Operation ENDURING FREEDOM in Afghanistan, Japanese vessels provide fuel and logistical support to American ships plying the Indian Ocean and the Arabian Sea. And Japan has renewed this naval support for another six months.

Japan's superb leadership as co-sponsor of the Afghan Reconstruction Conference last January resulted in $4.5 billion in pledges from sixty countries, $296 million from the United States in this fiscal year alone. Japan itself pledged over half a billion dollars to Afghan reconstruction over the next several years. At the Tokyo Conference, I will never forget Hamid Karzai, the head of Afghanistan's Interim Authority, as he listened with quiet dignity as nation after nation pledged to help his people build a future, a future built on freedom and hope. As nation after nation pledged that they would never again abandon Afghanistan back to chaos and terror. And I guarantee you tonight that we will not. We will be there for Afghanistan. In Afghanistan today, Australians fight shoulder-to-shoulder and wing-to-wing with us in the war against terrorism, just as the Australians have done in every war of the last century. Indeed, the first non-American serviceman to die in Operation ENDURING FREEDOM was a sergeant in Australia's Special Air Service. Troops from New Zealand also serve alongside us in Operation ENDURING FREEDOM and in the International Security Assistance Force in Afghanistan. A South Korean medical unit cares for the ill and the injured. Thailand is now preparing to send peacekeepers, a military commitment that I hope others in Asia will make.

Beyond their efforts in Afghanistan, Asian nations are contributing to the global anti-terrorism campaign by tightening law enforcement, border controls and intelligence cooperation to make it harder for terrorists to move about, to communicate and to plot their evil deeds against us. We also deeply appreciate the efforts of a number of Asian countries to deny funds to terrorist groups that operate under the guise of legitimate businesses or charities. In their own backyards, the governments of Malaysia, Thailand and Singapore are cracking terrorist cells, arresting terrorism suspects and uncovering new leads, cooperating fully with us in the campaign against terrorism. The Armed Forces of the Philippines fight courageously against indigenous terrorist organizations that clearly have international ties. I am proud, so proud, that American forces are helping to train and equip their Philippine Army counterparts to combat groups such as Abu Sayyaf, a terrorist organization which regularly kidnaps, as you know too well, civilians for ransom. Just last week, Philippine forces encountered the Abu Sayyaf holding two American missionaries, Martin and Gracia Burnham, and a Filipina nurse, Ediborah Yap. The Burnhams had been hostages for over a year. Tragically, despite the best efforts of the Government of the Philippines to secure a safe release of the hostages, Martin Burnham and Ms. Yap died in the firefight that followed and Gracia Burnham was wounded. Seven Philippine servicemen also were wounded. Mrs. Burnham is now back in her home in Kansas. And wonderful, gracious lady that she is, despite the loss of her husband, and despite what she must have gone through over the past year, she was gracious enough in her grief to express her appreciation and admiration for what the Philippine Government had done. Vicious groups like Abu Sayyaf stop at nothing. They fear no one. The murderous example of Abu Sayyaf shows how right President Bush has been to lead a global campaign against all terrorists, all forms of terrorism, and not just against al-Qaida. We recognize the domestic concerns that exist that make some Asian states with large Muslim populations oft times reluctant to confront terrorism. They fear that taking action against terrorists will create martyrs. This fear stems from a popular misconception, fed by extremists, that the global campaign against terrorism is a war against Islam. Nothing could be further from the truth. It is not we who threaten Islam. It is the terrorists who murder, who murder men, women and children and violate Islam's fundamental precepts of tolerance and peace. They threaten Islam. They do a disservice to a proud and noble religion.

Far, far greater dangers come from ignoring the problem of terrorism and letting radical minorities drive domestic politics, rather than taking strong action against terrorists and their sympathizers. Among the 3,000 innocent souls murdered in the September 11 attacks were people from South Korea, China, Taiwan, the Philippines, Thailand, Malaysia, Indonesia, Australia, New Zealand and Japan. They were not the first Asians to die at the hands of terrorists, and, tragically, we know they won't be the last. We have only to remember the sarin gas attack in the Tokyo subway in 1995. Terrorism, without doubt, is a worldwide problem that will continue to require a resolute response from nations of every continent and creed, every region and religion.

If the complexities of combating terrorism and other 21st century scourges make you pine for the simpler, Cold War days, the black-and-white days, North Korea will snap you to your senses. North Korea's dangerously deluded policies drag its people further and further into a hell of deprivation and oppression.

North Korea's rulers have strangled its economic development and squandered what few resources the country has left on maintaining a massive offensive military capacity. They grow missiles and weapons of mass destruction instead of food for their starving and destitute people. Another generation of North Koreans should not have to live in fear, in hunger and in cold. A warming light can now shine where darkness quite literally prevails every day and night. We want the people of North Korea to be exposed to a whole wide world of ideas and we want them to join the growing community of free peoples. That is why we wholeheartedly support South Korea's sunshine policy. And to move this process forward we believe that Pyongyang should quickly live up to the promises it made to Seoul. It should establish industrial zones. It should implement military confidence-building measures. It should reunite more separated families. Extend the rail link to the South. Earlier this year, President Bush stood at a gleaming new railroad station built by the South Koreans at Dorasan near the 38th parallel. The railroad track ends abruptly at the DMZ at this beautiful station. It ends up abruptly, waiting, waiting, waiting to be met by a rail line from the North. I hope that day comes soon. Working with South Korea and Japan, the United States is prepared to take important steps to help North Korea move its relations with the U.S. toward normalcy. We expect soon to have meetings with the North Koreans to explore these steps. However, progress between us will depend on Pyongyang's behavior on a number of key issues. First, the North must get out of the proliferation business and eliminate long-range missiles that threaten other countries. It must take itself off the preferred-supplier list of rogue states. Secondly, it must make a much more serious effort to provide for its suffering citizens. America continues to be the world's biggest donor of humanitarian assistance to North Korea. Just last week President Bush authorized a further donation of 102 thousand metric tons of food aid for North Korea. We will continue generously to support the World Food Program's operations there, but we want to see greatly improved monitoring and access so we can be sure the food actually gets into hungry mouths. Third, the North needs to move toward a less threatening conventional military posture. We are watching closely to see if Pyongyang will live up to its past pledges to implement basic confidence-building measures with the South. And finally, North Korea must come into full compliance with the International Atomic Energy Agency safeguards that it agreed to when it signed the Nuclear Nonproliferation Treaty. The United States remains committed to the Agreed Framework which freezes and ultimately dismantles North Korea's dangerous old nuclear reactors in exchange for safer light water reactors. As President Bush made clear in Seoul this February, we hope for a peaceful transformation on the Korean peninsula. But no matter what the future holds, American forces remain prepared to defend with their lives the people and the democracy of South Korea. This is not just rhetoric to me, I have lived the experience and have seen the sacrifices that people make to keep South Korea free. There should be no doubt in anyone's mind that America's commitment to Asia's security and stability is an enduring one, for Asia's sake and for our own. We are a Pacific power. We will not yield our strategic position in Asia. Though we will constantly review our posture and consider sensible adjustments, we will maintain our forward-deployed forces in the Asia-Pacific for the foreseeable future. We will continue to meet the security obligations that geography and history have thrust upon us. We will also work to strengthen the various regional forums in which we participate. Though they are less numerous and cohesive than Europe's, Asia's regional organizations contribute to stability and we strongly support their continued institutional development. The ASEAN Regional Forum, Asia's only venue for regional security discussions, is tackling new threats ranging from terrorism and narcotics trafficking to human trafficking and HIV/AIDS. And I look forward to participating in the next ASEAN Forum in Brunei next month. The American people have invested more than taxpayer money and military hardware in a stable, prosperous Asia. Our sons and daughters—many of them Asian-American—have shed blood for it. We will continue to provide the essential security that not only promotes growth in Asia but also the global growth upon which our own prosperity depends. Under the protection of America's security umbrella, two-way trade between the

United States and East Asia and the Pacific has risen to $700 billion annually, larger than our trade with Europe. Between 1990 and 2000, exports of American products to Asia grew by over 80 percent and imports to the United States from Asia went up 150 percent. United States direct investment in Asia nearly tripled during the past decade to over $200 billion, roughly equal to the amount Asians have invested in the United States. Today, American teens buy Malaysian-made skirts at The Gap, drink coffee brewed from East Timor beans and email their friends with computers loaded with chips from Taiwan. Asian teens buy cookbooks from Amazon.com, see the latest Hollywood blockbuster on the same day it premiers in the United States and take vacations to Hawaii on American-built planes. Asian consumers support American jobs. Asian competitors keep our firms efficient and healthy. Asian savers provide capital to American businesses. Asian companies generate employment for over a million American workers. Asian innovators contribute significantly to technological advances to the world. Without doubt, America has earned dramatic returns on its investment in the security and the prosperity of Asia. The Asian financial crisis taught all of us, however, that balancing the books can be as important for regional stability as the balance of power. For this reason, we are working with our Asian trading partners and within regional and international institutions to promote financial restructuring and lay the foundation for a sustained recovery. The benefits of reform are clear. Korea carried out the most extensive financial reforms and has achieved the greatest progress: an average GDP growth of almost 9 percent in the past three years. We also recognize the role of trade and investment in promoting growth. To this end, the United States is working globally, regionally and bilaterally to achieve greater liberalization of Asian economies. Globally, through the new World Trade Organization round. Regionally, through APEC. And bilaterally through efforts such as our free trade agreement negotiations with Singapore. But there are still, notwithstanding all of this progress, some economic trouble spots. Japan in particular has been suffering through difficult economic times. We see high levels of government and private debt. There is a large burden of non-performing corporate and financial sector assets. Rates of bankruptcy and unemployment remain at near record levels. Deflation has been protracted. If this economic deterioration continues, Japan's important leadership role could be undermined. Our distinguished ambassador to Japan, our dear friend Senator Howard Baker, works these issues every single day. The Japanese government has declared that the recession finally has bottomed-out. We hope that is the case and that Prime Minister Koizumi can now accelerate implementation of the reforms that he has outlined to his people and that he has outlined to President Bush. That means letting markets function. Clearing bad loans from the banks.

Restructuring corporations to make them more profitable. And deregulating the economy to create new business opportunities. I am confident that the Japanese people will overcome these difficulties as they have so many others. As President Bush observed during his February speech to the Japanese Diet, Japan transformed itself into a modern economy during the Meiji Restoration at the end of the 19th century. In the postwar period of the last century it produced an economic miracle. And Japan will transform its economy again to ensure success in this new century. In China, market dynamism clearly has replaced dogmatism. China is no longer in the throes of Cultural Revolution. It is no longer exporting communism. It is no longer an enemy of capitalism. Though China still has huge economic problems and other problems, it has become the world's fourth largest trading power, after the European Union, the United States and Japan. It is now a member of the World Trade Organization, accountable to a law-based international order. Our bilateral relationship with China has come a long way in just a year. Last spring, we were in the midst of the EP-3 crisis, the reconnaissance plane crisis. And some wondered if the Chinese had brought down not just the plane, but had brought down the hope of a productive relationship. This spring, rather than our relationship being sunk by that incident, we are exploring new and promising new areas of cooperation with the Chinese, from counterterrorism to trade liberalization and stability in South Asia. In the past year, I traveled to China three times, twice with President Bush. We saw how China's skylines have been transformed by the entrepreneurial drive of its citizens and a flood of foreign investment, much of it American. Expectations have risen with the skylines. People aspire to cars, not bicycles. American banks and insurance companies are rushing to provide Chinese consumers with everything from financial services to convenience stores. In turn, China's growing economy benefits American shoppers, workers, farmers and business owners. I have no doubt, at the same time, that the Chinese military intends to use part of China's new wealth to modernize itself. As China trades with other countries and updates its military forces and equipment, it needs to work with us. It needs to work with us to show us and its neighbors transparency, to show us what they are doing, thereby building trust and reducing tensions. We remain deeply concerned about continued Chinese involvement in the proliferation of missile technology and equipment. And there is a gap between China's promises and its fulfillment of those promises. President Bush made clear at the Beijing summit that China's fulfillment of its nonproliferation commitments would be crucial to determining the quality of the United States–China relationship. An arms buildup, like those new missiles opposite Taiwan, only deepen tensions, deepen suspicion. Whether China chooses peace or coercion to resolve its differences with Taiwan will tell us a great deal about the kind of relationship China seeks not only with its neighbors, but with us. The differences between China and Taiwan are fundamentally political. They cannot be solved by military means.

On the subject of Taiwan, America's position is clear and it will not change. We will uphold our "One China" policy and we continue to insist that the mainland solve its differences with Taiwan peacefully. Indeed a peaceful resolution is the foundation on which the breakthrough Sino-American communiques were built, and the United States takes our responsibilities under the Taiwan Relations Act very, very seriously. People tend to refer to Taiwan as "The Taiwan Problem." I call Taiwan not a problem, but a success story. Taiwan has become a resilient economy, a vibrant democracy and a generous contributor to the international community. The People's Republic of China and Taiwan are both evolving rapidly. The constant in their cross-strait relationship is a common, long-term interest in the bloodless resolution of their differences. We wish them well as they work directly with one another to narrow those differences. They're doing pretty well. Taiwan has invested $80 to 100 billion in the mainland. Several hundred thousand Taiwanese businesspeople and their families live and work in the greater Shanghai area. Over 500,000 telephone calls cross the Strait every day. The two sides are building a foundation for a peaceful, shared future, and we applaud that. Ultimately, how China uses its increasing wealth at home and growing influence abroad are matters for China to decide. The United States wants to work with China to make decisions and take actions befitting a global leader. We ask China to collaborate with us and with our allies and friends to promote stability and well-being worldwide. To pressure governments that sponsor or harbor terrorists. To bring peace to regions in crisis. To become a global partner against poverty and disease, environmental degradation and proliferation. The experience of many other Asian countries suggests that as China continues to prosper and integrate itself into the international community, its citizens will demand ever-increasing personal and political freedom. Some think China is different—that its culture, history and size mean that ordinary Chinese people do not care about human rights and that democracy cannot develop there. I disagree. The desire for freedom is hard-wired into human beings. Freedom is not an optional piece of software, compatible with some cultures but not with others. No "Great Firewall of China" can separate the Chinese people from their God-given rights or keep them from joining an ever-growing community of democracies. The Chinese people want what all people want: respect for their fundamental human rights. A better life for themselves and their children. A real say in the future of their country. Again and again in Asia, the development of large middle classes has generated growing demands for more accountability, pluralistic governance. This pattern has been repeated in places with very different cultural and religious make-ups—Confucian, Christian and Muslim.

Again and again we have seen authoritarian regimes give way to tides of democratic reform: the Philippines in 1986, Taiwan in 1987, South Korea in 1988, Thailand in 1990, Mongolia in 1992. In 1998, Indonesia embarked on a democratic path. And just this month, as Dick Holbrooke noted, East Timor celebrated its independence and swore in its first democratically elected government. What we have seen in East Asia and the Pacific over the past half century, then, is a region undergoing historic transformations, all of them interrelated. A vast and varied region engulfed in hot and cold wars and rife with internecine conflict being transformed into one of new and unprecedented stability. To be sure, peace has not come to the Korean peninsula. Many other disputes within the region have yet to find political settlement. And how China will choose to exercise its growing power remains an open question. Still and yet, the East Asia–Pacific is more pacific now than ever. The change on the economic front has been just as dramatic. Some Asian economies got their start earlier, some later. But in just a few generations, Asian countries that have embraced the market have gone from near universal poverty to unprecedented new levels of prosperity. Indeed, Asia's economic transformation from dominoes to dynamos has become cliché. However, the transformation is not complete. Asian countries must undertake the reforms needed to spur their recovery from the 1997 crisis and to ensure their sustained success. Asia's transformation toward greater political freedom can be traced from Thailand to Taiwan, from Indonesia to South Korea. This transformation, too, is incomplete. We see new cause for hope in Burma as Aung San Suu Kyi re-enters the political process. Cambodia is strengthening a fragile democracy through more free and fair elections and the consolidation of democratic institutions. China, Laos and Vietnam have opened their economies but have yet to open their political systems. North Korea remains the chronic outlier. But I have no doubt, no doubt whatsoever, that Asia's great transformation from dominoes to dynamos, and from dynamos to democracies will only accelerate in this new century. There will be setbacks and dangers ahead for sure. I am equally sure that they will be surmounted by the determination and ingenuity of the peoples of Asia. And as they build a future of peace, a future of prosperity, a future of freedom for themselves and their children, the men and women can count on the essential and enduring support of the United States. We are a Pacific nation. We are an Asian nation. And we will remain so. And under the leadership of President Bush, I guarantee that to you tonight. Thank you very much.

Reference:

Powell, Colin L. 2002. "Remarks at Asia Society Annual Dinner." Available at http://www.state.gov/secretary/rm/2002/10983.htm (accessed 30 May 2004).

Dr. Condoleezza Rice Discusses President's National Security Strategy (1 October 2002)

Much of the international community became concerned about U.S. unilateralism as heard emanating from U.S. government official speeches in the months following September 11. Dr. Rice, as national security advisor, had a primary responsibility in developing the administration's approach to nation-building, as well as national security strategy in general.

I am honored to deliver this year's Wriston Lecture. And happy to be in New York. It is important for government officials to venture beyond Washington, to get out, talk to—and listen to—Americans from every corner of our vast, great country. The President said it best when talking about the National Security Strategy that he sent to Congress ten days ago. He was very clear that he wanted the document written in plain English, not academic jargon. He said, "This is the . . . Security Strategy of the [entire] United States. The boys in Lubbock ought to be able to read it." Manhattan is not Lubbock, but it is that same spirit that brings me here tonight to speak plainly about some of the great issues facing our country. Foreign policy is ultimately about security—about defending our people, our society, and our values, such as freedom, tolerance, openness, and diversity. No place evokes these values better than our cities. Here in New York, about a third of the population was born abroad. Across the street from here is St. Bartholomew's, a Protestant Church. Go three blocks to the east from here and there the Sutton Place Synagogue. Go a couple of blocks to the west, and you'll come to St. Patrick's Cathedral. Over the bridge in Queens, you'll find a Hindu temple. Go uptown a few blocks from where we are and you come to the Manhattan Won Buddhist Temple on East 57th. Keep going north and you will run into the Islamic Cultural Center on East 96th.

These facts stand as living rebukes to the extremism of our enemies, and the mindset that prevails in too many parts of the world that difference is a reason to hate and a license to kill. America is proof that pluralism and tolerance are the foundations of true national greatness. And today—385 days after September 11, 2001—it is clear that our commitment to our ideals is stronger than ever. The fall of the Berlin Wall and the fall of the World Trade Center were the bookends of a long transition period. During that period those of us who think about foreign policy for a living searched for an overarching, explanatory theory or framework that would describe the new threats and the proper response to them. Some said that nations and their militaries were no longer relevant, only global markets knitted together by new technologies. Others foresaw a future dominated by ethnic conflict. And some even thought that in the future the primary energies of America's Armed Forces would be devoted to managing civil conflict and humanitarian assistance. It will take years to understand the long-term effects of September 11th. But there are certain verities that the tragedy brought home to us in the most vivid way.

Perhaps most fundamentally, 9/11 crystallized our vulnerability. It also threw into sharp relief the nature of the threats we face today. Today's threats come less from massing armies than from small, shadowy bands of terrorists—less from strong states than from weak or failed states. And after 9/11, there is no longer any doubt that today America faces an existential threat to our security—a threat as great as any we faced during the Civil War, the so-called "Good War," or the Cold War. President Bush's new National Security Strategy offers a bold vision for protecting our Nation that captures today's new realities and new opportunities. It calls on America to use our position of unparalleled strength and influence to create a balance of power that favors freedom. As the President says in the cover letter: we seek to create the "conditions in which all nations and all societies can chose for themselves the rewards and challenges of political and economic liberty." This strategy has three pillars:

- We will defend the peace by opposing and preventing violence by terrorists and outlaw regimes.
- We will preserve the peace by fostering an era of good relations among the world's great powers.
- And we will extend the peace by seeking to extend the benefits of freedom and prosperity across the globe.

Defending our Nation from its enemies is the first and fundamental commitment of the Federal Government. And as the world's most powerful nation, the United States has a special responsibility to help make the world more secure. In fighting global terror, we will work with coalition partners on every continent, using every tool in our arsenal—from diplomacy and better defenses to law enforcement, intelligence, cutting off terrorist financing, and, if needed, military power. We will break up terror networks, hold to account nations that harbor terrorists, and confront aggressive tyrants holding or seeking nuclear, chemical, and biological weapons that might be passed to terrorist allies. These are different faces of the same evil. Terrorists need a place to plot, train, and organize. Tyrants allied with terrorists can greatly extend the reach of their deadly mischief. Terrorists allied with tyrants can acquire technologies allowing them to murder on an ever more massive scale. Each threat magnifies the danger of the other. And the only path to safety is to effectively confront both terrorists and tyrants. The Iraqi regime's violation of every condition set forth by the UN Security Council for the 1991 cease-fire fully justifies—legally and morally—the enforcement of those conditions. It is also true that since 9/11, our Nation is properly focused as never before on preventing attacks against us before they happen. The National Security Strategy does not overturn five decades of doctrine and jettison either containment or deterrence. These strategic concepts can and will continue to be employed where appropriate. But some threats are so potentially catastrophic—and can arrive with so little warning, by means that are untraceable—that they cannot be contained. Extremists who seem to view suicide as a sacrament are unlikely to ever be deterred. And new technology requires new thinking about when a threat actually becomes "imminent." So as a matter of common sense, the United States must be prepared to take action, when necessary, before threats have fully materialized. Preemption is not a new concept. There has never been a moral or legal requirement that a country wait to be attacked before it can address existential threats. As George Shultz recently wrote, "If there is a rattlesnake in the yard, you don't wait for it to strike before you take action in self-defense." The United States has long affirmed the right to anticipatory self-defense—from the Cuban Missile Crisis in 1962 to the crisis on the Korean Peninsula in 1994. But this approach must be treated with great caution. The number of cases in which it might be justified will always be small. It does not give a green light— to the United States or any other nation—to act first without exhausting other means, including diplomacy. Preemptive action does not come at the beginning of a long chain of effort. The threat must be very grave. And the risks of waiting must far outweigh the risks of action. To support all these means of defending the peace, the United States will build and maintain 21st century military forces that are beyond challenge. We will seek to dissuade any potential adversary from pursuing a military build-up in the hope of surpassing, or equaling, the power of the United States and our allies. Some have criticized this frankness as impolitic. But surely clarity is a virtue here. Dissuading military competition can prevent potential conflict and costly global arms races. And the United States invites—indeed, we exhort—our freedom loving allies, such as those in Europe, to increase their military capabilities.

The burden of maintaining a balance of power that favors freedom should be shouldered by all nations that favor freedom. What none of us should want is the emergence of a militarily powerful adversary who does not share our common values. Thankfully, this possibility seems more remote today than at any point in our lifetimes. We have an historic opportunity to break the destructive pattern of great power rivalry that has bedeviled the world since rise of the nation state in the 17th century. Today, the world's great centers of power are united by common interests, common dangers, and—increasingly—common values. The United States will make this a key strategy for preserving the peace for many decades to come. There is an old argument between the so-called "realistic" school of foreign affairs and the "idealistic" school. To oversimplify, realists downplay the importance of values and the internal structures of states, emphasizing instead the balance of power as the key to stability and peace. Idealists emphasize the primacy of values, such as freedom and democracy and human rights, in ensuring that just political order is obtained. As a professor, I recognize that this debate has won tenure for and sustained the careers of many generations of scholars. As a policymaker, I can tell you that these categories obscure reality. In real life, power and values are married completely. Power matters in the conduct of world affairs. Great powers matter a great deal—they have the ability to influence the lives of millions and change history. And the values of great powers matter as well. If the Soviet Union had won the Cold War, the world would look very different today—Germany today might look like the old German Democratic Republic, or Latin America like Cuba. Today, there is an increasing awareness—on every continent—of a paradigm of progress, founded on political and economic liberty. The United States, our NATO allies, our neighbors in the Western Hemisphere, Japan, and our other friends and allies in Asia and Africa all share a broad commitment to democracy, the rule of law, a market-based economy, and open trade. In addition, since September 11 all the world's great powers see themselves as falling on the same side of a profound divide between the forces of chaos and order, and they are acting accordingly. America and Europe have long shared a commitment to liberty. We also now understand that being the target of trained killers is a powerful tonic that makes disputes over other important issues look like the policy differences they are, instead of fundamental clashes of values. The United States is also cooperating with India across a range of issues—even as we work closely with Pakistan. Russia is an important partner in the war on terror and is reaching towards a future of greater democracy and economic freedom. As it does so, our relationship will continue to broaden and deepen. The passing of the ABM Treaty and the signing of the Moscow Treaty reducing strategic arms by two-thirds make clear that the days of Russian military confrontation with the West are over. China and the United States are cooperating on issues ranging from the fight against terror to maintaining stability on the Korean peninsula. And China's transition continues. Admittedly, in some areas, its leaders still follow practices that are abhorrent. Yet China's leaders have said that their main goal is to raise living standards for the Chinese people. They will find that reaching that goal in today's world will depend more on developing China's human capital than it will on China's natural resources or territorial possessions. And as China's populace become more educated, more free to think, and more entrepreneurial, we believe this will inevitably lead to greater political freedom. You cannot expect people to think on the job, but not at home. This confluence of common interests and increasingly common values creates a moment of enormous opportunities. Instead of repeating the historic pattern where great power rivalry exacerbates local conflicts, we can use great power cooperation to solve conflicts, from the Middle East to Kashmir, Congo, and beyond. Great power cooperation also creates an opportunity for multilateral institutions—such as the UN, NATO, and the WTO—to prove their worth. That's the challenge set forth by the President three weeks ago to the UN concerning Iraq. And great power cooperation can be the basis for moving forward on problems that require multilateral solutions—from terror to the environment. To build a balance of power that favors freedom, we must also extend the peace by extending the benefits of liberty and prosperity as broadly as possible. As the President has said, we have a responsibility to build a world that is not only safer, but better. The United States will fight poverty, disease, and oppression because it is the right thing to do—and the smart thing to do. We have seen how poor states can become weak or even failed states, vulnerable to hijacking by terrorist networks—with potentially catastrophic consequences. And in societies where legal avenues for political dissent are stifled, the temptation to speak through violence grows. We will lead efforts to build a global trading system that is growing and more free. Here in our own hemisphere, for example, we are committed to completing a Free Trade Area of the Americas by 2005. We are also starting negotiations on a free trade agreement with the Southern African Customs Union. Expanding trade is essential to the development efforts of poor nations and to the economic health of all nations.

We will continue to lead the world in efforts to combat HIV/AIDS—a pandemic which challenges our humanity and threatens whole societies. We will seek to bring every nation into an expanding circle of development. Earlier this year the President proposed a 50 percent increase in U.S. development assistance. But he also made clear that new money means new terms. The new resources will only be available to countries that work to govern justly, invest in the health and education of their people, and encourage economic liberty.

We know from experience that corruption, bad policies, and bad practices can make aid money worse than useless. In such environments, aid props up bad policy, chasing out investment and perpetuating misery. Good policy, on the other hand, attracts private capital and expands trade. In a sound policy environment, development aid is a catalyst, not a crutch. At the core of America's foreign policy is our resolve to stand on the side of men and women in every nation who stand for what the President has called the "non-negotiable demands of human dignity"—free speech, equal justice, respect for women, religious tolerance, and limits on the power of the state. These principles are universal—and President Bush has made them part of the debate in regions where many thought that merely to raise them was imprudent or impossible.

From Cairo and Ramallah to Tehran and Tashkent, the President has made clear that values must be a vital part of our relationships with other countries. In our development aid, our diplomacy, our international broadcasting, and in our educational assistance, the United States will promote moderation, tolerance, and human rights. And we look forward to one day standing for these aspirations in a free and unified Iraq. We reject the condescending view that freedom will not grow in the soil of the Middle East—or that Muslims somehow do not share in the desire to be free. The celebrations we saw on the streets of Kabul last year proved otherwise. And in a recent UN report, a panel of 30 Arab intellectuals recognized that for their nations to fully join in the progress of our times will require greater political and economic freedom, the empowerment of women, and better, more modern education. We do not seek to impose democracy on others, we seek only to help create conditions in which people can claim a freer future for themselves. We recognize as well that there is no "one size fits all" answer. Our vision of the future is not one where every person eats Big Macs and drinks Coke—or where every nation has a bicameral legislature with 535 members and a judiciary that follows the principles of *Marbury vs. Madison*. Germany, Indonesia, Japan, the Philippines, South Africa, South Korea, Taiwan, and Turkey show that freedom manifests itself differently around the globe—and that new liberties can find an honored place amidst ancient traditions. In countries such as Bahrain, Jordan, Morocco, and Qatar, reform is under way, taking shape according to different local circumstances. And in Afghanistan this year, a traditional Loya Jirga assembly was the vehicle for creating the most broadly representative government in Afghan history. Because of our own history, the United States knows we must be patient—and humble. Change—even if it is for the better—is often difficult. And progress is sometimes slow. America has not always lived up to our own high standards. When the Founding Fathers said, "We, the people," they didn't mean me. Democracy is hard work. And 226 years later, we are still practicing each day to get it right. We have the ability to forge a

21st century that lives up to our hopes and not down to our fears. But only if we go about our work with purpose and clarity. Only if we are unwavering in our refusal to live in a world governed by terror and chaos. Only if we are unwilling to ignore growing dangers from aggressive tyrants and deadly technologies. And only if we are persistent and patient in exercising our influence in the service of our ideals, and not just ourselves. Thank you very much.

Reference:

"Dr. Condoleezza Rice Discusses President's National Security Strategy." Available at http://www.whitehouse.gov/news/releases/2002/10/print/20021001-6.html (accessed 16 January 2004).

George W. Bush, "State of the Union 2003"

President Bush made clear his concerns about the imminent dangers posed by Iraq and the post-Saddam environment the United States sought to create. In the aftermath of the "war period" (March through late April 2003) and the subsequent upheaval as the United States sought to establish and stabilize a "democratic Iraq," much debate about the efficacy, planning, and understanding of this speech has transpired.

. . .The qualities of courage and compassion that we strive for in America also determine our conduct abroad. The American flag stands for more than our power and our interests. Our founders dedicated this country to the cause of human dignity, the rights of every person, and the possibilities of every life. This conviction leads us into the world to help the afflicted, and defend the peace, and confound the designs of evil men.

In Afghanistan, we helped liberate an oppressed people. And we will continue helping them secure their country, rebuild their society, and educate all their children—boys and girls. In the Middle East, we will continue to seek peace between a secure Israel and a democratic Palestine. Across the Earth, America is feeding the hungry—more than 60 percent of international food aid comes as a gift from the people of the United States. As our nation moves troops and builds alliances to make our world safer, we must also remember our calling as a blessed country is to make this world better.

Today, on the continent of Africa, nearly 30 million people have the AIDS virus—including 3 million children under the age 15. There are whole countries in Africa where more than one-third of the adult population carries the infection. More than 4 million require immediate drug treatment. Yet across that continent, only 50,000 AIDS victims—only 50,000—are receiving the medicine they need.

Because the AIDS diagnosis is considered a death sentence, many do not seek treatment. Almost all who do are turned away. A doctor in rural South Africa describes his frustration. He says, "We have no medicines. Many hospitals tell people, you've got AIDS, we can't help you. Go home and die." In an age of miraculous medicines, no person should have to hear those words.

AIDS can be prevented. Anti-retroviral drugs can extend life for many years. And the cost of those drugs has dropped from $12,000 a year to under $300 a year—which places a tremendous possibility within our grasp. Ladies and gentlemen, seldom has history offered a greater opportunity to do so much for so many.

We have confronted, and will continue to confront, HIV/AIDS in our own country. And to meet a severe and urgent crisis abroad, tonight I propose the Emergency Plan for AIDS Relief—a work of mercy beyond all current international efforts to help the people of Africa. This comprehensive plan will prevent 7 million new AIDS infections, treat at least 2 million people with life-extending drugs, and provide humane care for millions of people suffering from AIDS, and for children orphaned by AIDS.

I ask the Congress to commit $15 billion over the next five years, including nearly $10 billion in new money, to turn the tide against AIDS in the most afflicted nations of Africa and the Caribbean.

This nation can lead the world in sparing innocent people from a plague of nature. And this nation is leading the world in confronting and defeating the man-made evil of international terrorism . . ..

In all these efforts, however, America's purpose is more than to follow a process—it is to achieve a result: the end of terrible threats to the civilized world. All free nations have a stake in preventing sudden and catastrophic attacks. And we're asking them to join us, and many are doing so. Yet the course of this nation does not depend on the decisions of others. Whatever action is required, whenever action is necessary, I will defend the freedom and security of the American people.

Different threats require different strategies. In Iran, we continue to see a government that represses its people, pursues weapons of mass destruction, and supports terror. We also see Iranian citizens risking intimidation and death as they speak out for liberty and human rights and democracy. Iranians, like all people, have a right to choose their own government and determine their own destiny—and the United States supports their aspirations to live in freedom.

On the Korean Peninsula, an oppressive regime rules a people living in fear and starvation. Throughout the 1990s, the United States relied on a negotiated framework to keep North Korea from gaining nuclear weapons. We now know that that regime was deceiving the world, and developing those weapons all along. And today the North Korean regime is using its nuclear program to incite fear and seek concessions. America and the world will not be blackmailed.

America is working with the countries of the region—South Korea, Japan, China, and Russia—to find a peaceful solution, and to show the North Korean government that nuclear weapons will bring only isolation, economic stagnation, and continued hardship. The North Korean regime will find respect in the world and revival for its people only when it turns away from its nuclear ambitions.

Our nation and the world must learn the lessons of the Korean Peninsula and not allow an even greater threat to rise up in Iraq. A brutal dictator, with a history of reckless aggression, with ties to terrorism, with great potential wealth, will not be permitted to dominate a vital region and threaten the United States. . . .

Tonight I have a message for the men and women who will keep the peace, members of the American Armed Forces: Many of you are assembling in or near the Middle East, and some crucial hours may lay ahead. In those hours, the success of our cause will depend on you. Your training has prepared you. Your honor will guide you. You believe in America, and America believes in you.

Sending Americans into battle is the most profound decision a President can make. The technologies of war have changed; the risks and suffering of war have not. For the brave Americans who bear the risk, no victory is free from sorrow. This nation fights reluctantly, because we know the cost and we dread the days of mourning that always come.

We seek peace. We strive for peace. And sometimes peace must be defended. A future lived at the mercy of terrible threats is no peace at all. If war is forced upon us, we will fight in a just cause and by just means—sparing, in every way we can, the innocent. And if war is forced upon us, we will fight with the full force and might of the United States military—and we will prevail.

Reference:

Bush, George. 2003. *State of the Union 2003*. Available at http://www.whitehouse.gov/news/releases/2003/01/20030128-19.html (accessed 12 February 2004).

Remarks by the President on U.S. Humanitarian Aid to Afghanistan

President George W. Bush's war against terrorism began with ousting the Taliban government from Afghanistan in late 2001. At the same time, the administration began to address questions of what would replace that government and what type of assistance was required to achieve a reconstructed Afghanistan. The lessons that he outlines in this speech apply to the many cases of nation-building facing the international community around the world, with varying degrees of emphasis on each point. It was a stunning change from the views of candidate Bush in the 2000 presidential election.

The President: Welcome. Please be seated, thanks for coming. Laura and I appreciate you coming today, and it's a chance to talk about our vision for our friends in Afghanistan. It was a year ago that American forces were just beginning the liberation of Afghanistan. And on this date last year, a year ago today, I asked the children of America to contribute one dollar to provide food and medical help to the children of Afghanistan. In a year's time after making that request, we've really accomplished a lot. We have. We have seen, of course, the tremendous skill and character of a United States military. We have seen the courage of our allies and our Afghan friends. We have seen the spirit of the Afghan people, who long for freedom. We've seen the great generosity of our fellow Americans extended to men, women, and children on the other side of the Earth. And yet, today I want you all to know, and our fellow citizens to know, there's still a lot left to do. There's still a lot of work to do in Afghanistan to achieve our dreams—and more importantly, the dreams of the Afghan people. Today, America affirms its full commitment to a future of progress and stability for the Afghan people. I appreciate so very much the Ambassador for being here. Mr. Ambassador, I want to thank you for your service. The Ambassador is a—was an American citizen until recently. He decided he wanted to serve his country, the land of his birth; renounced his citizenship so he could become the official Ambassador from Afghanistan to the United States. And Ambassador Shahryar is a—is a great man who serves a wonderful example of putting your country above yourself. And so, Mr. Ambassador, we're honored you're here. I want to thank you— where is he? Oh, Ambassador, you'd think they'd have given you a better seat. I'm proud of you, I really am. I'm also proud of Andrew Natsios, who is our Administrator of USAID. I want to thank him. I'll talk about some of Andy's fellow employees here in a minute and what they're doing on behalf of the American people to help Afghanistan children. Sharif Faez is the Minister of Education—Higher Education. He, too, used to live in America. He's now serving his country. He shares our vision and understanding of the need to make sure the educational systems are strong and available, so that people can have hope in his country. Mr. Minister, thank you for your service, and I'm honored you're here with us.

I appreciate the members of the Congress being here. Dana, thanks for coming. Members of my national security team who are working hard on Afghan policy, whether it be Condi Rice, who's the boss; or Zal—where are you, Zal? Thank you, Zal—he knows a lot about Afghanistan; after all, he was from there. Elliot Abrams, members of my team who care deeply about our policy to make sure that our policy is complete. The—it's very important for our fellow Americans to remember that—keep in mind about the Taliban. They were the most brutal and oppressive governments—one of the most brutal and oppressive governments in modern times. It's hard for us to understand in America, but these are people who attempted to control every mind and every soul in the country. They, obviously, had a vast network of terrorist camps available to train extremists from around the world. Thanks to America, and thanks to our friends, thanks to people who love freedom for everybody, the oppressive rule has been lifted. They're no longer in power. They're on the run—along with a bunch of other ones over there, too. Afghanistan has entered a new era of hope. And we want to be a continued part of the new era of hope in Afghanistan. One of our dear values, one of the values we hold close to our heart is the respect and beliefs of all peace-loving people, no matter what their faith may be. Islam is a vibrant faith. Millions of our fellow citizens are Muslim. We respect the faith. We honor its traditions. Our enemy does not. Our enemy don't follow the great traditions of Islam. They've hijacked a great religion. But it's important, as we lift that veil, to remember that they are nothing but a bunch of radical terrorists who distort history and the values of Islam. Islam is a faith that brings comfort to people. It inspires them to lead lives based on honesty, and justice, and compassion. We've also got a great tradition, not only of recognizing freedom of religion and respecting religion, we've got a great tradition of liberating people, not conquering them. It's very important for our citizens to remember that as we upheld that doctrine that said, if you harbor a terrorist, you're just as guilty as the terrorists, that we went into Afghanistan to free people, because we believe in freedom. We believe every life counts, everybody has worth, everybody matters, whether they live in America or in Afghanistan. And so we are helping the people to now recover from years of tyranny and oppression. We're helping Afghanistan to claim its democratic future, and we're helping that nation to establish public order and safety— even while the struggle against terror continues in some corners of that country. There's still al Qaeda killers roaming around Afghanistan.

We're working closely with the government to rout them out, not only to make sure that Afghanistan is more safe, but also to make sure America is safe, as well. A year ago, it was really hard to find security and safety anywhere in Afghanistan. Just ask the citizens who were there. Now, America is helping to form a new Afghan national army. We are committed to an Afghan national army. The idea is to train 18 battalions of over 10,000 soldiers and finish the task by the end of next year. I'm proud that Germany is helping, as well, to bring civil order by helping to build a police force. The International Security Assistance Force, what they call the ISAF, led by coalition countries, is helping to keep the streets safe in the city of Kabul. Security is a requirement for recovery and development. Can't have recovery and development unless there is a secure society. America and other nations will continue working with the Afghan government to build security, so the Afghan people can live their lives without violence and without fear. A year ago, Afghans were living under history's first-ever terrorist-sponsored regime. These people had found a parasite. And in June of 2002, history will show that Afghanistan reversed its history by having a Loya Jirga and created the most broadly representative government in Afghanistan's history. There are two women serving in President Karzai's cabinet. The institutions of free debate and free press are taking hold. New commissions on human rights and the drafting of a new constitution will lay the groundwork for democracy and for the rule of law. The institutions necessary for the development of a peaceful, hopeful country are going to be put in place soon. We will stay the course to help that country develop—in their image, not in ours. A year ago, millions of Afghans lived in fear of famine and disease. In the time since, America has delivered food and medicine to the Afghan people. We are committed to the health of the Afghan people. Over the last year, UN. World Food Program, with the support of the United States, has provided 575,000 metric tons of food to nearly 10 million Afghans. The United States has also provided seed and fertilizer in time for the spring planting season. The United States joined with other nations to support UNICEF's vaccination of more than 8 million children against measles. American health care officials are helping with other efforts to improve public health, including the fight against polio and malaria, HIV and tuberculosis. These relief efforts have put hunger and disease on the retreat. We got the Taliban gone. We'd like to get disease and hunger gone, as well. More than 2 million Afghan refugees have returned back to the country since November. That is a positive sign. It's a good sign that people are sensing their country is a better place to live and more secure, a better place to raise a family. One American bringing hope to Afghanistan is Sergeant First Class Victor Anderson. Victor is with us today. Sergeant Anderson spent seven months traveling in Afghanistan. He visited hospitals and clinics, provided medical care from his car. He never turned down anybody who asked for help. He treated broken bones; he treated gunshot wounds; he treated cuts and diseases. He treated a small child who was bitten by a donkey. Sergeant Anderson, your service brings great credit to the Army and to America, and the nation is really grateful for your work. A year ago, the children of Afghanistan were suffering greatly in a nation beset by war. It's not hard to imagine children suffering in a nation beset by war, and it's really sad. The children of America responded with great compassion. America's Fund for Afghan Children has collected more than $10.5 million. That's a dime at a time, or a dollar at a time; that's a lot of kids working hard to collect money. It has allowed the Red Cross to deliver emergency medical supplies to help serve 60,000 people. This fund has helped provide winter clothes to 8,000 children, to help rehabilitate hospitals in Kabul. Today, we've got representatives of the fund, twins: Sarah and Alexander Ahmad. Together, they've raised $12,000—$12,000—that's a lot of money. Nearly 25 years ago, Sarah and Alexander's dad came to America from Afghanistan, from wartorn Afghanistan. Today, the family is helping to give peace a chance in their ancestral home, and as importantly, showing the world the generous heart, the great heart, of the American people. I really appreciate the example you're setting, and thank you for joining us today. And by the way, the fund still exists. And I hope the American children understand there are still people in Afghanistan who hurt a lot. And if you've given once, it's okay to give again to make sure we continue to help the people in Afghanistan. America will continue to provide that country with essential short-term relief. We also understand that Afghanistan needs long-term economic reconstruction help. And we will meet this commitment, as well. Starting with the Tokyo Conference last January, the United States and 60 other countries have pledged $4.5 billion over five years to work on reconstruction projects. America is delivering on our pledge; we're writing our checks. We're currently implementing more than $300 million worth of reconstruction and recovery projects. The nations who have made pledges, the other nations, they need to be good on their pledges. If you say you're going to help the Afghan people, do it. If you've made a pledge, write your check. It's important. America and our partners are helping rebuild roads and bridges and waterways and buildings. Last month, the United States and Japan and Saudi Arabia committed $180 million to rebuild the highway connecting Kabul, Kandahar and Herat. It's an important project. President Karzai spoke to me about it in the Oval Office. He said, it's important that we show the people that we're—that we can work together to restore the historic link, to make sure that commerce and trade flow more freely and that people are able to find work. I want to thank the Saudi Arabians, the Japanese for joining us in this highly visible and highly important project. We're also helping to rebuild schools and hospitals and clinics. Some of the first rebuilding is being done by the U.S. Army Civil Affairs soldiers, who are working with relief agencies to rebuild dozens of schools. With us today is Captain Britton London, who enlisted friends, family members, church groups to supply Afghan students with thousands of pens and pencils and notebooks. Captain London is a man after my own heart. He started a—he got the equipment necessary to start the first post-Taliban baseball league. He brought me a ball—two balls signed by the Eagles—the Eagles, the Eagles, the mighty Eagles of Afghan baseball. And they practice—they're practicing now, and the games are held once a week.

Our soldiers wear the uniforms of warriors, but they are also compassionate people. And the Afghan people are really beginning to see the true strength of our country. I mean, routing out the Taliban was important, but building a school is equally important. Across Afghanistan, U.S. aid will help build and refurbish several hundred more schools over the next two years. We're also in the process of training hundreds of teachers. In March, many girls walked into a classroom for the first time. And our country has provided them, as well as the boys, with millions of new textbooks. It's hard to believe—I know it's hard for some in America to believe that the Afghan people were living under a government that would not let girls go to school. It's just hard to imagine in America. But it's reality. And now we've got a lot of work to do to make up for lost time. Everybody counts, everybody has worth, everybody matters. Spearheading our back-to-school efforts are Lisa Hartenberger and Nitin Madhaf. They work for USAID. They're a part of the—they're a part of the new army in Afghanistan—these are army of compassionate souls who are on the front lines of making sure that the Afghan people understand our commitment is real; that when we talk about freedom we understand that freedom is more than just a word. Freedom is a chance for people to get a good education; freedom is a chance for people to get good health care; freedom is a chance for people to realize their dreams. And I want to thank—I want to thank these two fine public servants that work for—with Andy, for your service to the country in service of Afghanistan. Thank you, Lisa. Thank you, buddy. Last year when the Taliban fell, I know I remember it and I'm sure a lot of our fellow Americans remember, the images of celebration that took place in the streets. People came out to celebrate freedom. It reminded us that the whole world—in the whole world there is a huge appetite for freedom. People love to be free. And it's important—as we stay in Afghanistan, it will be important for other brave people, whether they live in Muslim countries or in the Middle East, people who stand for tolerance and the rule of law and equal rights and freedom of expression, to see our commitment to freedom; that our commitment for freedom is complete, and it's real, and it's sincere. It's also important for people to know we never seek to impose our culture or our form of government. We just want to live under those universal values, God-given values. We believe in the demands of human dignity that apply in every culture, in every nation. Human beings should have the right to free speech. Women deserve respect and opportunity. All people deserve equal justice, religious tolerance. This is true in America. This is true in Afghanistan. These rights are true everywhere. We've seen in Afghanistan that the road to freedom can be hard, it's a hard struggle. We've also seen in Afghanistan that the road to freedom is the only one worth traveling. Any nation that sacrifices to build a future of liberty will have the respect, the support, and the friendship of the United States of America. May God bless the people of Afghanistan and of America. Thank you all for coming.

Reference:

"President Highlights Humanitarian Efforts in Afghanistan." Available at http://www.whitehouse.gov/news/releases/2002/10/20021011–3. html (accessed 15 March 2004).

Background Briefing on Reconstruction and Humanitarian Assistance in Postwar Iraq

This is a fascinating off-the-record briefing on reconstruction and humanitarian operations, which preceded the war by seven days. It speaks to the assumptions about how welcome the U.S. forces would be upon the ouster of Saddam's regime.

Presenter: Senior Defense Official, Tuesday, 11 March 2003—10 a.m. EST

Staff: This is going to be a background briefing on the Office of Reconstruction and Humanitarian Assistance. We're going to have about 30 minutes to answer your questions. I know a lot of you have a lot of questions. This is our first opportunity to meet a lot of the media.

Our two people up here, for those people on background only, and I'll introduce our first Defense spokesman.

Senior Defense Official: I asked to talk to you. I asked [staff] to put this together and let me talk to you for several reasons. Number one, there's a lot of information coming out that's, to me, not quite right, and I wanted to tell you what I know; and what I don't know, I'll tell you that I don't know. And then I want to give you the background on how we got started, where we are today, what our goals are, and then we kind of take this into a dialogue and the two of us will field whatever questions you have for the time we have remaining.

On the—about the 20th of January, the president signed a directive that established our office, and it was to deal with the post-Saddam conditions in Iraq. And we began putting a group together from the interagencies. DOD was given the responsibility for putting the office together, and that's why the organization ended up here in this building. We started out very slowly. The first week we only had three or four people. And as these things occur, it began building, and now we have close to 200 people from the military and from the interagency process. We've taken all the plans—well, not all—all the plans that we know of, that have been prepared by the interagency—and there's been a—there was an awful lot of work done by the interagency. We brought all those together and we read them—we haven't changed any—we've read them, and we began trying to connect the dots on all of them. In fact, I think we have connected the dots on most of them. And what our focus was to take the good work that had been done and to begin to operationalize that work so you could execute those plans in a post-Saddam environment in Iraq. We began that process toward the end of January. Our team worked real hard on it. And then we had a rehearsal, facilitated by National Defense University over at McNair; we had a rehearsal that was very intense, lasted two days, went over all the plans. And that was on the 21st and 22nd February. That was a Friday and a Saturday. We had, at any one time, we've had anywhere between 150 and 200 people from the interagency in that, attended by many of the assistant secretaries of each one of departments. It was a good rehearsal. It brought out many, many issues—as you would think it would—as you begin to peel back the onion to look at how do you actually implement this plan. Is the team in place? Is the money there to do what you want to do? How long will this take? What is the lead [tackling ?]? When do they get there? Who do they report to? Are the communications set up where you could do that? Do they have the transportation? Et cetera, et cetera, et cetera.

So since that period of time, what we have done is gone through all of these issues and every day you uncover more issues, as you would expect. But it's been a good process, it's been a healthy process and it's been a process of team work. And it was good with us because it began to bond our team. And as you would expect, there is a little angst at the interagency coming into the Pentagon to do their work. And so we bonded together, I think, an extremely good team. And I'll go over that team with you in a few minutes. Our goal from day one has been to put together as solid set of plans that we could implement with a goal of going into country, implementing those plans, staying as long as necessary to be able to stand up a government in Iraq and get out as fast as we can. And our goal is to turn Iraq over to the Iraqi people, but with a government that expresses the free will of the people of Iraq. We intend to immediately start turning some things over, and every day, we'll turn over more things. I believe that's our plan . . .

Senior Defense Official: . . .I'll tell you how we're fixed here. Let me walk you through the three boxes. The first one is a reconstruction coordinator. And what you see listed under there are the functions that he's going to be most involved with. And the reconstruction coordinator is a very experienced USAID official who, after he gets in country, he will initially stand up all the USAID functions in country— done a lot of this; very experienced. The civil administrator—under him you see all the functions that he's responsible for. He is a DOD official—has a great deal of experience also.

Senior Defense Official: It's premature right now.

Senior Defense Official: Okay. The humanitarian assistance coordinator is a former ambassador. Excellent, excellent man . . .

Senior Defense Official: . . .So what you see in those three boxes are the functions that have to be accomplished in country. Now each one of those is almost a vertical stovepipe, and what we needed was something that horizontally allowed these vertical stovepipes to work. So my friend here put together an operations group, and that operations group is responsible for the logistical functions, the operational functions, the staffing, transportation, all the things it takes to make an organization move. Now below that you see three other boxes, and those are three coordinators. Because Iraq is so large, what we're going to have to do is have coordinators in the country, and so we have a coordinator for the northern part, and you have under him a core staff of about 12 people. And then we'll have the same thing in the South. And in the central [portion] we'll have a coordinator who— about 80 percent of their time will be spent on just the city of Baghdad. Each one of them will have a small staff, and what we're trying to do is we're working now to hire and enlist free Iraqis, from the United States, from Britain, from democratic European countries, that represent the provinces, each of the 17 provinces and Baghdad, that we can use to go down to the provinces and form groups from the people of each one of those provinces that begin to nominate to us things that they—that need to be done in terms of reconstruction, in terms of humanitarian aid. Now that process—I had great hopes for that process, but that's not going to—it'll happen, but it's not going as fast as I wanted. We've hired several free Iraqis, but we need to hire over a hundred, and we haven't approached that number yet. We're putting them under contract, and they are for a short period of time, somewhere between 90 and, at the most, 180 days. What we're doing is we're—the reason we're bringing them in is because they have lived in a democratic country now. They understand the democratic process. And as we use them to facilitate what's going on, we think that that's a good recipe— to have people that were born and raised in those provinces but now have lived in a democracy. And they can explain things to the people there, who have been oppressed for the last 30 or so years. These coordinators will then set up committees in each of the provinces. Like I said before, those provinces will nominate to us work that they want to see done. Now, as you know, this is a very labor-intensive business when you get into this type thing. So one of our goals is to take a good portion of the Iraqi regular army—I'm not talking about the Republican Guards, the special Republican Guards, but I'm talking about the regular army—and the regular army has the skill sets to match the work that needs to be done in construction. So our thought is to take them and they can help rebuild their own country. We'd continue to pay them. And these committees will nominate work for them to do, do things like engineering, road construction, work on bridges, remove rubble, demine, pick up unexploded ordnance, construction work, et cetera, et cetera. That also allows us—and using army allows us not to demobilize it immediately and put a lot of unemployed people on the street. So it works a pretty good process. They're working to rebuild their country. It's reestablishing some of the prestige that the regular army has lost over the years, and it allows us to get a lot of good things done for the country. The other thing we're trying to do with free Iraqis is bring in two to three with the right skill sets for each of the 21 or 22 ministries; say, from public health, bring in a free Iraqi that's an expert in public health. Now in the ministries, the Iraqis are going to continue to run the ministries, as—they run it now. And we're going to have them keep running it and we're going to pay them, pay them their salaries. But what we want to do is bring in a free Iraqi who understands the democratic process to help us facilitate making that ministry more efficient. The time frame right now is to be ready to go when called or when directed. Our time frame in country is to get in there as soon as we can and begin this work, and end it as fast as possible, but at the same returning to the Iraqi people a set of things that weren't as good when we got them and are better now and begin the democratic process and to have, like I said, a government that represents the free will of the people . . .

Senior Defense Briefer: Just one statement of the obvious, and that is this all assumes a decision by the president of the United States to execute military operations . . .

Question: Is the United States willing to accept anything other than a Western style democracy and a capitalistic economy for Iraq?

Senior Defense Official: I think what the United States is willing to accept—this me talking now—is any government that expresses the—any elected government that expresses the will of the people.

Question: That would include an Islamic-based government?

Senior Defense Official: Well, it's an Islamic country, right . . .

Question: Could you explain a couple of things?

Senior Defense Official: I'll try.

Question: One, security is not laid out in much detail here. This horizontal line to General Franks, what exactly is the chain of command between your organization and CentCom?

Senior Defense Official: Yeah, right now—right now my organization coordinates with CentCom. But as soon as we come into country, we'll work with CentCom. General Franks will be my boss.

Question: And the other question is, you know, the Iraqi National Congress last week put together this six-person group that they said was going to be the core of a new government. Is that the way you see that group as well?

Senior Defense Official: I think that's going to evolve over time. I think you're going to see a lot of people putting forth groups, and eventually we will evolve a process that leads to a democratic style government . . .

Question: How much of this plan here, how many of these players are actually in place now with you, ready to move? And two, how much of this plan is drawn from lessons learned based on experiences in Afghanistan?

Senior Defense Official: Well, I think the plans are based on experiences learned all throughout the '90s, since we've been involved in this. I've got about 180 people with me now, but we have a lot of people in country. The DART team is already in place. The coordinator that runs reconstruction is deployed; he deployed a little over a week ago with portions of his team. He's deployed an advance party that left last Friday, that we speak to daily. So when you get in—when we get in there, it will not only be all these people that I just talked about, but it will also be the mechanisms they set up to do the work, such as contracting.

Question: But they're already staging in the region, so they're ready to move immediately?

Senior Defense Official: Large bulks are already stationed in the region, you're right . . .

Question: Could you tell us about money that you guys have figured that you're going to need, what your budget is? And then there's a couple—I had heard that there was going to be maybe an international person put between you and CentCom, someone from the coalition—

Senior Defense Official: I don't know, but if you find out who that is, let me know, because I'd like to know about that.

Question: . . . .And have you established the coordinators? Are they going to be U.S. military or are they going to be—

Senior Defense Official: They're all civilian. They're all U.S. and they're all civilian.

Question: U.S. and civilian.

Senior Defense Official: Mm-hmm.

Question: And the budget?

Senior Defense Official: The budget's a function of the supplemental.

Question: Okay. And I'm sorry, one more thing. The INC members. Do they count as free Iraqis? Or are you really only looking for Americans and British—

Senior Defense Official: They count, but we're not trying to hire any of them right now. Okay?

[Clarification: DoD is not hiring or contracting with the Iraqi National Congress (INC) members as such, but some of the Iraqi expatriates working with DoD may be INC members. The INC has played an important role over the years in getting various Iraqi opposition groups to cooperate with one another. The U.S. government admires the INC's successes in organizing the endorsement by those groups of principles that the USG favors for the creation of a new democratic government for Iraq.] . . .

Question: Could you explain—is your office going to be in charge of the immediate humanitarian relief that the military supposedly is going to provide? Or how are you planning on interfacing, if you are, with—

Senior Defense Official: Well, what we have—as you know, the military has Civil Affair brigades that get involved in them. We have embedded DART teams that really are part of the humanitarian assistant coordinator.

Question: DART teams.

Senior Defense Official: Uh-huh.

Question: DART teams?

Question: Could you explain what that is? How that—

Senior Defense Official: They're the teams from USAID; they're the Disaster Response Teams. They're already in place. They're in place in Kuwait now.

Question: And in terms of resources? I mean, there's projections that, you know, millions of Iraqi children are going to need therapeutic feeding and all that. I mean, is that something that you're confident you have—

Senior Defense Official: I'm not—no, I'm not—

Question: [o]r is that something that's going to be—I'm just unclear on who does what.

Senior Defense Official: I'm sorry; I'm not following you. Maybe I'm not connecting with you here. I—

Question: Well, you've got people embedded with the military—

Senior Defense Official: Right.

Question:—from USAID.

Senior Defense Official: Right.

Question: Their responsibility is humanitarian assistance.

Senior Defense Official: That's right.

Question: I'm just trying to get a sense of how you're planning—

how that's going to coordinate and what the resource levels are at this point for that aid.

Senior Defense Official: If I could—that coordination will go on between our organization and the organization; if hostilities break out, that we'll prosecute those hostilities—that—what's called the CFLCC (ph). And all of that Civil Affairs structure is embedded in that military organization. We will be coordinating on our level with the commander of CFLCC (ph) and providing him every—all the information we have with regard to those kinds of issues that you suggest will generate early in the process. The resources to support those will flow from the UN, from ICRC, from all the NGOs and IOs and use the assessment capability extent in the DART teams, the Civil Affairs brigades and all of those other agencies that are out there looking at what the requirements are.

Question: Okay. So you're primarily functioning as communications and liaison—

Senior Defense Official: On the front end of this.

Senior Defense Official: On the front end.

Senior Defense Official: On the front end, that's correct.

Senior Defense Official: And every day, move more and more into the execution piece of this.

Question: If I could just follow up on that point—

Senior Defense Official: Now wait a minute. Wait a minute. He's been trying to ask—

Question: Thank you. Can you talk generally about how you plan to manage oil—in particular, what the plan is for—what you do with revenues, that income, and how you manage how much of that goes to reconstruction and how much not?

Senior Defense Official: Okay. Number one, the oil belongs to the Iraqi people. I see my involvement in oil to be to repair—begin the repairs of anything that's damaged, to ensure that the refineries are capable of doing what they need to do, to look at the pipeline, begin the initial repairs on the pipeline. But I don't intend to be the guy that sells Iraqi oil. That's—I think the oil belongs to the Iraqi people. Whatever the UN does in resolutions to allow more use of revenues, I think that ought to be very transparent, widely audited, and it ought to go to work for the Iraqi people. So I'm not getting into the sale of oil business.

Question: Having said that, do you anticipate the U.S. having to pay for everything that you're about to undertake on its own, or do you anticipate some of that revenue, because it's Iraqi, being used for Iraqi reconstruction?

Senior Defense Official: I would think, as we go down this road—this is my thought—that over time, some of that revenue will go for the reconstruction of Iraq, to build schools, to build hospitals, to put in better power grids, improve roads . . .

Question: On the issue of budget, I know that you said that it's part of the supplemental, but do you have any working estimates of how much it's going to cost to pay all the people in the ministries and the Iraqi military, et cetera, et cetera?

Question: What are you asking for?

Senior Defense Official: The—we've had a number that's been dancing on the—what we need to do up front is pay the people in the ministries, be able to pay the army and be able to pay the law enforcement agencies and the court system. We spent a lot of time trying to establish what that pay scale is, what are they getting now and how much should they get. And when you do that, you have to factor in the fact that over 60 percent of them are receiving food, and so if they receive less food in the future, the wage scale has to be higher.

So we about completed that. That's still in the works. And there are several that—they're looking at several places for those revenues. One of them is frozen Iraqi assets, and I think that's being discussed this week.

Question: Any—

Senior Defense Official: But I don't have an answer for you right now. I'd just tell you it's a work in progress . . .

Question: I hardly know where to begin.

Senior Defense Official: I don't either, so—

Senior Defense Official: If you figure it out, come up and—.

Question: As you look at the ministries, I mean, some of them are benign, health ministries, and some of them are not so benign.

Senior Defense Official: Some of them go away.

Question: Interior ministries, the ministry of prisons and stuff like that, some of which you actually need to continue to have function. So are you going to go in and gut some of the less benign ministries? How do you—

Senior Defense Official: Let me throw them into a couple categories, okay? I think to begin with, you have to have a face, a U.S. face, a government, interagency face for every ministry. Then the ministries begin to fall in categories. One of them is those that you're probably not going to keep and don't want to keep, but you still have to have some oversight ability because you have to have a way of dismantling it. The second category would be those that you can turn over pretty quick, hand back to the Iraqi people. The third category are those that will take a while longer to turn over but you're going to work on turning them over as fast as you can. The last category would be the ones that are difficult to turn over. An example of that might be defense. And that may end up over time being turned over to an international agency or somebody else. But our intent is to keep the ministry people in place, have them continue to function in ministries until we either, A, disestablish that ministry or, B, turn it back over to the Iraqis.

Question: You have now described several different parts of the government that you are going to pay salaries for—army, court system—

Senior Defense Official: Right. Somebody is going to pay salaries.

Question:—and some of the ministries. There are other chunks of the government that—if you can help us out—do you plan on keeping schools and hospitals? Do you plan on paying teachers? I mean, how deep are you going to go with this largesse of pretending to have revenue flowing in—not pretending, having revenue flow in? What other institutions will you support with revenue, with money?

Senior Defense Official: I think, Jack, when I say ministries, and you take education, yes, I think that flows all the way down the school system. You take public health, yes, that flows all the way down into the medical system.

Question: So it's not the ministries you're trying to [keep afloat?], you're trying to keep the whole school system.

Senior Defense Official: When you talk about ministries, we're talking about probably in the neighborhood of 2 million or more people.

Question: You're describing a vastly more invasive and widespread operation than even is remotely going on in Afghanistan. And we've been told that in Afghanistan there is no time set when the troops might come out; they'll be there for a long, long time. I know the answer is "as long as it takes," but are we talking months, years, decades?

Senior Defense Official: I'm talking—I'll probably come back to hate this answer, but I'm talking months. But in Iraq you do have a somewhat more sophisticated country and a somewhat more structured country than you do in Afghanistan. And that—and I think also, that—even though it's been an oppressed country, it has the structure and the mechanisms in there to run that country and run it fairly efficiently. At one time, it was probably one of the most efficient countries in that part of the world, and a lot of that talent's still there. So I think it's hard to try to put an Afghan template over Iraq. I don't think you'll be able to do that.

Senior Defense Official: There's a—my view is that there's a couple of branches that could occur here. First of all, remember that this organization we would call the interim transitional civil administrator. And so the branches that could come off of that could be that one could have an international flavor. I think someone here raised the question of, will there be an international figure? That is one branch. This could, hopefully sooner rather than later, be internationalized to deal with this issue. And the other branch is one that had a more U.S. face, but that was a civilian face, and interagency face so that you have more people from the other very capable departments of the U.S. government involved. But if you look at this from our standpoint, it's a short term effort to get this started, just put the wheels in motion, and then to hand that off to one of those two branches. I think probably everybody would agree that a larger international face would be better than a smaller international face. It would deal with some of—[name omitted]—issues that he talked about in terms of, okay, who's going to pay the bills over time. And I think the other thing is, everyone's focused on, you start with the oil program. Okay, the oil program feeds the food issue in the country, and you need to make sure it continues to feed that process. As he said, you got 60 percent of the people getting a large amount of their food out of that process. You can't shut it down and turn that revenue in some other direction, even if it's all for the Iraqi people. So you got to deal with that. But as you go forward, then, you know, the natural resources of the country begin to kick in . . .

Question: On the issue—on the issue of free Iraqis, you said you're trying to hire a number of them to go to different provinces; you're hoping to have some of the [ministers?]. Could you talk a little bit more about who these people will be and what exactly—how you're choosing them?

Question: And did you say they wouldn't be INC? You weren't seeking to hire them?

Senior Defense Official: Wouldn't be what?

Question: INC.

Question: You said earlier—INC.

Senior Defense Official: We haven't gone out to hire people from the INC, okay.

Question: You haven't.

[Clarification: DoD is not hiring or contracting with the Iraqi National Congress (INC) members as such, but some of the Iraqi expatriates working with DoD may be INC members. The INC has played an important role over the years in getting various Iraqi opposition groups to cooperate with one another. The U.S. government admires the INC's successes in organizing the endorsement by those groups of principles that the USG favors for the creation of a new democratic government for Iraq.]

Senior Defense Official: We have not, no. The free Iraqis—it started out with the Michigan bunch, and it's kind of expanded now to free Iraqis throughout the United States, throughout Britain. There's—we—

Question: [Off mike]—the Michigan bunch—

Senior Defense Official: There's a lot of free Iraqis that live in Michigan. On that—yeah.

Question: And are they trying to—[off mike]?

Senior Defense Official: Yeah. And we've been contacted by Iraqis in Switzerland and Iraqis in Sweden, some in Germany. First thing we do is we give them a fairly quick security check, to the degree that we can, for whatever knowledge we have on them. The second thing we do is we don't bring them on for a very long period of time, because we don't want them in Iraq as competitors to indigenous Iraqis. And the third thing is, the ones we talk to—their kids were born—a lot of their kids were born here. Their jobs are here. They want to come back here when it's over. They just want to go—they want go back home. They want to help their country for a couple of months. And so what we've done is we've written a letter to their bosses, saying, "If this is a—we need this person's skill set, talents, and we'd like for you to give them a leave of absence for a specified period of time," up to, I think, 120 days. But the boss picks out that period of time, or the Iraqi themselves.

Question: Are some of them from the State Department's Freedom of Iraq—Future of Iraq Project? Do you know?

Senior Defense Official: Yes, we have Future of Iraq people.

Question: May I follow up on the month—you said it would take a month to complete. Just exactly what are you envisioning in that month period? Is it—and is it going to set the government on track in that month period? And who exactly is going to guide them on what sort of government to set up? Just U.S.?

Senior Defense Official: No. It'll be greater than that. We're—the reason I kind of danced from you a little bit—we're still coming up with the governance process. It's being worked right now in the interagency mechanism, with the deputies and principals.

[Clarification: U.S. policy is for the Iraqis to mange their own constitutional commission to devise their own governmental institutions. The U.S. government envisions a post-Saddam Hussein Iraq as being governed by broad-based, representative institutions that will put Iraq on a democratic path toward safeguarding the rights of all Iraqis.]

Question: So you're trying to come up with a sort of government for them?

Senior Defense Official: The deputies and principals will come with that, and we'll execute that—

Question: So on the international aspect, who would be the international face? It would be someone from the UN.?

Senior Defense Official: I don't know.

Question: Would General Abizaid play a role? He has been mentioned in—

Senior Defense Official: Certainly eventually he will . . .

Question: Sorry. My second question, on international—yesterday there were bids—companies, U.S. companies, were mentioned for reconstruction. Would you be then open to other countries or—in the second phase? Or how do you envisage that?

Senior Defense Official: I don't know the answer.

Senior Defense Official: I don't know the answer to that either. In fact I found out about that two days ago, when I heard it on NPR or something . . .

Senior Defense Official: Our—the one thing I want to try to do with that is, as you come contract for work in Iraq, it'll be our goal to make sure that you must first try to find an Iraqi subcontractor to do that. And the reason for that is to—number one, is to begin to jump-start the economy; begin a process of economic development; and number three, to broaden the employee base for people to—for more jobs.

Question: What are you going to do if you get in a region that already is fairly well-organized, like the Kurdish area? They come up after a war and they say, "Okay, these are the guys we want to have in charge. We've got"—[off mike]. You bring in your guy, and they say, "Uh-uh. Don't want him. We've got ourselves organized. We don't need your"—

Senior Defense Official: What guy are you talking about?

Question: Your free Iraqi person—

Senior Defense Official: We're not—I should—we're not doing that up north. We're not doing that in the Kurdish—in the three Kurdish provinces.

Senior Defense Official: We're not bringing a free Iraqi person in there to run things. We're bringing him in as an advisor, a technical advisor, a technocrat; someone who can assist what's already there—

Senior Defense Official: A hometown boy or girl—

Senior Defense Official:—help us shape what it ought to look like in the future. But not to be in charge.

Question: Will they maintain their autonomy, though, in the north?

Senior Defense Official: Well, there will be one unified Iraq when this is all over. Now, I would think that in the governance process, the differences between the three Kurdish provinces and the remaining 14 would be worked out as part of the new Iraqi government.

Question: But your people are not going in there—you're not going in there at all?

Senior Defense Official: Sure we are. We'll be up there doing reconstruction and whatever humanitarian. But we're—hey, but we're not going to tell the—we're not going to try to re-design the ministry system and the governmental system that the Kurds have put in. We'll let the Kurds and Iraqis do that as they work out their own government. Thank you, folks. Thank you.

Reference:

This transcript was prepared by the Federal News Service, Washington, DC. Federal News Service is a private company. For other defense-related transcripts not available through this site, contact Federal News Service at (202) 347–1400. Available at http://www.pentagon.gov/news/Mar2003/t03122003_t0311bgd.html

U.S. Department of Defense
News Transcript: Coalition Provisional
Authority Live Briefing from Iraq

This is a similar briefing, but on the record, three months into the nation-building phase. The questions and answers illustrate a number of the problems facing U.S. forces as they work with Iraqis, international assistance workers, and even within the U.S. government.

Presenter: Army Maj. Gen. Carl Strock, Monday, 7 July 2003
(Video-teleconference briefing from Baghdad, Iraq. Participating were Army Maj. Gen. Carl Strock, deputy director of operations for the Coalition Provisional Authority, and Andrew Bearpark, director of regional services for the Coalition Provisional Authority.)

Bryan Whitman [deputy assistant secretary of defense for public affairs (media operations)]: Well, thank you again for joining us early this morning. Today we would like to bring into focus some of the many efforts under way in Iraq to improve the infrastructure and services in and around Baghdad. And with us today from Baghdad are two individuals that are deeply involved in those activities and are leading the coalition efforts in that regard. Major General Carl Strock is a professional military engineer with decades of experience with the U.S. Army Corps of Engineers. He currently is the deputy director of Operations for the Coalition Provisional Authority. With him is Mr. Andy Bearpark, who is a veteran overseas development and humanitarian aid official for the British government, with experience in field postings all over the globe. He serves as the CPA's director of Regional Services in Baghdad. And yes, they did return to the camera. With that, gentlemen, I will turn it over to you. And I think you might want to say something before we get into the questions.

Strock: Yes, thank you very much. As you said, I'm Major General Carl Strock. My normal job is director of Civil Works for the U.S. Army Corps of Engineers. Here in Baghdad I'm currently serving as deputy director of Operations for the Coalition Provisional Authority. I'd like to spend a few minutes here talking about Iraq's infrastructure, the challenges that it presents and the progress we've made since the end of war. I'll then turn it over to Mr. Bearpark, who will talk more about where we're headed from this point. We have an enormous job here to do to help rebuild this country. Combat damage was comparatively light, due to careful targeting and the use of precision weapons. But the real problem here is decades of neglect to this infrastructure, lack of investment in operations and maintenance, and also the looting and sabotage that's occurred since the end of fighting. We've made incredible progress in the last 12 weeks since the war ended. We are engaged in a very wide range of reconstruction and rehabilitation projects all over the country. In the last six weeks, we've committed almost a billion dollars in several thousand projects, from high-impact, relatively low-cost things that brigade commanders are doing out in the field to large infrastructure investments that will have a huge impact on the future. When I say "we," I'm talking about the collective efforts of the coalition military, the U.S. Agency for International Development and their British counterpart, DFID. We're talking about the private sector, nongovernmental organizations. But most importantly, we're talking about the Iraqis themselves. We have found here that the Iraqi public servants are wonderfully competent and remarkably committed to serving the Iraqi people. They have worked under some very, very tough circumstances both during and after the war, and yet they continue to stay at their posts and provide services to the people. It really has been gratifying. What I'd like to do now is just run through each of the sectors very quickly, and at the end of this I'll take whatever questions you have on any detail. Electricity is probably the most important thing we're doing right now, because without it, nothing else works in the country. It's an antiquated system. It's basically 1960s technology. It's an amalgamation of systems that, due to a number of circumstances, the Iraqis have not had a consistent investment approach, and they have a wide variety of manufacturers and types of systems that make up the electrical system. Hence, it is very complicated and difficult to maintain. The capacity of this system is about 7,800 megawatts. And the real important figure here is the fact that due to its age and condition, they can only generate about 4,500 megawatts. The national demand right now is about 6,000 megawatts, and so you can see that right away, there will be shortages of electricity. And this always has been for the Iraqi people. It's something they're used to. So that just means that we have to do a program of load shedding, which essentially is rolling blackouts, so that people have their power cut off at different times during the day. It's very difficult to control because the control systems they did have in place were largely looted and destroyed following the war. The distribution system which moves power around the country is also very unstable and not very reliable, so it's difficult for us to give any predictability to the Iraqi people about when their power will be on or when it will be off.

The fuel system is also in fairly poor condition. They rely heavily on the oil industry and direct feeds from refineries to power the generators. And with the shutdown of the oil system and also the lack of maintenance in that system, getting fuel to the generators has been a real challenge to us. So, as I say, we have accomplished quite a bit here. On 12 April when we arrived in the city of Baghdad, it was a complete blackout. And through a very, very complex process, working with the Iraqis, we were able to bring up the electrical system. We now have

39,000 electrical workers back on the job. We have today about 3,200 megawatts of power being generated, and by the end of the month we'll have about 4,000, which is about where they were prewar. We should continue to see rises in power as we make additional investments and repairs in the system. We've also reconnected the national grid, which has been very important in moving power around the country. Where water and foods are concerned, again, the electrical system is the real key there to power pumps and move the commodities through the system. Here in Baghdad, before the war we were getting about 200 million liters—I'm sorry, 2,000 million liters per day of drinking water, right now we're about 1,400, and we should be back to 2,000 in the next three months or so. In the southern part of the country, about 60 percent of the people in the urban population have access to drinking water, and about 30 percent of the rural population. Those are about the numbers they had prewar. But we are going to continue to improve on those, and we think we'll get it up to about 80 percent by the end of October. No one is really going without water. We are supplementing with tankers, wells and river water to purify, and feed the people. Sewage is a big problem, especially here in Baghdad. None of the sewage here in the city is being treated, because of damage to the sewage treatment plants following the war. It's going to be several months before we are able to get up any level of sewage treatment. This certainly has some down-river consequences, which we're very sensitive to, but so far we haven't had any significant outbreaks of disease as a result of that. Our big challenge is just to continue to move the sewage through the system. Roads and bridges. The highway network here in Iraq was in fairly good shape before the war. It did suffer some neglect, and that's been, really, the focus of our effort, is to maintain some of those damaged sections of road. Thirty highway bridges were knocked down during the war, by both us and the Iraqis. Ten of those are very high priority, and we're building on five of them right now. The other five are being covered by temporary military bridging. So no real significant issues on roads and bridges at the moment. The rail line is an important transportation network for the Iraqis. They moved all commodities from their port of Umm Qasr all the way up to Mosul in the north. That line is now open. There is one section of the road that is being worked on, about a 70-kilometer stretch south of Nasiriyah, so we're investing about $20 million in doing that. The ports, both air and sea ports, obviously, are very important as we get the country back on its feet. The port of Umm Qasr is open and, in fact, has a higher capacity than it's had in many years. We're dredging the port, removing wrecks, and we've got it pretty much down to 12.5 meters. So we can get deep-draft vessels in here to bring in relief supplies and begin to stimulate the economy. We're also quite busy removing wrecks that are in the waterway there. Air traffic should be reinitiated here in about two weeks. It will be the first time we've had commercial air traffic here coming into Baghdad in 12 years, so it's a big event for the people. It will then be followed very closely by the airport at Basra opening, and then eventually up at Mosul in the north. In irrigation, agriculture is very important to the people here. And again, that system has suffered from years of neglect. And we have a specifically focused program to put people back to work in the irrigation sector. So we're going to have about 100,000 people at work over the next couple of months clearing about 5,500 kilometers of irrigation system. We've surveyed the major dams throughout the country. We found some structural problems, which we're addressing with the Army Corps of Engineers and with USAID. We've restarted a number of irrigation projects that were put on hold for various reasons. We're also doing a significant amount of environmental work and investigation, particularly down in the Mesopotamian marshes, in the Shi'a area. This is a very social and—socially and politically charged issue. Saddam drained the marshes down there in—as a way of punishing the Shi'as and essentially changed a thousand—many thousand-year-old culture in the process. He has also, in the process, caused us problems with fresh water down in the Basra area. So we're looking into how we can restore those marshlands. The communications network was—really took some beating during the war. We are currently replacing four switches in Baghdad. We're putting in an international gateway, and we're putting in a fiber-optics backbone, which would connect about 75 percent of the users in the nation here with access to telephones. Government buildings have been a huge problem for us, especially here in Baghdad, but throughout the nation, with hospitals, schools, police stations, fire stations and so forth. So we've [got ?] a very, very large effort, about $150 million so far, in putting those facilities back on-line. One of the most important ones is—are the schools, and we're going to fix about 1,350 schools in 12 different cities over the next few months. So when they open schools in the fall, the children will have a much better learning environment. And in the process, we'll put about 1,500 people to work on those jobs. The oil infrastructure I won't spend a great deal of time on, but simply to recognize that like electricity, without oil, this company—this country does not run. Again, we are gratified with the small amount of damage done to the oil fields. They had a wonderful military campaign that was able to capture the system impact, in spite of some of the Iraqis' attempts to destroy it. But the oil infrastructure also suffers from looting and vandalism following the war. We're pleased to announce that we had the first oil out of Turkey on the 20th of June and out of Mina al-Bakr terminal here in Iraq on the 28th of June. So the system is now up and functioning. We're able to produce about 800,000 barrels of crude a day. And by the fall, we should break the million-dollar—million-barrel mark and begin to really stimulate the economy here. Let me close by just saying a few words about security. I know there's been a lot of reporting about this lately. There have been attacks, and this is not surprising or unexpected. As conditions improve, the opposition is going to get more and more desperate in their attempt to destabilize the country and to discredit the coalition and our efforts here to put the nation back on its feet. We have in recent weeks put a lot more effort into security of infrastructure, particularly the linear lines of communications for power and oil, and I think we're beginning to see the benefits of that. I think these saboteurs fail to recognize that these are really viewed by the Iraqis as attacks on the Iraqi people, not on the coalition, and increasingly, they are alienating the people they're trying to gain the support of. So hopefully that'll be something that they recognize here pretty quickly and they'll turn their attention elsewhere. Thank you very much for the opportunity to share with you some of the challenges and successes we've had here. With that, I'll turn it over to Andy, and I look forward to taking your questions. Thank you.

Bearpark: Okay. Good afternoon. My name's Andy Bearpark, and I'm the director of Operations here for the CPA. I just want to follow on from General Strock with a few remarks about the wider context and the context going a little bit further out in terms of time. The first point I'd make is that we've always got to remember that the reconstruction we're talking about is nothing really to do with war damage. What we're talking about is 30 years of criminal neglect of maintenance, and then we have the criminally and politically motivated sabotage of the last few weeks. Problems like that are going to take a while to put right. We're talking several years to build a new power station. You can't just build one overnight. So we've got to work, and we've got to work with the people of Iraq to get those long-term improvements. Now the coalition already has an excellent record. There are many, many immediate achievements of which people can be proud. But what we've got to do is move forward and move onward to get these bigger economic improvements. That's going to take several years. But we haven't been idle during these last few months. As well as doing the immediate emergency projects, the ones that General Strock's been describing, we've also been doing the big engineering assessments to see what's going to be required. And so we're now ready, over the next few weeks, to move in, if you like, that second phase of things where the benefits will be visible in months and years ahead—in other words, building new transmission lines, getting things up and running that have never run before, putting in new bits to the water system. And that's a big effort. It's going to require a lot of money. But most of all, it's an effort that comes with the Iraqi people. It's not something that we can do by ourselves. And those projects that'll be coming under way have a long-term economic benefit, yes, but they also have a short-term economic benefit, in that they'll be providing tens of thousands of jobs immediately to the people of Iraq. So we do have progress on infrastructure, and we do have a path forward. But it's not just about infrastructure. That's important, but what we're doing is looking at Iraq as a whole, and we're moving forward on political issues; on, if you like, social issues; and on economic issues. And I'll just give you three of the examples of where things really are moving forward. The 32 members of the Baghdad Interim City Advisory Council took up their posts today. They've been elected—they've selected in a fair and transparent manner, the first time that's ever happened in this place. So that's real political progress. We've got a rewards program up and running, not just for Saddam Hussein, but also for information on others who are attacking the coalition, who are sabotaging utilities. I know that Bernie Kerik, the ex–New York police commissioner, was describing one part of that program the other day. We've got a whole program like that that's moving forward now. And just a few moments ago, the administrator, Ambassador Bremer, announced the introduction of the new Iraqi bank notes that will be coming in October. So infrastructure is vitally important, but it's part of the overall structure of the Iraq that we're helping to build against a background of all of those years of neglect and oppression. So yes, an awful lot has been achieved already, and we're on the right path to achieve more. Yes, there are going to be problems. There are going to be problems all the time. But we're moving forward at the moment and that's the way it's going to continue. Thanks very much.

Whitman: Let's go ahead and get started with some questions. Charlie?

Question: General and Mr. Bearpark, this is Charlie Aldinger with Reuters. I'd like to get a better picture of the oil exports, if you could. In terms of money for Iraq, what—the 800,000 barrels-a-day exports which you say are going out now, what does that mean? And you say that will go up to 1 million. How does that compare to what Iraq will be able to export in the days ahead—in the years ahead? Sorry.

Strock: Charlie, we're actually producing about 800,000 barrels of oil today. Iraq uses about 20 percent of that for internal consumption through the refineries. We are not at the moment exporting any of that oil. We sold about 7.5 million barrels to Turkey at the end of June, and we emptied the storage banks at Mina al-Bakr here just recently. So we're now in the process of recharging the storage tanks. In terms of the ultimate capacity, we think that we can get up to over 2 million barrels per day—2.2, 2.5, something like that—in about a year's time. And that is about the normal export level that the Iraqis have been accustomed to.

Question: What does that mean in terms of money? How much did Turkey pay for the 7.5 million barrels?

Strock: Well, I think the price is somewhere in the 21, 22 dollars per barrel. So, you know, it's a—I think they sold about $200 million worth of oil. The proceeds from the oil flows will go into the Iraqi development fund, the Development Fund of Iraq, which is a UN fund that's been set up. And it will be administered by the administrator here. I think that if—our projections are that for the remainder of the year, if we can continue to make improvements as they now stand, Iraq should realize about $5 billion by the end of this year.

Question: General, Tom Bowman with the *Baltimore Sun*. Could you expand a little bit on what you said about there's a lot of effort on the security, the infrastructure? Can you talk about the numbers of soldiers that have this duty, or percentage of soldiers? And you could also get into the sabotage as well. Are you seeing an increased amount of sabotage? Has it plateaued, or has it decreased because of the added soldiers for the security situation?

Bearpark: Well, I think I got your question. But forgive me, I missed a bit of it. When we talk about sabotage, at the moment we're talking about the sabotage of public utilities. We're talking about hundreds and hundreds of miles of power cables, hundreds and hundreds of miles of pipelines and all the associated facilities. And there just aren't enough tanks in the world to put one tank on every electricity pylon. So when we look at security for that system, what we're looking at is a holistic approach. We're looking at the incredible efforts being made by the U.S. military and other coalition forces. But we're also looking at local Iraqi security forces, the new Iraqi police force, in due course we're looking at the new Iraqi security force as well, but also we're looking at the ordinary Iraqi people, because the only way you can protect a system of that size in any country in the world, but obviously here, is by the whole network of everything from starting at the top with security forces to getting right down to the bottom to having people who will give you a tip-off and say, Look, I've heard that somebody may be thinking of attacking that facility, or, I've heard this rumor or that rumor. So what we've got at the moment is that integrated network of, if you like, components coming together to increase the protection against sabotage. It's a complicated network, and some bits of it only come out fairly slowly. And the new Iraqi police force is only now beginning to be stood up. So the U.S. forces and the other coalition forces are taking a large share of the burden at the moment, but the other bits of it are coming into being now.

Strock: May I also add that another aspect of security is to reduce the vulnerability of the systems through these investments we're making. As I said, it's a very fragile system, does not have a lot of redundancies, so when it does get attacked, it can have catastrophic impact. So the work we're doing in making these investments will make the infrastructure less vulnerable to attack. And we're also putting into place a response mechanism with the Iraqi work crews to be able to respond quickly and get things back on-line when we do have interruptions of utilities. Thank you.

Question: With these incidents of sabotage, can you quantify that in any way? And also, how many more U.S. troops are being dispatched for this kind of duty, either the numbers or a percentage?

Bearpark: Just in terms of the incidents in sabotage, we've been seeing increasing sabotage over the last few weeks. I haven't seen any increase over the last few days. But I think we may now be seeing—I don't want to be too optimistic too soon, but I think we may be seeing ordinary Iraqi people assuming that this activity is actually directed at them, not at us—that they're the ones who have been suffering from lack of electricity or lack of water. So I think we may—I hope we may—we're beginning to see that sort of reaction now, so maybe we'll see a stronger reaction against sabotage. In terms of numbers, I mean, I don't go in for numbers. This is the network of all the things that have to come together. And the point I'd like to emphasize is that there's no point in protecting one thing and protecting it incredibly well. When you've got such an amazing network and such an array, what you've got to do is have the overall thing. If you protect one bit too well, all that happens is the saboteurs can go somewhere else. So it's this network of levels of security that's important to us.

Question: Sir, Martha Raddatz from ABC News. You talk about this network of security and the sabotage and that the Iraqi people are now thinking these attacks are against them. What is it you expect them to do about that?

Bearpark: What I expect is that people will begin to take responsibility, insofar as they can, for the results of these things. The very easy example I was given a few moments ago was that, say, a couple of weeks ago, if somebody had information about possible sabotage, the odds were that they still felt too afraid to come and tell us about that. Now, I sense that they're becoming a bit more confident, so they're prepared to come along and face the coalition to give us that information, which enables us to prevent that piece of sabotage taking place before it actually does. That's where I think we're seeing a change. I—so I don't want to be too optimistic. It may take a bit longer, because when you've lived in a repressive regime for so long, it takes a while to understand that you can speak freely. In the beginning, people were bound to think, "Well, we've had this awful regime, where we didn't dare speak openly. Surely we can't now." But I think now ordinary Iraqis are beginning to sense that they can talk to the coalition and that we can then use that information for their benefit.

Question: Basically, they're not expected to do any sort of security or police themselves. It's—this is basically if they know of some sort of sabotage attack—they're sort of your intelligence network, in other words.

Bearpark: Yeah, I'm certainly not expecting the ordinary Iraqi housewife or worker to go out there and fight off a saboteur. When I talk about the network, I'm saying that people like that, ordinary people, can certainly pass on information. Then I'm saying that in the other extreme, you've got U.S. troops; that in between, you've got an awful lot of other levels. You've got the security guards who are now being employed by the ministries themselves to protect some facilities. You've got the Iraqi police. So what I'm saying is that you've got that entire network, that entire range of tools, if you like, in your toolbox, to help you fight against these very, very difficult subjects.

Question: One final—you say that they're beginning to trust that they can come and talk to the coalition, and yet they're seeing attacks all over the country on not only coalition troops, but Iraqis who turn people in or who help coalition troops. Isn't there a sense of fear as well?

Bearpark: I recognize what you say, and there have been some terrible incidents, I know. But I think that the two things don't exactly equate. I think that people are beginning to feel that slightly greater sense of ability to talk freely. In parallel with that, yes, there are certainly absolutely tragic incidents happening every day, whether these—the incidents involving coalition troops or local Iraqi workers. Hopefully they will start to decrease very soon. Every single incident is one incident too many. But I think that's a separate process from a slightly growing—a slowly growing confidence that we are actually here to help them help themselves and that this is a joint venture; that we can't impose economic development, we can't impose utilities. It's something that we do together.

Question: Eric Schmitt with the *New York Times*, gentlemen. I was under perhaps the mistaken understanding that the electricity and water levels were back to prewar levels and had been. It sounded like, from the numbers that General Strock gave, though, however, you're still not quite there. Had you ever reached that point and then fallen back, or you'd always been kind of striving to get to that level? And the second question, General Strock, if you could just address the earlier question of how many U.S. forces are now conducting some kind of security duty, either in numbers or in percentage. Thank you.

Strock: Eric, thank you. It's been awfully difficult for us to really understand exactly what level of service the Iraqis had prior to the war. There's never been enough electricity to go around, and Saddam definitely used the provision of utilities as a political tool to reward those he wanted to reward and punish those he wanted to punish. So it's been awfully difficult for us to really get at exactly what the average Iraqi had. We know, for example, that here in Baghdad they typically enjoyed 23 to 24 hours of power. But there are other places in the country that got two. And as we have brought the system back on-line, we've tried to get more equitable in the distribution of that power. So what you're seeing here is the people of Baghdad are receiving less than they did before, but the—but about 80 percent of the population is receiving more. In terms of the numbers, we think that last year they were able to get to about 44 megawatts, 4,400 megawatts at the peak.

And we're—we hope to get to about 4,000 by the end of July. So we will not be where they tell us they were last year. But it should not be a crisis situation, because much of the nation's power demands have been diminished. For example, the military is no longer drawing the huge amounts of power that they did before the war. So I think what we'll see here by the end of July is the status quo ante bellum with the exception of the people of Baghdad, who will begin to feel the pinch, because power is being shared throughout the country more so now than it was before.

I also am reluctant to talk, really, numbers, first of all because I don't have the specific numbers on troops involved in security. I can say just generally, though, that this is called a security and stability operation. And every one of our soldiers is providing some sort of security, whether it's point security or presence patrol, if he's moving around and being seen in the community. So all of our soldiers are involved in that. We—I don't know that we have a—put more troops on specific point security roles than we have. We have changed some of our procedures and don't want to go too much into those because that tells the enemy what we're doing differently now, and we'd prefer for him to find that out on his own. But I can tell you that the number one job right now in the security sector is the protection of these lines of communication. Thank you.

Question: General, just one more follow-up—Eric Schmitt again. Do you need more American forces or coalition forces to provide security to do what you need to do?

Strock: That's really not my question to answer. I don't want to dodge the question, but that's really for General Sanchez, the commander of the coalition force. And I think he's been pretty clear about that.

Question: General, hi. This is Esther Schrader with the *Los Angeles Times*. A number of the attacks on U.S. soldiers have taken place when they have been, as you've said, moving in and through the community. I wonder if that is causing you to reassess some of the instructions that you give to the troops there? Do they have to—is it limiting their mobility? Are they being asked to pull back or being asked to take extra caution as they move through the community? Can you give us anything on that?

Strock: Well, Esther, I think that answer is, every time that we have a contact, we analyze it and try to learn something from it. So certainly every time one of our soldiers is attacked, we look at our procedures and whether or not we need to adjust those. I think what's really happening here is that the—after the cessation of hostilities, the enemy's had a little bit of time to regroup, so we're seeing more deliberate types of attacks. We have not seen any sort of central or national orchestration of those. But we do see more sophisticated attacks, a combination of explosive devices and direct fire, for example.

And we're adjusting to those tactics. What I think we're also seeing here is a response to our more offensive operations. We are going after the enemy using the sort of information that Andy referred to, that we're getting from a lot of Iraqi civilians. We are seeking the enemy out. And when you get in that kind of a situation, you're going to stimulate more action just by the nature of our tactics. We're not sitting still and waiting for them to come to us, and hence more things are going on. I think that's part of the reason you're seeing an increase in the number of attacks. Again, I don't want to get too far out of my lane here. I'm an engineer and not a war-fighter at the moment. But that's my personal assessment of what's going on. Thank you.

Question: General, Richard Sisk, *New York Daily News.* Can you give us an idea of the role, the involvement of the Bechtel, Halliburton, private contractor people that are over there? Do they work on their own? Do they work on their own separate projects? Do they work overseeing Iraqis in what they do? And do they carry sidearms?

Strock: Sir, they do not work on their own. They are under contract with the Agency for International Development. We have about an $800 million contract out here, which is being managed by the U.S. Army Corps of Engineers on behalf of Bechtel [*sic*]—I mean on behalf of USAID. The priorities are really set by the Coalition Provisional Authority on what they're going to work on, and they have a very clear picture of that. And AID then gives the instructions to them on how to carry out their work. So they're very definitely working for the coalition here. They do not carry sidearms. They rely on us for the provision of security. And they also are instructed to employ local Iraqi firms to the greatest extent possible so that the money that is spent in this country stays in this country.

Question: General, I'm interested in the policy you have about the power in Baghdad, in redistributing it, since that's where the lion's share of the attacks on U.S. soldiers is occurring and it seems that's where you would have cause for more people to be unhappy about the services that they're receiving. Are you seeing any correlation between those two? I've heard news reports over the weekend that the tolerance for the attacks, if not the attacks themselves, seems to be coming from people in the cities who feel like they're not being taken care of. And it occurs to me, when you say that Saddam Hussein punished people by withholding power or utilities, do you think they feel that they're being punished?

Bearpark: I think people certainly don't react—[Inaudible.]— happily when they're getting more power. So first of all what we've got is people who were getting very little power before getting a lot more now. But of course, the ones who are getting less power, the people in Baghdad, are unhappy about it. That's obviously understandable. What we've had to do is have a big information campaign over the last week or so to explain the reasons why there's been less power, to explain that it has been because of sabotage. In a place like Baghdad, there are always rumors, and so I'm quite sure there were people out there who thought the coalition was stealing the electricity, as if we could steal it and send it back to the United States. So what we've had is a big campaign to explain why it is that the power has been less over the last week or 10 days. And what we are moving towards now over the next week or 10 days is a more reliable load-shedding system, as one gets elsewhere in the world, to say, "No, we can't give you 24-hour-a-day power in Baghdad at the moment, and these are the reasons, but what we can do is give you power for, say, 20 hours a day, and we can help you predict when the four hours a day are when you won't be getting power." So I think with that sort of information campaign, that people are, if you like, trusting us more and understanding more what the problem is.

Question: Could you give us a little bit more information about the information campaign? Is it radio? Television? Fliers? How is that being put out? And you could you also update us on the status for the interim Iraqi government and the constitutional convention?

Bearpark: Okay. As far as the information campaign is concerned, the simple answer is that we use any means that we find, because the infrastructure for the media here is much less complete than one would wish. It was, of course, completely and utterly state-controlled by Saddam Hussein. A lot of elements of that have quite likely now vanished. And it's taking time for things like new television stations, new radio transmitters to come up, and for newspapers. And people here are very poor at the moment. So not all of them can afford to buy newspapers. So with every information campaign that we do, my guiding principle is we do absolutely everything: we do flyers, we do posters, we do word of mouth, we do television, we do radio, we do anything we can, because at this stage of the game you can't be confident that any one media outlet is going to hit the audience that you're looking for. As far as the political process is concerned, as I said earlier, things are moving, and they're moving very rapidly now. I think Ambassador Bremer spoke a week or so ago about his ambitions for standing up the interim authority, the political process, and then the constitutional process. I don't think I'd be going into any more detail at this stage, but I'm sure he will be making further announcements as and when appropriate.

Whitman: If George's question is not too complicated, we'll take his and one other.

Question: George Edmonson with Cox Newspapers. You and others have talked about the fact that most of what you're repairing is a result of neglect over the years, not war damage. Can you tell us how good the prewar assessment was of the status of Iraq's infrastructure, how much did you find that you were anticipating and how much have you been surprised by that you didn't anticipate and didn't get information on?

Strock: You know, I'm afraid I don't know much detail on the initial assessment coming in. I think we were surprised at—and I know we were surprised with the state of the infrastructure. The—as I mentioned earlier, the Iraqis are very, very competent, and it's remarkable what they've done with very few resources. But what we've seen is while they were getting power, for example, in Baghdad, as we look at—look into the system, we find that there are very few transformers, very few circuit breakers and the sorts of things you need for a stable and reliable system. So it's been a cobbled-together system, and I think that surprised us a bit, that they were able to make it work as effectively as they had. We are doing the sorts of investments, though, that are both correcting that lack of investment, and we're investing in new infrastructure in parallel with the Iraqis. We're bringing on new generation, for example, to supplement what was here before.

Whitman: No, let's go ahead and finish up. Go ahead. We'll have one more here.

Question: I'm Carl Osgood. I write for *Executive Intelligence Review*. If I understood your opening comments properly, it sounds like most of the reconstruction efforts, the projects are direct—it's a directed effort. That is, you identify a project, and then you marshal the resources to get it done. But the U.S. and British economies have both been characterized by deregulation and privatization over the last two or three decades. I'm wonder if, over the long term, you plan to bring these kinds of concepts into the Iraqi economy.

Bearpark: I think that the current activities are exactly as you say, directed activities to deal with immediate infrastructure problems. And whatever one's future economy, you know for sure that you need to have clean drinking water for people, and you know for sure that you need reliable electricity. And in the very short term, you know that you've got to mend what you've got, because that's the only way of delivering. So a directed program in that way is obviously correct. But as we look to the future, just as the future of Iraq is in democracy, so the experience of the European Union, of the United Kingdom, of the United States of America is indeed that a free market economy is the one that works. So indeed, that is the direction in which I am quite sure the economy of Iraq will be going over the coming years. And yes, in addition to the immediate work that we're doing, the longer-term planning work focuses on that. But I would stress that that longer-term planning work is not imposed. I think nobody would object if we imposed a water system on Baghdad. That's perfectly okay, because everybody wants the results of that water system. But when we're talking about longer-term development, we're talking at the moment about partnership with the Iraqi people, and of course a partnership in which they're increasingly taking the responsibility. But on the specifics on the free market economy, I think it's been proven around the world pretty well that it's the only model that works.

Strock: May I also add, there's a pragmatic aspect to this, and that is that the system we found here when we got here was one of many, many state-owned enterprises. Virtually every ministry has companies associated with it that are described as business entities, but they're clearly state-owned and are not private sector. For us to get anything done in the short term, we really have to rely on the existing mechanisms. And there is a process in which we're beginning to really assess which of those state-owned enterprises need to stay as state-owned and which need to privatize, and how we can get to a free market economy without bringing the country to its knees. If we simply cut off all of these enterprises now, we're putting a lot of people out of work and creating perhaps bigger social problems in the short term that we'd be correcting in the long term. So it is—it has been a very difficult process to work through that.

Whitman: General Strock, Mr. Bearpark, thank you for taking the opportunity today to bring us up to date on the progress that you're making and the many challenges that lie ahead of you. And we appreciate your time. We know you're very busy. Thank you.

Bearpark: Thank you.

Strock: Thank you.

Reference:

http://www.defenselink.mil/cgibin/dlprint.cgi?http://www.defenselink.mil/transcripts/2003/tr20030707–0342.html

Media contact: media@defenselink.mil or (703) 697–5131

Public contact: http://www.dod.mil/faq/comment.html or (703) 428–0711

U.S. Military Commitments and Ongoing Military Operations Abroad

This is testimony by one of the most senior Department of State officials about U.S. activities overseas in nation-building. Note the vast number of places the United States is engaged in nation-building. There are other places around the world where other states work on the same issues but often with significantly less public scrutiny or debate.

Mr. Chairman and other members of the Committee, thank you for your invitation to appear today. The State Department is committed to supporting, in every way, America's men and women in uniform. And I thank you for your support of the 46,000 men and women of the State Department who defend our country every day in 258 diplomatic posts around the world. After the defeat of the Taliban in Afghanistan, State Department people volunteered to staff our reopened Embassy in Kabul, where they endured, and still do endure, hard living conditions and danger.

Thirty-three State employees joined General Garner in Iraq in April. Forty-seven of my colleagues are there now with Ambassador Bremer, and 22 more are scheduled to go out in the next few weeks. Altogether, 282 have volunteered to go since July. That so many people have gone or volunteered to go to Iraq is a tribute to the professionalism and patriotism of State Department employees, civil and foreign service. Last September, the President signed the National Security Strategy of the United States. This document is the basis for the conduct of US foreign policy as well as military policy. It says that the primary aim of America's security strategy is to make the world not just safer, but better. In order to bring about political and economic freedom, peaceful relations with other states, and respect for human dignity, the President has designated a number of tasks. As Secretary Powell highlighted in his speech at George Washington University last Friday, these include strengthening alliances to defeat global terrorism, building cooperative partnerships with the other major powers, including Europe, Japan, Russia, China, and India, working with other nations to defuse regional conflicts, and preventing our enemies from threatening us, our allies, and our friends, with weapons of mass destruction.

America is not alone in its desire for a better and safer world, and so at the President's direction we seek partners and allies because it enables us to better achieve our national objectives. You asked in your letter about cooperation with individual countries, with NATO, the UN and other multinational organizations.

All NATO countries contribute to the Global War against Terrorism. Indeed, Afghanistan represents an historic first out-of-area operation for the Alliance as a whole. We work with the United Nations on Iraq. The UN has a vital role to play in the reconstruction of that country, and the criminal bombing of the UN headquarters in Baghdad only further shows the importance of galvanizing international support for Iraq's reconstruction. As the President announced to the nation Sunday, we seek a new UNSC resolution on Iraq to build on UNSCRs 1441, 1483 and 1500. This resolution should:

(1) Invite the Iraqi Governing Council to submit a plan and a timetable for them to write a constitution, develop political institutions, and conduct free elections, leading to the Iraqi peoples resumption of sovereignty over their own country. (2) Authorize a United Nations multinational force under a US commander. (3) Afford the United Nations a more comprehensive and active role in the transition back to Iraqi sovereignty. We are also working with friends and partners around the world for a successful Iraq donors' conference in Madrid in October. This conference should further mobilize international efforts to help the Iraqi people reconstruct their country and rebuild their lives. In addition to using structures like NATO and the UN, we have reached out to our friends and allies, including many new partners, in order to attain the goals that are crucial to our national security and that of other nations in the world. We are in constant coordination with the Combatant Commands to find out what is needed, and then we approach our friends to try to meet those needs. We have sought troop contributions and for basing and staging rights, material support, overflight permission, and refueling. The task of working with foreign governments intensifies with the termination of major combat, as both Afghanistan and Iraq have shown. In both these places we continue to call on our friends and allies to support stabilization and reconstruction. Many countries which were not in a position to offer combat troops have offered humanitarian and reconstruction relief. As the President highlighted Sunday night, we do not underestimate the challenges: terrorists and Saddam loyalists have done great harm in Iraq; in Afghanistan, al-Qaeda and Taliban fighters seek to regroup and have attacked coalition and Allied forces and NGO workers and others trying to stop the essential work of reconstruction. Our work at the State Department has two other dimensions that are key: we are working with allies and partners to help them to solve regional conflicts; and working with partners to address the internal security problems that can lead to terrorism and other transnational threats. As you requested in your letter, I would like now to highlight some of the activities that I have just mentioned, in particular, Iraq, Afghanistan, and Liberia. Iraq: Forty-nine nations publicly declared their support for our policy by joining the Coalition for the Immediate Disarmament of Iraq. A number of other countries quietly cooperated with and supported the military operation in various ways. In total, there were 45 countries that provided access, basing, and/or over-flight rights, and

24 countries that contributed military assets in one form or another for operations in Iraq.

Additional countries have joined the stabilization effort. A total of 29 countries have now deployed approximately 23,000 troops for stability and humanitarian operations in Iraq; three more countries are in the process of deploying additional troops. We are in discussion with approximately ten other countries concerning additional potential contributions. We have followed a clear strategy: we have taken the needs of the US military and the Coalition Provisional Authority as we seek to help the Iraqi people build a democratic and secure Iraq and have then sought assets other countries might be able to provide to meet those needs. These contributions have not only been support for US efforts. Other countries, such as Spain, Italy and Ukraine have taken key roles in providing brigade headquarters in the UK and Polish divisions. Other countries have offered to take on support functions such as engineering that contribute to reconstruction. And we continue to talk to a range of foreign governments about the possibilities for further contributions. Afghanistan: In the wake of 9/11, the international community worked with us in the fight against Al Qaeda and the Taliban regime. Over 70 countries joined our coalition and over 34 countries have contributed forces to Operation ENDURING FREEDOM and to the International Stabilization Force for Afghanistan (ISAF). In an historic milestone for the North Atlantic Alliance, NATO as an organization has recently taken over the lead role in ISAF after supporting NATO members Germany and the Netherlands in their co-leadership of the force. Currently, 15 NATO countries make up ISAF, providing some 5,800 troops on the ground. The main contributors to this force include Canada with almost 900 soldiers, France with more than 500, and the UK with approximately 400 troops. It is crucial for Afghanistan's long term security and prosperity that Afghan citizens themselves be prepared to take responsibility for maintaining peace and order in their own country. This will require a national army that is multi-ethnic, subordinate to civil authority, subject to rule of law and international norms of human rights. The Afghan National Army (ANA) Train and Equip Program, initiated for this purpose, will establish a Central Corps of sufficient size and military capability (10,000+ soldiers) to provide security for the June 2004 elections and eventually relieve the International Security and Assistance Force and OEF elements of security duties. With over two dozen countries contributing to the establishment of the ANA we have made significant progress toward our goal of a Central Corps by June 2004. One crucial project is the establishment of Provincial Reconstruction Teams. The U.S. has already set up three of these, in Gardez, Bamiyan, and Kunduz. The U.K. has recently opened a PRT in Mazar-e-Sharif, and New Zealand will relieve U.S. forces in Bamiyan later this year. The mission of the PRTs is to provide additional stability to provincial areas, allowing for increased reconstruction and assisting the expansion of central authority and linkage to local governments. Each team includes State Department and AID officers working side by side with military personnel. Against these efforts we face al-Qaeda and Taliban fighters determined to regroup and to attack coalition and Allied forces, NGO workers and the international community. Recent attacks on the critical Kandahar-Kabul highway and killing of international workers show us the threat continues.

Liberia: The Liberian civil war has generated unrest and misery throughout West Africa. Hundreds of thousands of people are displaced internally and in neighboring countries. Participants in the Liberian conflict have destabilized Liberia's neighbors, and gross violations of human rights have occurred. With the departure of Charles Taylor and the decision by the parties to sign the Accra peace agreement, there is an historic opportunity to restore peace to Liberia and to the region. On August 1, the UN Security Council passed Resolution 1497, authorizing deployment to Liberia of a Multinational Force (MNF) under Chapter VII of the UN Charter and a follow-on UN PKO. The West Africans have stepped up to the challenge, using their regional Economic Community of West African States (ECOWAS), providing the MNF that will help restore order and separate the parties pending the arrival of UN peacekeepers. Led by Nigeria, over 3,000 troops from Ghana, Mali, Senegal, Togo, Gambia, Guinea-Bissau, and Benin are deploying to the region with US assistance and will likely be subsumed into the UN mission. Because of this positive action by ECOWAS, and since the UN is planning to take over responsibilities from ECOWAS by October 1, there has been a decreased need for the U.S. to send troops. An Amphibious Readiness Group comprised of 3 ships and more than 4,000 service members is standing by off Monrovia to respond to emergencies, but our work has been primarily in logistics support and diplomatic coordination. We have assisted with the deployment and sustainment of the West African troops, and expect to continue to do so until the transition to the UN PKO is complete. To date, the U.S. has committed over $15 million for this effort. We are in the process of identifying additional resources to ensure the ECOWAS force is able to fulfill its mission until the UN PKO is in place.

Bosnia/Kosovo: The U.S. remains committed to ensuring peace and stability in the Balkans and remains an active participant in the NATO-led operations in Bosnia and Kosovo. Through intense diplomatic activity and coordination with our allies, we have been able substantially to reduce the number of U.S. troops in the region as the security situation in the region improves. In January 2001, the U.S. provided 9,600 of the roughly 56,000 troops in the Balkans. Today, the United States contributes 4,050 troops to those same missions—1,800 U.S. troops in Bosnia and 2,250 U.S. troops in Kosovo. The total size of the forces will drop below 30,000 by the end of the year. In recent years, the U.S. has generally tried to keep our forces in the Balkans at

approximately 15 percent of the overall, although, originally, we
provided one-third of the forces in Bosnia. We continue to work within
NATO to restructure and reduce the forces, lowering our contributions
in line with the overall reductions of the Alliance. At present, the
French, German and Italian contribution to KFOR surpass that of the
U.S. In Bosnia, where the U.S. commands SFOR, we are among the
largest contributor of troops. There are many other areas in which we
work to support the President's vision in the National Security Strategy.
North Korea. Colombia. The Philippines. Georgia. I would be glad to
discuss these with you if you wish during the hearing.

Resources: As the President indicated in his recent address, $87
billion will be needed to accomplish Administration goals in Iraq and
address other complex contingencies. We welcome the opportunity to
work with you to make that pledge a reality. We also welcome your
support for our Foreign Operations budget request, which has passed
the House and is awaiting floor action in the Senate. The world is a
dangerous place. The President has made it clear that we will do what
it takes to make it safer and better, by working to rid it of terrorists and
tyrants who threaten the United States, their neighbors, and their own
people. By fostering democracy and rule of law, by building coalitions
with allies and friends, and by pursuing regional stability through
funding military aid programs and training, the State Department
actively pursues the President's goals of peace and security. Together
with the Department of Defense and our military colleagues, we are
committed to these goals and will continue to work unceasingly to
attain them. Released on 10 September 2003

Reference:

Grossman, Marc. 2003. "U.S. Military Committments and Ongoing Military Operations Abroad." Testimony before the Senate Armed Services
Committee, Washington, DC, 9 September. Available at http://www.
state.gov/p/23940.htm (accessed 20 May 2004).

Reconstruction Activities in Iraq

*The role of the U.S. Agency for International Development in nation-
building has been a long one. The administrator illustrates the problems
that the current activities in Iraq pose for the foreseeable future.*

Mr. Ereli: Good afternoon, everyone. Welcome to the State
Department briefing room, where we have a special guest, Director
Andrew Natsios of the United States Agency for International
Development, will be briefing us on reconstruction in Iraq. Director
Natsios will be bringing to us what we think are some really

newsworthy success stories of partnership and progress in Iraq with U.S. assistance and Iraqi, sort of ingenuity, know-how and commitment.

With that, I'll introduce Director Natsios, who will have a few remarks of introduction, and then take your questions.

Administrator Natsios: School starts tomorrow in Iraq, on the 4th, and when kids return to school they'll find the following things that are very new: 1,595 schools have been completely rehabilitated and reconstructed. These schools, in many cases, had been abandoned for years; in other cases, they had been looted; in other cases, simply, they had fallen into disrepair—the electrical wiring had been ripped out, the plumbing had been ripped out, the water systems were not functional, there was no electricity; the ceiling fans, which are critically important, what's in 125 degree temperature in the schools in many months during the year, which if the fans don't function, it's difficult for the kids to stay awake.

We have repaired all of that. Much of the window glass was broken in many of the schools. I went to many of these schools myself in June, when I was in Iraq for six days. To have rehabilitated that many schools over a five month period is, I think, a great indication of the rate at which the reconstruction is progressing.

We have also begun to train 5,000 school administrators and principals and school superintendents in more modern ways of managing schools, in a more collaborative and less autocratic way. There are about 65,000 teachers in the country and we have begun a master teacher program, where we teach democratic methods ("small d"), systems of instruction that are less reliant on rote learning and more reliant on debate and questioning and more—what we call pupil-focused educational system.

We have been running those seminars now for four months. We also today are announcing three grants, which will be three in a series of grants, with American universities and universities in Europe, partnering with universities in Iraq. For example, just giving you one example here is, SUNY, the State University of New York, will partner with Baghdad University and Mosul University and Basra University; and there is a consortium under SUNY with Columbia University, Boston University and Oxford University, and they will be focused on archeology and environmental research.

In agriculture, we've got a new award of $3.7 million to the University of Chicago's Tropical Agriculture and Human Resource Department, with University of Mosul's Agricultural School.

We can go through them all, but DePaul University in Chicago—is it Chicago—DePaul University, wherever it is—

Administrator Natsios:—law school has an Institute on Human Rights, which will be working with an Italian university with the University of Baghdad. This will be for professors to go back and forth.

One of the things I noticed—I had dinner with a number of university professors around the country, many of them had never in their entire lives been outside of Iraq, not just to the West. They had never been to Saudi Arabia, or even Kuwait, or Turkey or any neighboring countries, and they felt an enormous sense of isolation. Some of these are even older men and women who had never traveled.

And so they want to see what other universities are, how they're run, what the student bodies are like, what methods of pedagogy are used in those universities. And so there's a series of these higher education programs that we'll be doing to link our civil society with their civil society, so we have three of those grants today; 1.5 million schoolbook—schoolbags were distributed to the children who are returning to school, to secondary schools, in other words, high school students, and you have a picture of this here in your packet.

So every kid in high school goes back with that. We've worked with UNESCO and UNICEF on redoing the textbooks, which were full of vitriol and Baathist party propaganda. And we've now printed 76 math and science textbooks that UNESCO has done, I think, for high school students, if I'm not mistaken; 3 million have been printed already, and another 1.5 million will be shortly printed, and they are being distributed now.

So school buildings, curriculum, teachers, and then the university system that trains the teachers are all part of this effort. So in the area of education, I think we have some accomplishments, not promises, for the people of Iraq.

I might also add that one of the first things that we like to do in societies that have gone through a period of deterioration where the kids aren't in school—because, apparently, only about 55 percent of the kids who were of school age were in school prior to the war on a regular basis. There was just—school enrollment declined dramatically, particularly girls' school—girl children's enrollments went down.

What we notice in those societies, there is a tendency toward more social disorder. If the kids are not in school with an ordered schedule, it causes problems. Certainly the period earlier in the year was somewhat chaotic for kids, and getting them off the streets into schools will increase the stability and the security of the society.

And children are, essentially, very conservative ("small c"), in their habits. They like order in their day. If they don't have it, they can become disruptive in any society, north or south, east or west. And so a matter of simply rehabilitating the kids and ordering their day better will add to the security and the social order in Iraq.

Anyway, those are some of the things we've accomplished. And I think there's another—one piece here, which you can see some of the statistics, and then there are some case studies in the back.

Are there any questions from anybody?

Yes, sir.

Question: Total dollar figure on everything you just put together?

Administrator Natsios: I can tell you what the contract is for education, not including the reconstruction of the buildings. And that's—I believe it's $60 million, is the education contract?

A Participant: Sixty-seven, I think.

Administrator Natsios: Sixty-seven? Let me just see if there's a figure here.

Question: It seems that the figure is 63.

Question: Sixty-three.

Administrator Natsios: Sixty-three million is for the training, the textbooks—training for the teachers, the textbooks and the schoolbags. It does not include the reconstruction of the buildings. It does include new desks because most of the schools didn't have desks. The kids were on the floor or—I saw some of the old desks, it's rather difficult to believe people sat in them.

The Bechtel contract includes money for the actual reconstruction. Bechtel did about 1,000 schools in the NGOs, and I guess one of the— the education contractor did do—or no, it was a local government contractor did some of the schools as well.

In some towns, we gave—we have given about 850 small grants to city—these new city councils and town councils have been formed, in order for them to decide what the priorities in their village, and many towns and villages chose the school as the first thing they would rehabilitate; and therefore, in those towns we didn't do the rehabilitation ourselves.

Does that answer your question?

Question: Do you know roughly how much—what the school rehabilitation was then?

Administrator Natsios: I can get, get a figure for you. Do you know what the breakout from—the task order for Bechtel for the schools was?

A Participant: For Bechtel it was a portion of $50 million, but it wasn't all because that was clinics and some other public works as well.

Administrator Natsios: Okay. We can get a figure for you if you'd like it.

Yes.

Question: You talk about this Master Teacher Program and teaching new ways of—

Administrator Natsios:—right.

Question:—kind of teaching. But who is in charge of determining the curriculum? Is it the teachers, themselves, or are you having a hand—or the administrators?

Administrator Natsios: No, no, it's not the teachers. It's the Ministry of Education.

Question: Okay, but is it in collaboration with the CPA? I mean, okay—

Administrator Natsios: Yes. All of this—we report, just so it's clear, AID reports to Ambassador Bremer and the CPA. And the CPA has in it, the Iraqi Minister of Education and the American advisors to the ministry. And they went, worked with UNICEF and UNESCO in redoing these textbooks with our contractor, Creative Associates, and with the NGO community, as well. But the teachers were involved in this, the Ministry of Education was involved in this, they had to approve all of this before it would go out.

Question: I guess what I'm trying to get at is you're teaching them how to—new ways of how to teach, but you're not kind of dictating to them what to teach?

Administrator Natsios: No, no, no. The training is not in subject matter, it's in methods. Because in autocratic, and particularly, totalitarian societies, the system is highly centralized, and literally everybody will be on the same page of the book in every school in the whole country on the same day. That's how the old Soviet system was built.

And you had to—you know, if kids were more interested in this subject than others, it is completely irrelevant. You have to be on this page for this hour of the day. That is not a helpful way of tying what you're teaching to the needs of the children. And so western systems—and I might add other, more progressive Arab systems, like the Jordanian and Moroccan educational systems—we have just been through a whole reform process in Alexandria, Egypt, where parent/teachers associations were formed, which is another thing we intend to do, but I don't think that was done. That hasn't been done yet, Ross, has it?

A Participant: It's in the beginning, but it hasn't gotten off the ground very far.

Administrator Natsios: Okay. We find in all countries, north and south, that when there are parent/teachers associations involved in the governance of the school, that the learning levels of the kids go up because parents will ask, "Well, what's your homework tonight, and did you get it done, and how can I help you with it?" Parents/teachers associations get the children's parents involved in their own education, which will increase achievement levels.

So those—there are things that we have learned, not in terms of the subject matter, but just in terms of school governance, in terms of the methods by which material is presented, where there is discussion and people can ask questions, where people just—the kids don't just learn by rote. They have to reason their way through and use critical reasoning. And these techniques improve the quality of education, regardless of what the subject matter is.

Yes.

Question: Since these buildings have been completely, for the most part, as you've said, just totally devastated for a good period of time, does this also include monies for maybe libraries or computer internet, so that if a library isn't at hand, they can—

Administrator Natsios: There are no school libraries. In Iraq— people think of schools in the United States and they compare them to schools. And the schools, all of the schools I went to in Iraq were simply classrooms, and there was one room for the headmaster or the principal of the school. There's no gymnasiums, there are no lunchrooms, there are no libraries, there's nothing else except the classrooms.

Our plan was not to reconstruct all the schools of the country. We were taking what was there already and making it functional. We're not intending to transplant all of our infrastructure into Iraqi society. We think that would be inappropriate. It would also take a very long time and we're not sure that would be the best use of money right now.

We have introduced internet cafés, but not in the schools. They have a system, a chain, of telephone—I guess they're sort of related to the post office in many European countries and the Middle East—and we opened our first one. I went to it in Umm Qasr. It was very interesting because they did not have links to the internet in Iraqi society, except at a very certain number of universities in a very controlled way.

And I watched while an older man learned how to read Arab newspapers from other countries on the internet. And he sat there, and he said he was just astonished. He had heard that there was this sort of magical device that you could take the Cairo newspaper from that morning and read it on this electronic device, and of course, it appeared in front of him, and he read it and he was just astounded. He said, "Our society has been cut off from the world for 20 years, and now we're reconnected."

Question: Sorry to interrupt. They were that isolated?

Administrator Natsios: Yes. Oh, yes.

Question: I mean, you hear stories—I mean, certainly that they get, you know, the Arab satellite channels, and things like that. I guess that's for a very small number of the elite?

Administrator Natsios: And if you were caught with a satellite, you could get arrested. Now—I'm not talking about under Saddam— now there are disks all over the city; apparently, this is one of the big boom businesses.

Yes.

Question: Just for the record, when is the first, normal first day of school in Iraq? And then on the question of—

Administrator Natsios: It's the beginning of October.

Question: It is normally now? And then about curriculum, you said it's just methods, but there wasn't any changes in the actual material itself, such as—

Administrator Natsios: Yes. Our UNICEF and UNESCO are working with the Ministry of Education under grants from AID through the CPA, to redo the whole curriculum, but it will take a while. This is a vast curriculum for 27 million people.

Question: But, the actual factual stuff is being changed?

Administrator Natsios: Only one kid in six in Iraq had textbooks prior to the war. They simply—and most of them were, like 20 years old, or 15 years old, they're falling apart. I've seen some of them. And so these are the first texts many kids have ever seen in school.

Michael.

Question: I'd like to ask about electricity generation, just to clarify some of the numbers. In your September 30th testimony, you referred to 3,927 megawatts that it had reached on the 28th. The CPA's request for funds refers to 3,600 megawatts. Is it—

Administrator Natsios: It goes up. It's been going up.

Question: Is it now—I mean, is it now at—

Administrator Natsios: It's over 4,000 now.

Question: It's over 4,000 now, okay.

Administrator Natsios: Yeah. There was a plan put in place with the CPA. There was an electricity task force that Ambassador Bremer put together and he asked us to serve on with our people from Bechtel and our engineers on the AID staff. And they designed a plan to bring electrical generation up to the level that it was prior to the war and we're just about there, not quite there, but we're just about there.

Question: Well, it was 4400 megawatts, right?

Administrator Natsios: Right.

Question: So can you just give an account of—what is it exactly that has prevented us, several months after the end of major hostilities, from even reaching the level that it was at before the war?

Administrator Natsios: Sure. When I was in Iraq in June, there were 65 transmission towers down. Bechtel did a survey by helicopter on May 15th, a month earlier, and there were 15 down. Do you know how many transmission lines are down now? 650.

So it was 15 at the end of the war, it was 65 in mid-June, and it's now 650. These are the towers, the transmission towers, not the poles.

Question: So it's almost entirely sabotage?

Administrator Natsios: It's not sabotage. Almost none of it is sabotage. There's some around Baghdad. Most of it is a criminal gang called the Garumsha (ph). The Iraqis told me about it, the British office has told me about it, the Iraqis in the streets said, "Oh, the Garumsha (ph) are at it again."

Apparently, they're sort of a criminal mob that's been around for a long time. They make their living by stealing stuff. They have no interest in politics. They don't shoot at our soldiers or anything. They're selling the copper from the wiring, and because of it, there's been such a flood in the market in the Middle East of copper tubing from Iraq's electrical system that the price for copper is now depressed in the Middle East.

Question: So how do you spell that name of the group?

Administrator Natsios: I don't know how to spell it. I'm sorry.

Question: We'll get it for you. And so what exactly has Bechtel been doing since it made that initial survey?

Administrator Natsios: It's been focused on the electrical generating plants themselves.

Let me just tell you that the transmission system is not necessary for people to have electricity in their houses, it is necessary for stability in the system. The way our system works or works most of the time, as we had a little incident this summer as you know, the transmission system is designed to increase the reliability and the stability of the electrical system. I was in the industry for two years. I know I'm not an expert on this.

But the reason for the transmission system is it links all of the generating plants together with the distribution systems. And what it does is, if there is a plant that goes down somewhere in the United States, because there's always excess amount being produced, then the electricity simply will flow from the excess areas of the system. But the linking of the system increases the reliability so you never have outages—or you're not supposed to.

Until we can restore those transmission lines, there will be instability in the system. Now, one of the interesting effects of this is because Baghdad got 23 hours of electrical power before the war for 10 years or 20 years. No matter what was going on, they got their power because it was the center of a totalitarian state.

Basra had an average of three to four hours. Basra now has 23 hours of electrical power. And the reason is, is because Basra has been de-linked from Baghdad because the transmission lines are down. So the people in Basra might not want the transmission lines back up.

Question: I don't understand something. The transmission—I mean the generating capacity has not really been affected by this criminal gang, too?

Administrator Natsios: No. There have been—there is a huge problem with the quality of the—I went through several of the plants. And I, again, was in the industry for a couple of years. I have never seen anything in such horrendous condition. The stuff is rotting out. I was amazed the stuff was functioning as it was. And they would have outages constantly in the old order, because there was never any replacement equipment. They would go to the dumps to scavenge stuff.

Let me just tell you, there was a little—

Question: But they're still producing 4400 megawatts, which we're not at yet. And if the criminal gang is hitting the transmission line—

Administrator Natsios: But what we're doing—

Question:—but doesn't affect the generating capacity, why is the generating—

Administrator Natsios: Because we're taking the plants down that are unstable or on the edge of collapse and we're repairing them. And this article you saw in a major newspaper earlier last week—late last week, which interviewed an engineer at a particular electrical generating plant, who said, "We've been waiting for six months." That guy's going to be waiting for the next six months, because that is the—we triaged that plant, it was in such horrendous condition.

Our engineers—we also have, by the way, the Corps of Engineers overseeing the Bechtel stuff with us. We have them doing part of this, too. But this is a CPA effort. Bechtel and AID have a leading role in it with the Corps. And we categorized all the plants in the whole country. We've done a complete survey of the condition of all the generators and all the plants in the country, and the ones that can be fixed the fastest, that have a regular supply of gas or oil and can be fixed the cheapest are the ones done first.

The ones that have an erratic or unreliable source of energy cost a huge amount of money and will take two years to fix were put in the bottom and they were, frankly, triaged. We're not going to do them for probably another six months to a year. And the one that was—the guy who was interviewed in that article, which annoyed me a lot to be very frank with you, I'm not sure the reporter understood it, but that plant was on the bottom of the list.

It was never going to be repaired and we've never told the engineers at that plant that they're just going to have to wait because they're probably one of the worst—plant in the worst condition in the country.

Question: Just one final question on this. Is it—have there been any attacks, whether it's with a criminal gang, whether it's any saboteurs, anyone, attacking any of these generating plants?

Administrator Natsios: Yes. Yes, we have had—

Question: How many incidents have you had?

Administrator Natsios: We have had three or four instances of sabotage at electrical generating plants. Isn't that correct, Ross?

Ross: Not external attacks, but, yes, sabotage inside.

Administrator Natsios: Inside sabotage.

Question: Okay. And have those completely taken down those plants?

Administrator Natsios: Yeah, temporarily, and then they get put back up again, which is why plants go on and off. They go on and off for several reasons, that's one of them. Another thing we're doing, which is a very interesting thing from a security perspective, you can do reconstruction in a way that increases the security of public services.

Right now—and I had it happen to me in my—supposed to take a shower the next morning when I was in Baghdad—what happens, the electricity goes out, we knew it was going to go down. But guess what else went down? The water system and the sewer system, the pumps don't work.

So what we are now methodically doing in the larger cities, is deconnecting the water pumping stations, the water purification stations, the sewer pumping stations, and the treatment plants from the electrical grid. They have their own generators. And it's much easier to protect through point security, a facility than a transmission line. So even though electricity may go down for whatever reason at some point in the future, water and sewer services will continue.

Yes, sir.

Question: That gang you mentioned, is there a—I don't know if it's your area—but is there a strategy for going after—either going after them, or preventing the copper from making it to market or some way to stop it?

Administrator Natsios: We actually were considering intervening in the copper market, to pour copper in to depress the price, but it's already happened. Most of it was going to Iran, apparently, and they're melting it down into bars. The British brigadier down in—I think it was the second in command down in Basra, told me that they closed just that week I was there six copper smelts that had been—black market copper smelts—that had been set up to melt these wiring down.

I went by a—

Question: Where in the country, you say?

Administrator Natsios: Sorry?

Question: Where in the country?

Administrator Natsios: In Basra, the city of Basra, down at the—the southerly most city in the country.

And so they have actually now, I think, closed down about 40 or 50 of them. They're doing it on a regular basis because it's a little difficult to hide them.

Yes, sir.

Question: Looking over your September 30 testimony, it wasn't clear to me you've got—

Administrator Natsios: People actually read my testimony?

Question: Well, parts of it at least.

[Laughter.]

Administrator Natsios: I shouldn't have said that, I think.

[Laughter.]

Question: It wasn't clear to me whether you've actually gotten to, say, have commercial traffic on a regular basis in Umm Qasr and—

Administrator Natsios: Oh, yes, definitely.

Question: What is the situation with commercial flights going in and out of the airports?

Administrator Natsios: 600,000 tons of tonnage arrived in Umm Qasr in the month of September, and some of that was food—

Question: So the operation will be able to process up to 600 metric tons?

Administrator Natsios: Well, I believe it did last month. A lot of it's food from the Oil-for-Food program. But I was there when commercial—I was there the first day we opened it, the regional governor and I, and four commercial vessels arrived that were private when I was there.

Question: And the airports?

Administrator Natsios: In Umm Qasr.

Question: Yeah. And the airports?

Administrator Natsios: The airport of Baghdad is open to chartered commercial traffic, military traffic. I don't think any airlines are yet landing there. I think there were like 200 flights last month, or something like that, into Baghdad International Airport.

We've got to finish the tower. Almost all the work is done, but there's some of this equipment that—what do they call that?

Question: Air traffic—

Administrator Natsios: Air traffic safety control equipment that has been ordered that has not yet been installed in the tower. And we're now beginning work on Basra International Airport. We've got three airports to do that are important to the economy of the country, which is why Ambassador Bremer made them a high priority. They will affect commerce and the business community coming in to invest and that sort of thing.

Yes, sir.

Question: Mr. Natsios, you've mentioned the fact that there's children coming to school and the satellite dishes, but is there any implementation of the new radio and television type—either in network or local stations—to communicate to, obviously, people out in both the urban and rural areas?

And also, do many of these people—adults, as well as maybe teenagers, do they have portable radios where they can get communications and—

Administrator Natsios: They do.

Question:—if the rest of the infrastructure was ruined, any plans to perhaps build a cellular telephone system?

Administrator Natsios: Actually, we're building—we're rehabilitating—we're not reconstructing, we're rehabilitating the fiber optic cable system that goes from the north of the country down right to the south that ties the country together that had been destroyed during the war, and that will help with communications.

We're also putting up dishes that will allow the country to be tied together for—with cellular communication. That's a contract of—subcontract of Bechtel. This was also at Ambassador Bremer's insistence.

What was the first question?

Question: Well, I wanted to know, just because—

Administrator Natsios: Oh, about the television-radio station.

Question: Right.

Administrator Natsios: We're not in charge of running the stations, but we did reconstruct the looted radio and TV commission headquarters that was run by the state, that the CPA now controls, and I was there when they were broadcasting.

They have since, apparently, substantially upgraded those facilities so that Ambassador Bremer can speak to the people and they get outside news. And I guess programming from neighboring Arab countries is brought in from Lebanon and from Egypt to play, and I guess it's on the radio and TV.

There is also Radio SAWA, which predates the war. That's U.S. subsidized. It's a private radio station, but we subsidize it, I guess, and that reaches about 40 percent of the kids in the country—at least prewar—listen to it every day because it's got a lot of music on it and that sort of thing.

Yes, sir.

A Participant: I think we have time for just one more question.

Administrator Natsios: Who hasn't asked a question? Anybody hasn't?

Okay. Yes, sir.

Question: On the debate over the UN resolution, it seems that one of the issues at hand is that the—a lot of the other countries want the U.S. to put the reconstruction money through a common fund, and I'm wondering if maybe from your point of view you would explain why it is the Administration is really holding the line on this point? Why would that make the job more difficult for you, or what's the problem there?

Administrator Natsios: I'm not—I have to say the debate in the UN is something that Secretary Powell and the State Department deals with. International funds are generally useful for smaller countries that do not have large aid agencies and do not have a presence on the ground. That's why we set it up in Afghanistan, and also to provide monetary support to the Afghan Government.

That is not what we're facing in Iraq on a mass scale. There would be no point to us going through a fund like that with the large amounts of money we're dealing with because we're already spending it on the same things that would be spent through the fund, so—but I'm not an expert in the resolution. You'd really have to ask the State Department that.

Question: Can I ask one?

Administrator Natsios: Yeah, one last question. Maybe I'll regret this. What's the—

Question: You've got, obviously, a lot of big projects under way: telecommunications, electricity—how much of that work—what are the basic guidelines for allowing non-American companies to do some of this work? And I'm not referring only to the Iraqi ones. I'm thinking of, you know, the European ones—

Administrator Natsios: Sure.

Question: Siemens. Companies like that are expert in some of the—

Administrator Natsios: There are a very large number of British companies, for example, that have got contracts.

Question: Yeah. There's, but how much is—

Administrator Natsios: Ambassador Bremer—

Question:—"buy America" policy, you know, affected here?

Administrator Natsios: We have a new edict from, from Ambassador Bremer, which, as I thought about it when I was there, I fully agreed with him.

We are now employing 55,000 Iraqis doing the reconstruction work. If people are working, they're not shooting at us. So maximizing Iraqi business participation in this will increase the security of the country, keep people off the streets, particularly young men who, in any society, increase the level of instability if there are high unemployment rates.

So it's one of the things we always look for in a country that's unstable is, how many young men there are between 15 and 25 or 30? And what's the unemployment rate? And it's very high in Iraq. But Ambassador Bremer wants us to bring up total employment just through our contracts to $300,000 by next year. And we think we—I'm not sure we can do it as rapidly as he wants, but we're up to $55,000 now. That's a lot of people in five months to be working.

This is not just one day. Most of these people are working, you know, the wage is not great. The wage by our standard is $4 a day, $5 a day. But by Iraqi standards, that's a very good wage.

And so what he has asked us to do is make sure the subcontracts primarily go to Iraqi firms. And Bechtel made a commitment that they would get up to 70 percent of the subcontracting going to Iraqi firms. So there's a heavy emphasis on Iraqi companies.

We are noting, though, some of the Iraqi companies are—have joint ventures with Turkish companies or Egyptian companies or neighboring countries.

Thank you.

Reference:

Natsios, Andrew. 2003. "Reconstruction Activities in Iraq." Special Briefing to the Press, Briefing Room, Washington, DC: U.S. Department of State, 3 October. Available at http://www.state.gov/p/nea/rls/rm/24898.htm (accessed 20 May 2004).

Accelerate Reconstruction in Afghanistan, State Department Coordinator for Afghanistan, William B. Taylor Jr. Testimony before the U.S. Senate Committee on Foreign Relations Washington, D.C. (27 January 2004)

Taylor's testimony on the Hill indicates what more than two years' reconstruction has shown in Afghanistan. The task has proven more complex and vexing than originally expected.

Mr. Chairman, thank you for this opportunity to update the Committee on our program to accelerate reconstruction in Afghanistan.

Our objective in Afghanistan is clear: to help the Afghan people build a responsible, self-sustaining market democracy that will never again harbor terrorists. Our national security requires that we stay the course until we and the Afghan people have achieved this goal.

When I addressed the committee last October I offered my frank assessment of the hurdles we face as we work toward that objective but also of the progress we are making. At that time the glass was by no means full, but it was far from empty.

I am pleased to report today that while many hurdles remain, the glass is measurably fuller today than it was four months ago. Congressional support has been crucial. The supplemental funding approved by Congress last fall is helping to underwrite a far-reaching program to accelerate the reconstruction of Afghanistan—and that effort is already bearing fruit. The FY04 appropriation that you passed last week will also help. I seek your full support for the FY05 request that the President will send up shortly.

Mr. Chairman, we can usefully think of our effort in Afghanistan in two overlapping phases: stabilization and institutionalization. In each of the three tracks of reconstruction—political, economic and security—we need to stabilize the sector and then build lasting institutions. These institutions take time to build but are crucial if the Afghan people are to build a self-sustaining market democracy.

Political Reconstruction

The Bonn Agreement of December 2001 and the Emergency Loya Jirga in June 2002 began to stabilize governance in the immediate aftermath of the victory over the Taliban. Hamid Karzai was selected to head the transitional government and a cabinet was drawn from the many factions of Afghan society. The Constitutional Loya Jirga that finished up on January 4 represents a huge step forward to institutionalize political progress toward an Afghan democracy—part of our objective.

The new constitution took shape through a representative process. It was drafted by a nine-member committee of Afghans last winter, reviewed by a 35-member Afghan commission starting last March, revised following nationwide public consultations that began in June, and ultimately ratified by 502 Afghan delegates to the Constitutional Loya Jirga—an event that was beamed live on TV and radio to Afghan households. About 20 percent of the delegates were women, and the debates included hard bargaining on clauses relating to parliamentary powers and the rights of minorities, including official languages.

At the end of the day, the Constitutional Loya Jirga approved the first nationally mandated constitution in 40 years—a constitution that Afghans can be proud of and that can provide a solid framework on which to build the functioning elements of a stable democracy.

The next big step toward institutionalizing democracy is the election scheduled for this summer. Registration is underway, with the UN reporting that some 500,000 voters—out of an estimated 10.5 million—have been registered to date. The UN is already behind in registration—a million and a half voters should have been registered by now. The Afghan government, the UN, the international community and the U.S. government are now straining to pick up the pace of registration so that the election can take place in June.

Economic Reconstruction

To stabilize the economy, the international community has provided large amounts of foreign aid to jump start economic growth and begin to rebuild economic infrastructure. The Afghan economy grew at 30 percent last year and is growing at 20 percent this year—from an exceedingly low base. Since we last spoke in October, USAID completed a layer of pavement on the Kabul-to-Kandahar road, allowing vehicles to travel between the two cities in less than six hours. Survey and design work is already underway for the Kandahar-Herat stretch of the road and the topographic surveys of that section are 80 percent complete.

Also in December Afghanistan completed repair work on the Salang Tunnel, a critical mountain pass linking Kabul to its northern provinces.

It would be hard to overstate the significance of new roads in drawing the country together politically and economically and in offering Afghans a visible sign of progress and hope. Certainly the Kabul-Kandahar-Herat ring road has been a major priority for

President Karzai, so much so that he escorted a contingent of delegates from the Constitutional Loya Jirga to the ribbon cutting ceremony for the Kabul-Kandahar leg.

Over the last three months the impact of U.S.-funded irrigation projects has almost tripled, going from coverage of about 55,000 hectares to almost 150,000 hectares.

These projects have begun to stabilize the Afghan economy, but sustained economic growth requires massive, private-sector investment, investment that will not come until the economic foundations of a market economy are put in place. Investment law, a commercial code, banking laws, commercial standards, dispute settlement mechanisms—these establish the economic and regulatory framework necessary for real growth. Some are in place, but sustained effort to create the investment climate capable of attracting foreign and domestic investors will be necessary for years to come.

Security

In the security sector, stabilization requires the continued pursuit of terrorists who oppose and threaten the Karzai government, the steady removal of local strongmen who harass the Afghan people, the disarming of local militias and the firm crackdown on narcotics cultivation and trafficking. We have made progress—disarmament is picking up momentum—but stabilization in the security sector has a long way to go.

We have seen progress towards militia disarmament in recent months. In November, Japan and the UN completed the first DDR pilot program in Kunduz, disarming over 1000 combatants and collecting a corresponding number of individual and crew-served weapons. In the reintegration phase approximately two-thirds of the demobilized combatants requested agricultural assistance, job placement, or vocational training.

The Gardez DDR pilot program was completed in December, resulting in nearly 600 combatants registering and turning in their weapons. DDR has also begun in Mazar-e-Sharif, and is scheduled to begin in Kandahar next month.

We have also seen real progress in Kabul. On January 15, ISAF coordinated the transfer of over 100 heavy weapons belonging to the Northern Alliance out of Kabul, including multiple rocket launchers, anti-tank guns and artillery. Over 800 of the verified 2000 combatants identified for the pilot program have been disarmed and demobilized in Kabul.

Even as we continue to stabilize the security environment, however, we must be working to build Afghan security institutions.

We have trained an additional 1,300 Afghan National Army recruits since October putting ANA strength at 5,780 with over 2,100

more soldiers in training. We reached a major milestone just this
month: the capacity to train three battalions simultaneously. That
capacity is essential to our goal under the acceleration program of
reaching a troop strength of 10,000 by the time of elections this summer.

Over 1,200 new recruits are awaiting training in Kabul—an
ethnically diverse group representing 26 of 32 provinces. These recruits
are the result of a strengthened recruitment effort in the provinces. Ten
new recruitment centers are partly or fully operational and twenty-four
more are planned.

Our police-training programs also entered a new phase over the
last four months. With new resources available under the supplemental
appropriation, we are building seven new regional training centers for
national, border and highway police. The training center in Kabul is
already complete and centers in Mazar-e-Sharif, Gardez, Kandahar and
Konduz are under construction and will reach full capacity of 750
trainees by the end of next month.

All-told, since last October, German and U.S. police-programs
have trained over 2000 new national police officers and over 200
highway patrol officers. With the added capacity of the new training
centers coming on line, this puts us on track to reach our goal of
fielding 20,000 police officers by the time elections take place next
summer.

Provincial Reconstruction Teams

As I reported in October, we are also working with our partners in the
international community to deploy civil-military teams around the
country to enhance security, accelerate reconstruction and extend the
reach of the central government into the provinces. These provincial
reconstruction teams (PRTs) contribute to both stabilization and
institution building.

In December we established four new PRTs—in Parwan, Herat,
Kandahar and Jalalabad, bringing the total number of PRTs to eight. By
the end of next month we expect to establish another four PRTs—in
Ghazni, Asadabad, Khowst and Qalat. Over the last few months these
PRTs have been instrumental in facilitating preparations for the
Constitutional Loya Jirga, assisting voter registration teams, defusing
tensions among rival militias and supporting DDR efforts and police
training. We are examining options for expanding their number still
further and encouraging NATO/ISAF to establish additional PRTs.

Embassy Staffing

Finally, we are well on our way toward building the team at our
Embassy to manage the accelerated reconstruction effort. Ambassador
Khalilzad presented his credentials to President Karzai on November

27, 2003, and is being joined by a team of senior advisors to help him implement the acceleration program.

Conclusion

Mr. Chairman, we are still very much in the stabilization phase—hunting Taliban and Al Qaeda, jump-starting the economy. Even as these efforts continue, however, we are starting to build the institutions—a constitutional government, credible elections, loyal army and police forces—that will move Afghanistan toward the self-sustaining market democracy that we seek and the Afghan people deserve.

As the President said last week:

> *The men and women of Afghanistan are building a nation that is free, and proud and fighting terror—and America is honored to be their friend.*

As their friend, we need to assure the Afghan people that, this time, we will see this important mission through to success.

Thank you.

Reference:

"Accelerate Reconstruction in Afghanistan." Available at http://www.state.gov/p/sa/rls/rm/28599.htm (accessed 12 February 2004).

6

Organizations

This chapter provides basic information on organizations that aim to influence nation-building, to study it, to lobby for or against it, or to implement it. The organizations are broken into four types: those from the private sector that are not-for-profit, private sector for-profit, international organizations, and U.S. governmental organizations. It should be noted that this list is continually changing. Organizations that are not interested in nation-building today may take an active role when the activity is in a different place tomorrow. Every attempt has been made to make the list current.

A particular word on the for-profit private groups. This is only a representation of the many organizations that do contract work in nation-building around the world. The ones listed here are the largest and best known in the nation-building field. The list has been compiled in consultation with USAID personnel who have worked in the field. The Internet is a tremendous help in locating these groups, but the listings for them are not as complete as the not-for-profit or governmental groups because they are not reached by the public in the same manner. In trying to provide the maximum information, however, the data are as current and complete as possible.

Private Sector

Not-for-Profit

Afghans for Civil Society
30 Brattle Street
Cambridge, MA 02138
(617) 576-7104
E-mail: acs@afghanpolicy.org
Web site: http://www.afghansforcivilsociety.org

1501 Bolton Street
Baltimore, MD 21217
(410) 523-3034
E-mail: baltimore@afghansforcivilsociety.org

Afghans for Civil Society (ACS) attempts to create a new Afghan society based on the rule of law, meaning equal treatment and justice for men and women, Islamic and secular, rich and poor, with the ultimate goal that Afghanistan take its place in the community of states around the world. ACS acknowledges that the U.S. role in Afghanistan will be important to fulfilling the needs of the state. The organization works to promote partnerships among the United States and other foreigners, along with Afghans, making certain these groups are not merely funneling money to Western contractors. One of ACS's main projects is in the city of Khandahar, where it carries out a wide array of projects in creating an independent media, forming a society open to women, building institutions, repairing the physical damage to Afghanistan's civil and historic sites, and promoting education throughout the society. In promoting cross-cultural ties, ACS uses grant money from the U.S. Agency for International Development (USAID) and other grant-giving institutions. ACS also accepts donations from individuals.

American Enterprise Institute for Public Policy Research
1150 Seventeenth Street, N.W.
Washington, DC 20036
(202) 862-5800
Fax: (202) 862-7177
Web site: http://www.aei.org

The American Enterprise Institute (AEI) has been involved in public-policy issues since its inception in 1943 and is a major U.S.

think tank. One of its major focuses is foreign policy and the range of issues involved in nation-building. During the late 1970s and 1980s, international concern focused on escalating conflicts in Central America, and a subsidiary concern was nation-building. AEI representatives were frequently involved in the national debate. Public discussions on Iraq and Afghanistan were influenced by a number of prominent fellows associated with AEI, such as Reagan administration Department of Defense official Richard Perle, Vice President Richard B. Cheney, and former UN ambassador Jeane J. Kirkpatrick. AEI publishes the *American Enterprise,* a monthly journal. It also produces a range of reports on various topics.

American Friends Service Committee
1501 Cherry Street
Philadelphia, PA 19102
(215) 241-7000
Fax: (215) 241-7275
E-mail: afscinfo@afsc.org
Web site: http://www.afsc.org

The American Friends Service Committee (AFSC) is a Quaker group with a long-standing commitment to nonviolent solutions to international tensions. The committee was created during World War I, in 1917, as a conscientious objector group reaching grassroots supporters. It strongly opposed U.S. involvement in the conflicts in Southeast Asia and Central America and continues its opposition to military solutions to nation-building problems. In the case of Iraq, for instance, AFSC has a Web page entitled "Iraq Aftermath: The Human Face of War," which brings to light individuals who have been purged from government posts in Iraq or have been affected by the 2003 conflict. Other parts of the site include links to various on-line and print resources, information about U.S. government spending on the conflict, suggestions for volunteer opportunities, and testimonials from people working in the war zone.

The national office has many activities, including providing international resources and sponsoring the Nationwide Women's Program, the Peacebuilding Unit, and the Third World Coalition. Links with other Quaker organizations around the world mean that AFSC is engaged in nation-building efforts in all continents and in many countries. AFSC publishes news releases and opinion pieces in newspapers around the United States.

Amnesty International
322 Eighth Avenue
New York, NY 10001
(202) 807-8400
Fax: (202) 463-9193 or (202) 463-9292 or (202) 627-1451
E-mail: admin-us@aiusa.org
Web site: http://www.aiusa.org

International Secretariat:
1 Easton Street
London, WC11X 0DW
United Kingdom
44-2-07-413-5500
Fax: 44-2-07-956-1157
Web site: http://www.amnesty.org

Amnesty International (AI) is probably the world's best-known human rights organization, with offices in virtually all countries, allowing it to monitor human rights concerns regardless of borders. AI has raised international consciousness since 1961 about political prisoners around the world and the compliance of various states to the 1948 Universal Declaration of Human Rights. It considers human rights protection a basic concept in nation-building, and hence has continued its focus on places such as Afghanistan, Kosovo, Bosnia, and Iraq, where successive governments and government opponents have systematically ignored human rights over generations. In Iraq, AI has persistently argued that the nation-building process must be based on human dignity and the rule of law, not merely laws that are ignored. The Amnesty International USA office is one of the larger ones, but by no means the most vocal.

As the Web site points out, Amnesty International has had success in changing the international attitude toward prisoners of conscience. Its Web site notes various campaigns for individuals, addresses specific concerns in countries, and gives links to other sites, volunteer opportunities, and other concerns. AI issues an annual *Amnesty International Human Rights Report,* available online or from one of the offices. The organization issues reports on specific countries as appropriate. It also addresses immediate concerns in press releases.

Atlantic Council of the United States
910 Seventeenth Street, N.W., Suite 1000

Washington, DC 20006
(202) 778-4961
Fax: (202) 463-7241
E-mail: info@acus.org
Web site: http://www.acus.org

The Atlantic Council (ACUS) was created in the 1950s to educate the public about the importance of strong ties among NATO member states but has gradually grown into an organization with a broad national security base, including nation-building. Its interests in nation-building concern the broader public-policy issues of peace and stability around the world. Retaining its focus on trans-Atlantic relations, ACUS also considers Asia, the Middle East, and Central Asia. In those latter contexts, ACUS has devoted some resources to considering what would be required for good governance and stability in newly evolving portions of the world, such as in a post-Castro Cuba, in Central Asia, and in a post-Saddam Iraq. ACUS hosts conferences, symposia, and studies on relevant nation-building examples. The Council publishes *Atlantic Council Policy Papers* to offer prescriptions for policymakers in various instances.

Brookings Institution
1775 Massachusetts Avenue, N.W.
Washington, DC 20036
(202) 797-6000
Fax: (202) 797-6004
E-mail: brookinfo@brook.edu
Web site: http://www.brook.edu

One of the most venerable think tanks in the United States, the Brookings Institution (BI) has long studied good governance and now increasingly puts its resources toward the broad question of nation-building around the world. The institution was a World War I creation, and while associated with Democratic administrations through much of the twentieth century, is largely considered nonpartisan. Its policy concerns are as wide ranging as any in the United States, with an array of analysts, many with long-term U.S. government experience, who ponder issues from economics, international relations, political science, and other policy questions. With its prominence, BI is able to attract many scholars and analysts for frequent symposia, meetings, electronic town hall meetings, and various other events. In particular, BI has in the 1990s and early 2000s played a major role in debates on rebuilding efforts for the former Yugoslavia, Afghanistan, and, increasingly, Iraq. These areas complement its traditional focus on Europe and Northeast Asia, as well as the functional areas of defense, governmental studies, and economics. Brookings has an active, prestigious press with approximately fifty new monographs appearing annually. *The Brookings Review* is a quarterly journal concentrating on a range of policy questions, including nation-building. There are several other periodic publications, such as *Policy Briefs* and *Brookings Analysis and Commentary*, in print and on the Web. Materials can be ordered by phone or online.

CARE
Atlanta (headquarters)
151 Ellis Street
Atlanta, GA 30303
(404) 681-2552
Fax: (404) 589-2651

37 Temple Place, 3d Floor
Boston, MA 02111
(617) 338-6400
Fax: (617) 574-7345

70 East Lake Street, Room 1430
Chicago, IL 60601
(312) 641-1430
Fax: (312) 641-3747

13101 Washington Boulevard, Suite 133
Los Angeles, CA 90066
(310) 566-7577
Fax: (310) 566-7579

610 Carlson Parkway, Suite 1050
Minnetonka, MN 55305
(763) 473-2192
Fax: (763) 473-4042

650 First Avenue, 2d Floor
New York, NY 10016
(212) 686-3110
Fax: (212) 683-1099

114 Forrest Avenue, Suite 106
Narbeth, PA 19072
(610) 664-4113
Fax: (610) 664-4256

41 Sutter Street, Room 300
San Franscisco, CA 94104
(415) 781-1585
Fax: (415) 781-7204

1402 Third Avenue, Suite 912
Seattle, WA 98101
(206) 464-0787
Fax: (206) 464-0752

1625 K Street, N.W., Suite 500
Washington, DC 20006
(202) 585-2800
Fax: (202) 296-8695
(800) 422-7385 is for information on special CARE programs
(800) 521-CARE is for general information and donations
E-mail: info@care.org
Web site: http://www.careusa.org

CARE started in 1945 in the aftermath of World War II in the
midst of poverty and severe malnutrition around the world. It
has evolved into an international organization with twelve sub-
sets in states around the world, including Australia, Brazil,
Denmark, Canada, the Netherlands, Germany, Britain, Austria,
Japan, Norway, the United States, and France. CARE retains its
goal of alleviating poverty, although its work is now concentrated in those areas where nation-building is the primary
focus.

Carnegie Endowment for International Peace
1779 Massachusetts Avenue, N.W.
Washington, DC 20036-1840
(202) 483-7600
Fax: (202) 483-1840
E-mail: info@ceip.org
Web site: http://www.ceip.org

Established before World War I by steel magnate Andrew
Carnegie for the purpose of ridding the world of international

210 Organizations

conflict, the Carnegie Endowment for International Peace (CEIP) is a prolific scholarly institution, as well as one of the best-funded think tanks in the world. CEIP has programs and scholars focusing on the range of issues that promote peaceful resolution to conflict and generate peace in the international system. In particular, CEIP has programs relating to nation-building under the auspices of Democracy and the Rule of Law and U.S. Leadership, as well as embedded in some of their regional programs, such as China and the Middle East. Additionally, the endowment has a project, led by Martha Brill Olcott and Aleksei Malashenko, on Ethnicity and Nation-Building, with emphasis on the former Soviet Union. CEIP scholars are prolific at publishing, particularly opinion pieces in various newspapers around the globe, and timely reports. The endowment also hosts many conferences annually. The influential journal, *Foreign Policy*, began at the endowment in 1970 and retains strong ties. CEIP also publishes many Policy Briefs and produces many of its findings on-line through e-mail messages and on its Web site.

Catholic Relief Services
209 West Fayette Street
Baltimore, MD 21201-3443
(410) 625-2220 or (800) 736-3467
E-mail: webmaster@CatholicRelief.org
Web site: http://www.CatholicRelief.org

Catholic Relief Services (CRS) started in 1943 when U.S. Catholic bishops sought to assist the poor and destitute outside of the United States in accordance with the teachings of Christ. Long involved in Latin America because of its Catholic population, CRS is now engaged in nation-building through humanitarian operations in Latin America, Africa, Asia, the Middle East, and any other part of the world where conflict arises. CRS accepts donations for its work in more than ninety countries.

CATO Institute
1000 Massachusetts Avenue, N.W.
Washington, DC 20001-5403
(202) 842-0200
Fax: (202) 842-3490
E-mail: cklein@CATO.org
Web site: http://www.CATO.org

The CATO Institute is a Libertarian think tank. It advocates minimizing U.S. commitments overseas, including activities involved in nation-building. CATO's position is that nation-building is not only unnecessary for national security, but actually undermines security by exposing the United States to outside commitments, as well as diminishing its strength. CATO has a strong focus on national security interests, so it covers nation-building to a great degree. CATO holds conferences regularly. CATO produces an array of on-line and print publications in various lengths. Its *Policy Analysis* series is perhaps its most visible publication, with several past issues dedicated to nation-building. The institute also publishes a journal, *CATO Journal*, on public-policy issues.

Center for Defense Information
1779 Massachusetts Avenue, N.W.
Washington, DC 20036-2109
(202) 332-0600
Fax: (202) 462-4559
E-mail: info@cdi.org
Web site: http://www.cdi.org

The Center for Defense Information (CDI) was organized in the 1970s to question the basic assumptions underlying U.S. national security calculations, including those about nation-building. The center has a number of former defense officials and retired military officers (two former heads of the center were retired rear admirals), who often question the assumptions on which decisions are based. CDI has an active project on Iraq with all of the aspects of change examined. The Center does not take federal contract money but is financed by citizen contributions. This allows some flexibility in what it analyzes. CDI actively publishes its studies, such as the 16 April 2003 "Rumsfeld's Strategy: Fine for War, Now What about Peace?" by Marcus Corbin. It also hosts a weekly television show appearing in a number of television markets, including the nation's capital.

Center for International Policy
1775 Massachusetts Avenue, N.W., Suite 550
Washington, DC 20036
(202) 232-3317
Fax: (202) 232-3440
E-mail: cip@ciponline.org
Web site: http://www.ciponline.org

The Center for International Policy (CIP) originated in 1975 to encourage public discussion on national security issues, including Colombia and the nation-building efforts of the United States in that country. In general, CIP highlights demilitarizing public-policy options for international conflict, often taking positions critical of various U.S. policies. The center has a small staff, which mostly engages in opinion-writing for various newspapers across the country. CIP publishes *International Policy Report* on-line and in hard copy on various specific questions in international security.

Center for Security Policy
1920 L Street, N.W., Suite 210
Washington, DC 20036
(202) 835-9077
Fax: (202) 835-9066
E-mail: info@security-policy.org
Web site: http://www.security-policy.org

The Center for Security Policy (CSP) was founded in 1988 by Frank Gaffney, a major figure in the Reagan administration who has charged that U.S. security is eroding because of policy decisions in Washington. CSP has consistently taken one of the most "hawkish" positions on national security questions and consistently does so on nation-building. The center advocates policies that will promote "American strength" as a time-tested mechanism for preventing threats from harming the United States. CSP frequently sends short faxes to policymakers and policy analysts advocating its positions. On nation-building, CSP is guarded in its willingness to commit U.S. forces (such as proposed forces for Liberia's civil war) but often strongly supports procurements of modernized weapons that will support U.S. military strength while secondarily helping nation-building. The center currently concentrates most of its efforts on Iraq and the rebuilding and peacekeeping efforts under way there. The center does its work largely through faxes sent around the public-policy community rather than through traditional publications.

Center for Strategic and International Studies
1800 K Street, N.W.
Washington, DC 20006
(202) 887-0200
Fax: (202) 775-3199

E-mail: webmaster@csis.org
Web site: http://www.csis.org

The Center for Strategic and International Studies (CSIS) was founded in the mid-1960s as an outgrowth of the American Enterprise Institute and is perhaps the most active think tank in Washington. CSIS engages in public-policy discussions across the national security field, which includes nation-building. It has a large number of experts who can be called upon by the press in less than an hour to comment on issues. Many former policymakers from various presidential administrations are on the board of directors or serve as project directors. CSIS hosts numerous conferences that attract considerable international and domestic attention. It has a major project on rebuilding post-conflict Iraq, which has included at least a ten-day visit to the country. The nation-building studies relate to several cases involving the United States and include the military, political, economic, and social aspects of Kosovo, Bosnia, Russia, Afghanistan, Central Asia, and Somalia. CSIS has an impressive range of monographs, periodic reports, on-line reports such as *Comparative Connections* about Asia, and a widely cited journal, the *Washington Quarterly*.

Council on Foreign Relations
Washington Office
1779 Massachusetts Avenue, N.W.
Washington, DC 20036
(202) 518-3400
Fax: (202) 986-2984
E-mail: communications@cfr.org
Web site: http://www.cfr.org

New York Office
The Harold Pratt House
58 East 68th Street
New York, NY 10021
(212) 434-9400
Fax: (212) 434-9800

The Council on Foreign Relations (CFR) is probably the most prestigious think tank and public-policy discussion forum for national security, devoting considerable attention to nation-building and its attendant questions. CFR was established in 1921 to foster public debate and awareness about international issues in the aftermath of World War I. Council members are nominated and include prominent policymakers and scholars. It is not open to public membership. Its sessions and reports are frequently cited, but they are generally not available to the public. CFR has a number of large, ongoing projects. Currently prominent is Governance and Human Rights, which focuses on Iraq and the lessons learned from both the recent conflicts and the rebuilding effort, with fourteen experts in this field noted on the Web site. The nation-building issue also appears in other areas of CFR's work, including globalization, international organization, and national security and defense.

CFR hosts luncheons, lectures, and conferences at its Washington, D.C., and New York locations. Attendance is limited to members, but the council often issues reports afterward to give access to the remarks. CFR's flagship work is in the journal, *Foreign Affairs*. This bimonthly contains many articles on nation-building, such as those by Thomas Carothers and Paula Dobriansky that debate the promotion of democracy. CFR also publishes monographs and encourages its members and staff to write opinion pieces for various newspapers and to appear on television talk shows. Its Web site is quite informative.

Council on Hemispheric Affairs
1730 M Street, N.W., Suite 1010
Washington, DC 20036
(202) 216-9261
Fax: (202) 216-9193
E-mail: coha@coha.org
Web site: http://www.coha.org

The Council on Hemispheric Affairs (COHA) began in 1975 with a focus on Latin America. It was closely involved in the national debate about Central American policy in the 1980s and has a pivotal role in the discussions of nation-building efforts in Colombia today. It is often critical of administration policies. Its Web site and staff gives positions that COHA advocates as less injurious to the people of the region than current U.S. efforts in both nation-building and the promotion of neoliberal economic reform.

East-West Center
1601 East-West Road
Honolulu, HI 96849-1601
(808) 944-7111
Fax: (808) 944-7376

E-mail: ewcinfo@EastWestCenter.org
Web sites: http://www.EastWestCenter.org;
http://www.ewc.hawaii.edu

East-West Center Washington
1819 L Street, N.W., Suite 200
Washington, DC 20036
(202) 293-3995, ext. 19
Fax: (202) 293-1402
E-mail: Washington@EastWestCenter.org
Web site: http://EastWestCenterWashington.org

The East-West Center (EWC) has its primary location at the University of Hawaii at Manoa and is a congressionally mandated organization that researches, educates, and serves as a location for U.S. citizens to meet Pacific counterparts. Created in 1960s, the center has played a role in promoting better understanding of the changes occurring in the region, as well as in improving U.S. interactions with the Pacific community. The research portion of EWC includes a project on Politics, Governance and Society, on many of the themes included in the nation-building debate. While EWC emphasizes nation-building in the Pacific rim, the issues remain similar to those in other regions of the world. The center holds conferences and brown bag sessions and offers other opportunities for scholars to interact. The Web page for EWC also has a feature called the Pacific Disaster Center that gives data on typhoons, volcanoes, and other natural disasters that can seriously undermine nation-building efforts in the Asia Pacific region.

On 1 September 2001, the East-West Center Washington began to enhance relations between Washington and the countries and peoples of the Asia-Pacific region. The mission of this center is decidedly more linked to domestic U.S. debate on political and security issues affecting the Asia Pacific area. Specifically, some research topics are Civil Society and Political Change in Asia, Management of International Conflicts in Asia, and the Asia Security Order. It holds conferences, hosts guest fellows (such as through the Southeast Asia Fellowship Program), and works in conjunction with the Honolulu center, as well as other public policy research organizations in the nation's capital. Included among the works of EWC are *East-West Center Occasional Papers, East-West Center Special Papers, East-West Working Papers, Asia-Pacific Population and Policy, Asia-Pacific Issues, Contemporary Issues in Asia and the Pacific, NFHS Bulletin,* and *NFHS Subject Reports.*

Foreign Policy Association
470 Park Avenue
New York, NY 10016
(212) 481-8100
Web site: http://www.fpa.org

The Foreign Policy Association (FPA) has been committed from its beginnings in 1918 to educating the public about all the issues relating to national security. With some programs aimed at teachers and others at the public at large, the FPA is much changed from the Committee on Nothing at All or the League of Free Nations, as it has been called at various points in its history before being given its current name in 1923. Nation-building is an important component of the work of the FPA. The association is a membership organization that welcomes the public to its locally based councils. The FPA publishes a well-known series, *Great Decisions*, that introduces people to the debate about national security in specific contexts. The individual *Great Decisions* are written by academics with an ability to make complicated policy questions accessible to the public, regardless of their knowledge.

Foreign Policy Research Institute
1528 Walnut Street, Suite 610
Philadelphia, PA 19102
(215) 732-3774
Fax: (215) 732-4401
E-mail: FPRI@fpri.org
Web site: http://www.fpri.org

The Foreign Policy Research Institute (FPRI) was founded in 1955 as a nonpartisan, educational organization to concentrate on national security questions. It hosts many conferences, educates teachers, and offers students internships in the security field. While FPRI is not considered one of the major think tanks on nation-building, it does ponder U.S. military involvement overseas and the attendant questions that form the basis to much of the nation-building debate. The quarterly journal *Orbis*, begun in 1957, is a product of FPRI. The institute also produces the weekly *FPRI Bulletins* and the *FPRI Wire*.

Fund for Peace
1701 K Street, N.W., 11th Floor
Washington, DC 20006

(202) 223-7940
Fax: (202) 223-7947

665 Chestnut Street, 3d Floor
San Francisco, CA 94133
(415) 749-1409
Fax: (415) 749-1402
E-mail: comments@fundforpeace.org
Web site: http://www.fundforpeace.org

The Fund for Peace (FfP) has as its mission the prevention of war, working to wipe out the causes of conflict through education and research to find practical solutions. Founded by Ronald C. and Dorothy Danforth Compton in the 1960s, FfP works to enhance understanding as a means of preventing conflict. It has a research arm as well as an internship arm, allowing students to gain practical experience. Much of the focus is on what is now called nation-building, creating conditions that preclude war. Particularly noteworthy is the fund's project, Regional Approaches to Ending Internal Wars, that studies the conditions necessary to allow neighbors to help end conflict rather than turning to those from far outside a region. FfP publishes *Innovations* and *Reality Check*, two newsletters dedicated to real solutions to problems, especially the latter, which addresses internal wars. Additionally, FfP publishes occasional reports on topics of interest to its staff and membership.

Henry L. Stimson Center
11 DuPont Circle, N.W., 9th Floor
Washington, DC 20036
(202) 223-9604
Fax: (202) 238-9604
E-mail: info@stimson.org
Web site: http://www.stimson.org

The Stimson Center, named after former secretary of state Henry Stimson, describes itself as a "community of analysts" developing realistic solutions to international problems, increasingly including nation-building. The center has a large number of analysts with government experience who address topics from a practical as well as a theoretical bent. The center has a number of concentrations, including the Institute for Global Democracy and UN peace operations. It also focuses on China and South Asia as areas facing nation-building challenges. The center works to develop regional security through confidence-building measures and studies the issue of security in the new century. The Stimson Center puts out a newsletter, press releases, and various other materials on nation-building topics. Printed copies are available for a fee, but the Web-based material is largely available gratis.

Heritage Foundation
214 Massachusetts Avenue, N.W.
Washington, DC 20002
(202) 546-4400
Fax: (202) 546-8328
Web site: http://www.heritage.org

The Heritage Foundation (HF) is one of the most visible, best-funded think tanks in the United States, having risen to this prominence over more than three decades. Its base grew out of the interests of a number of wealthy, conservative public policy activists such as former Coors chairman Joseph Coors. A significant number of prominent members of the Reagan and Bush administrations have ties to the Heritage Foundation and its vast public policy agenda, which includes nation-building. While it has regional programs, the foundation also addresses issues relating to nation-building, such as democracy, use of U.S. force, peacekeeping, and homeland security. The Heritage Foundation has an impressive array of publications, including monographs, "Backgrounders," "Heritage Reports," "Heritage Memoranda," and "Heritage Lectures," each targeting a different constituency. These materials supplement the journal, *Policy Review,* which appears bimonthly on pressing policy concerns.

Hoover Institution on War, Revolution, and Peace
Stanford University
Stanford, CA 94305-6010
(650) 723-1754 or (877) 466-8374
Fax: (650) 723-1687
E-mail: horaney@hoover.stanford.edu
Web site: http://www-hoover.stanford.edu

The Hoover Institution on War, Revolution, and Peace was created by Stanford alumnus and U.S. president Herbert Hoover to study the issues that caused war in 1914. Located at Stanford, the institution eventually became part of the university, where it provides an environment for studying public policy questions relating to national security and free societies. Much of its nation-building work relates to ongoing processes in societies such as China and Russia where old political systems have either evolved or been completely wiped away and new approaches tried and tested. George W. Bush's national security advisor, Condoleezza Rice, was closely associated with the Hoover Institution prior to her assumption of the White House post in 2001. Hoover Institution scholars are some of the most prolific on nation-building and author articles and monographs regularly. The institution produces the *Hoover Digest*, *Weekly Essays* on nation-building, and other analyses of ongoing debates. Many of the publications appear on the institution's Web site.

Hudson Institute
Indianapolis Office
5395 Emerson Way
Indianapolis, IN 46226-1475
(317) 545-1000
Fax: (317) 545-9639
Web site: http://www.hudson.org

Washington Office
1015 Eighteenth Street, N.W., Suite 300
Washington, DC 20036
(202) 223-7770
Fax: (202) 223-8537

The Hudson Institute is now headquartered in Indianapolis but retains a significant presence in Washington, where it was established in 1961. Innovative thinkers such as Herman Kahn, Oscar Ruebhausen, and Max Singer searched for more realistic approaches to national security and accompanying public policy concerns such as nation-building. Much of its work retains its Russian flavor, reflecting the institute's beginnings at the height of the cold war, but its work now focuses on the global policy questions characterizing the complexity of the early twenty-first century. With its Washington presence and satellite facilities throughout the country, the Hudson Institute addresses not only broad policy questions but offers links to the public community at large through many internships and programs. Hudson Institute authors publish a range of materials, such as *Hudson Reflections* on specific policy questions. The institute also produces *Foresight*, which compiles in-house contributors' op-eds on a single topic.

Outlook is a sixteen-page analysis of a topic, while *Visions* is a quarterly on the institute and its staff. *American Outlook* is a bimonthly, with in-depth analysis of a couple of topics. Finally, Hudson authors produce many monographs on policy questions.

Human Rights Watch
350 Fifth Avenue, 34th Floor
New York, NY 10118-3299
(212) 290-4700
Fax: (212) 736-1300
E-mail: hrwny@hrw.org

1630 Connecticut Avenue, N.W., Suite 500
Washington, DC 20009
(202) 612-4321
Fax: (202) 612-4333
E-mail: hrwdc@hrw.org

11500 West Olympic Boulevard, Suite 445
Los Angeles, CA 90064
(310) 477-5540
Fax: (310) 477-4622
E-mail: hrwla@hrw.org

312 Sutter Street, Suite 407
San Francisco, CA 94108
(415) 362-3250
Fax: (415) 362-3255
E-mail: hrwsf@hrw.org
Web site: http://www.hrw.org

Human Rights Watch (HRW) is a significant player in the international community, pressing concerns on the treatment of political prisoners while trying to focus international attention on the protection of human rights. The organization is concerned with nation-building because human rights are a key component of any state's ability to build a viable, thriving society, and HRW encourages citizens to press their governments to both engage in and press other states to protect the building blocks of nation-building. HRW sometimes engages in campaigns on various aspects of its work, such as protecting refugees, that are essential to nation-building. HRW publishes reports, electronically and in print. The organization sponsors an international film festival to focus attention on human rights questions. It publishes a report,

Human Rights Annual, which receives international attention for its comprehensive, nonpartisan approach to this topic.

Institute for Conflict Analysis and Resolution
George Mason University
4260 Chain Bridge Road
Fairfax, VA 22030
(703) 993-1300
Web site: http://www.gmu.edu/departments/icar

The Institute for Conflict Analysis and Resolution (ICAR) at George Mason University focuses on the linkages between globalization and conflict, the various types of conflict at work in the international and domestic systems, and how to resolve those conflicts. Its work has expanded into both the theoretical and practical applications of conflict resolution, all of which is intimately tied to nation-building. Its location in Fairfax, Virginia, with close proximity to the nation's capital, allows it access to decision makers who participate in nation-building around the world. ICAR has an aggressive research agenda but also awards master's and doctoral degrees in conflict resolution. ICAR publishes a series called *ICAR Working Papers* and the *ICAR Newsletter.* Its publications are available in hard copy or can be downloaded from the Web site.

InterAction
1717 Massachusetts Avenue, N.W., Suite 701
Washington, DC 20036
(202) 667-8227
E-mail: ia@interaction.org
Web site: http://www.InterAction.org

InterAction is an alliance of nongovernmental humanitarian organizations from the United States. It consists of more than 160 members which operate around the world, including important projects in Liberia, Iraq, Ethiopia, Eritrea, Afghanistan, and other places where conditions require outside humanitarian assistance. Its role as a clearinghouse for information and coordination is extremely important to the nation-building community. InterAction also pushes for gender equality and works to see advantageous legislation passed in Congress to promote development around the world. InterAction works as a crucial interface between the Agency for International Development and the nation-building nongovernmental organization community.

Inter-American Dialogue
1211 Connecticut Avenue, N.W., Suite 510
Washington, DC 20036
(202) 822-9002
Fax: (202) 822-9553
E-mail: aid@thedialogue.org
Web site: http://www.thedialogue.org

The Inter-American Dialogue (IAD) was founded in 1982, during the highly charged atmosphere of political partisanship over Central America. It has functioned as an important arena for debate and the exchange of ideas on Latin America. Much of the discussion examines issues pertinent to nation-building. Membership includes high-ranking government officials from Latin America, individuals who are able to affect the policies of various countries. Programs include Democratic Governance, Inter-American Institutions, Social Equity/Education, and Trade and Economics, all of which have nation-building ramifications. The IAD also has outreach and educational activities aiming to enhance understanding of the region. IAD produces studies in Spanish and English, in print and on-line editions. It has a periodic newsletter, *Dialogue/Diálogo*, on issues relevant to the region, concentrating on nation-building and the meetings of the group.

International Institute for Strategic Studies
Arundel House
13–15 Arundel Street
London WC2R 3DX
United Kingdom
44-0-207-379-7676
Fax: 44-0-207-836-3108
E-mail: iiss@iiss.org
Web site: http://www.iiss.org

1749 Pennsylvania Avenue, N.W., 7th Floor
Washington, DC 20006
(202) 659-1490
Fax: (202) 296-1134
E-mail: taylor@iiss.org

The International Institute for Strategic Studies (IISS) was begun in 1957 by the British government to provide a range of discussion on the life-and-death strategic themes of the 1950s. It has evolved into perhaps the most prestigious international organization of thinkers and practitioners. With headquarters in London and an office in Washington, D.C., it focuses on strategic issues broadly defined, to include nation-building. The IISS increasingly looks at those regions of the world where nation-building concerns are evolving new theories and practices, such as the Singapore Dialogue with its concern regarding East Asia. IISS is primarily a research institution, although it does hold important meetings that air various views which are not always heard. It has always been a nonpartisan institution. Several IISS publications are generally viewed by the research community as reference standards: the *Military Balance* and *Strategic Survey*, global surveys that both appear annually. More relevant to nation-building are *The Adelphi Papers*, periodic analyses of roughly a hundred pages on specific questions such as nation-building, governance, and civil-military balances, and the more recent *Strategic Comments*, periodic short analyses on current public policy questions. The IISS journal is *Survival*, a refereed quarterly on strategic questions.

Inter-University Seminar on Armed Forces and Society
University of Maryland
College Park, MD 20742
(301) 405-6013
Fax: (301) 314-1314
E-mail: isu@socy.umd.edu
Web site: http://www.bsos.umd.edu/ius

The Inter-University Seminar on Armed Forces and Society (IUS) grew out of seminars held by Dr. Morris Janowitz and his graduate students examining civil-military relations around the world, starting in 1960. This basic element of nation-building remains the heart of the IUS, but the seminar also considers many other areas of the global nation-building experience. The IUS is primarily a research seminar, with a membership of just under a thousand Fellows from around the world, which hold biennial meetings to discuss research. The seminar began at the University of Chicago, became a Chicago-wide experience, and is now headquartered at the University of Maryland. But unlike other organizations making such claims, it truly is an international group in its membership. Supplementing the biennial meetings are more local, irregularly scheduled events around the world. Members tend to come from the academic fields of history, sociology, international relations, political science, and strategic studies, as well as from decision-making positions. The IUS journal, refereed and highly cited, is *Armed Forces and Society*, published by Transaction Books.

Jamestown Foundation
4516 43d Street, N.W.
Washington, DC 20016
(202) 483-8888
Fax: (202) 483-8337
E-mail: webmaster@jamestown.org
Web site: http://www.jamestown.org

The Jamestown Foundation (JF) is primarily concerned with ensuring that freedoms are guaranteed around the world, understanding that this is a crucial aspect to nation-building. The foundation was founded in 1983, during the Reagan era concerns about repression and deprivations in the former Soviet Union. The organization is now increasingly concerned with nation-building efforts in Russia, the former Soviet republics, China, and other places where these are required. JF prides itself on offering a realistic and sometimes critical understanding of nation-building around the world. JF has several important works. The *Fortnight in Review* looks at events in the former Soviet Union, with long essays on some specific concern in each issue. The weekly *Russia's Week* reviews events in Russia and the former Soviet republics. *Prism* examines political, cultural, economic, and social conditions in Russia by scholars, journalists, and other experts. The best known publication is *Monitor*, a daily appraisal of events in the former Soviet Union. Other publications, on-line, include *Chechnya Week, China Brief,* and *Russia Eurasia Brief.*

Johns Hopkins University Foreign Policy Institute
The Johns Hopkins University
Paul Nitze School of Advanced International Studies
1619 Massachusetts Avenue, N.W.
Washington, DC 20036
(202) 663-5773
Fax: (202) 663-5769
E-mail: fpi@mail.jhuwash.jhu.edu
Web site: http://www.sais-jhu.edu/centers/fpi

The Foreign Policy Institute (FPI) at Johns Hopkins University's northwest Washington, D.C., campus engages in various research aspects of foreign affairs. Housed in the Paul Nitze School of Advanced International Studies, FPI is a research arm that bridges the gap between public discussion and scholarly analysis. It considers many aspects of nation-building, including civil-military relations, governance, elections, and military operations such as peacekeeping. The institute holds conferences and seminars, as well as hosting visiting scholars. FPI publishes the quarterly journal, *SAIS Review*, one of the journals that most directly addresses those aspects of nation-building that receive public attention.

The Matthew B. Ridgway Center for International Security Studies
3J01 Posvar Hall
University of Pittsburgh
Pittsburgh, PA 15260
(412) 648-7408
Fax: (412) 624-7291
E-mail: goldy@pitt.edu
Web site: http://www.gspia.pitt.edu/ridgway/contact.html

The Ridgway Center for International Security Studies is probably the premier location in the United States for the study of transnational issues such as money laundering, drug trafficking, corruption, illegal movement of people, and other areas that undermine democratic systems in states undergoing nation-building efforts. The center's work is broader than just transnational concerns, but this is its primary focus at Ridgway. Ridgway is part of the Graduate School of Public and International Affairs at the University of Pittsburgh, created in 1988 to honor the memory of Korean War military leader General Matthew Ridgway. It offers a multidisciplinary approach to issues confronting the international community. Ridgway hosts conferences and produces many reports, while also educating graduating students. The Ridgway Center has an exhaustive, detailed Web site with links to government organizations and sites considering the "new" security issues that make up nation-building concerns. The center publishes *Ridgway Viewpoints* and is the editorial office for the refereed journal, *Transnational Organized Crime*.

Médecins Sans Frontières/Doctors without Borders
Rue de la Tourelle 39
1040 Brussels
Belgium
32-2-280-1881

Fax: 32-2-280-0173
Web site: http://www.msf.org

337 Seventh Avenue, 2d Floor
New York, NY 10001-5004
(212) 679-6800
Fax: (212) 679-7016

2525 Main Street, Suite 110
Santa Monica, CA 90405
(310) 399-0049
Fax: (310) 399-8177

A private humanitarian relief organization, Médecins Sans Frontières (MSF) began in 1971 with French doctors providing immediate health care to victims of armed conflict, regardless of creed, religion, race, or gender. Growing to include physicians from many countries around the world, MSF has become an increasingly important organization in the international humanitarian and nation-building arena. In the late 1990s, the organization received the Nobel Peace Prize for its efforts to provide relief in crisis areas. Taking volunteers as well as private donations to assist humanitarian needs in any conflict, MSF maintains a relief network in eighteen countries, and its 2,500 volunteers from the medical, logistics, and basic infrastructure replacement communities have been engaged in nation-building in more than eighty countries over the past thirty years.

Mercy Corps
Department W
3015 S.W. First
Portland, OR 97201
(800) 292-3355, ext. 250
E-mail: info@mercycorps.org
Web site: http://www.mercycorps.org

10 Beaverhall Road
Edinburgh, EH7 4JE
Scotland
44-0-131-477-3677
Fax: 44-0-131-477-3678
E-mail: admin@mercycorps-scotland.org

This humanitarian relief organization, based in Scotland and the United States, has been operating since 1979. Mercy Corps (MC) has distributed more than $710 million in assistance in seventy-nine countries around the world, working to establish sustainable, civil societies and to answer humanitarian crises. MC works with in-country partners wherever possible. This not-for-profit organization accepts donations and volunteer services. MC operations have been in Central America, East Asia, the Caucasus, Central Asia, the Balkans, the Middle East, and South Asia. The most recent conflicts in Liberia, Afghanistan, Eritrea, and Iraq have been areas where MC volunteers have worked.

Meridian International Center
1630 Crescent Place, N.W.
Washington, DC 20009
(202) 667-6800
Fax: (202) 667-1475
E-mail: info@meridian.org
Web site: http://www.meridian.org

The Meridian International Center offers a forum for people from the world to discuss issues, such as nation-building, with analysts and practitioners from the United States. The center hosts seminars, conferences, and other educational events across the United States. These events facilitate an exchange of ideas among people from several layers of the U.S. government and those from similar positions in other societies. There are cultural as well as academic exchanges.

Mershon Center of the Ohio State University
1501 Neil Avenue
Columbus, OH 43201
(614) 292-1681
Fax: (614) 292-2407
E-mail: herrmann.1@osu.edu
Web site: http://www.mershon.ohio-state.edu

The Mershon Center of the Ohio State University is an interdisciplinary institution for discussion on international security issues, including nation-building. The center was originally endowed by a retired army officer who wanted to create the best opportunity for collaboration across this major campus in the state of Ohio. The center hosts conferences and other activities to encourage public policy discussion and to encourage thinking in nontraditional approaches to solving tensions. The organization hosts the

Summer Institute for Political Psychology and has an international network of historians. It also endows some research by dissertation students and visiting scholars. *Mershon Center Review* appears three times annually.

Monterey Institute of International Studies
425 Van Buren Street
Monterey, CA 93940
(831) 647-4100
Fax: (831) 647-4199
E-mail: president@miis.edu
Web site: http://www.miis.edu

The Monterey Institute of International Studies (MIIS) is probably best known for its work on nonproliferation but is also a graduate school and research facility that enhances the links among business and scholarship across the global community. Located south of San Francisco, MIIS work concentrates on East Asia, with some coverage of Russia. Its work on nation-building is part of a holistic approach to these societies and their ongoing changes. MIIS may offer more languages than any other graduate school and is a solid link between business and other societal concerns.

MIIS has three research centers: the Center for East Asia and Pacific Affairs, the Center for Russia and Eurasian Studies, and the Center for Nonproliferation Studies. Embedded in each are aspects of nation-building. All three centers hold periodic, international conferences. The *NonProliferation Review* is the journal that MIIS produces periodically. Conference reports also appear irregularly. These and all publications are listed on the Web site.

National Institute for Public Policy
3031 Javier Road, Suite 300
Fairfax, VA 22031
(703) 698-0563
Fax: (703) 698-0566
E-mail: amy.joseph@nipp.org
Web site: http://www.nipp.org

The majority of work done at the National Institute of Public Policy (NIPP) since its inception in 1981 has focused on drawing public attention to the need to increase defense spending to alter the military balance. Part of the institute's work has also been helping other governments engage in military reform, such as the ongoing process in the former Soviet republic of Georgia. This sort of nation-building is both practical and theoretical because it illustrates the requirements necessary for change. The NIPP has good access to the U.S. bureaucracy and continues to keep the United States aware of potential threats. NIPP scholars most often publish in materials that are disseminated through other sources, such as *Defense News*. These are listed on the Web site, and are noted as available through the Web site or at Amazon.com.

National Security Archive
Gelman Library, Suite 701
The George Washington University
2130 H Street, N.W.
Washington, DC 20037
(202) 994-7000
Fax: (202) 994-7005
E-mail: nsarchiv@gwu.edu
Web site: http://www.gwu.edu/~nsarchiv/

The National Security Archive originated through efforts of former journalist Scott Armstrong, who sought a program that would allow access to public papers in the Reagan administration concerning the Nicaraguan *contrarevolucionarios* in the 1980s. Armstrong used the Freedom of Information Act (FOIA) of 1967 to analyze U.S. government intentions and actions. Established as the Central American Papers Project, the archive moved to its current home at George Washington University in 1995, allowing continued public access to the national security papers in its possession. A major archive goal is to assist those seeking to use the Freedom of Information Act to study the motives for U.S. actions, including those in nation-building.

The archive has a number of ongoing projects on Chile, China, the Chinese nuclear program, Cuba, Guatemala, Honduras, Israel, Iran, intelligence, Mexico, Pakistan-India, openness in Russia, and Japan. Additionally, the Parallel History Project, considering NATO and the Warsaw Treaty Organization, and the Cold War International History Project are nationally known. The archive also has ties to other decision-making projects throughout the world and has been able to help bring attention to U.S. nation-building efforts. This is particularly important for former Third World areas where U.S. policymakers have believed their actions would not only enhance U.S. national security directly by thwarting threats but would also help create thriving democratic systems. NSA provides access for scholars and citizens to its collections of public documents, through the Digital National Security Archive, as well as in twenty different microfiche collections. The archive was important in the publication of the *Tiananmen Papers* about attempts to alter the government in China through June 1989. The archive publishes Electronic Briefing Books, as well as monographs by its staff, on topics like intelligence, the evolution of South Africa, and other areas germane to its core interests in evolving U.S. policy. The archive also holds more than twenty published collections of U.S. national security policy papers from the collections of U.S. national security FOIA requests it has handled.

National Strategy Forum
53 Jackson Boulevard, Suite 516
Chicago, IL 60604
(312) 697-1286
Fax: (312) 697-1296
E-mail: nsf@nsf.org
Web site: http://www.nationalstrategy.com

The National Strategy Forum (NSF) began in 1983 with the imprimatur of attorney Morris I. Leibman, a Chicagoan with significant and enduring concern about national security. The NSF spends increasing amounts of time, largely through its luncheon series and various publications, on nation-building topics, including efforts in Iraq, Haiti, Liberia, and Indonesia. The forum publishes a quarterly, *National Strategy Forum Review*, which has short articles on many nation-building concerns.

RAND Corporation
1700 Main Street
P.O. Box 2138
Santa Monica, CA 90407-2138
(310) 393-0411
Fax: (310) 393-4818

1200 South Hayes Street
Arlington, VA 22202-5050
(703) 413-1100
Fax: (703) 413-8111

201 North Craig Street, Suite 102
Pittsburgh, PA 15213

(412) 683-2300
Fax: (412) 683-2800
Web site: http://www.rand.org

The Rand Corporation began in the late 1940s as the Research and Development Corporation of the newly created U.S. Air Force. Rand, along with the Center for Naval Analyses and a couple of other organizations, is a Federally Funded Research Center (FFRDC), a not-for-profit arm of the U.S. government engaging in independent, contract-driven research work on a wide array of subjects. Much of Rand's work today, with a stable of regional specialists as well as functional specialists on topics aligned with nation-building, makes it one of the most comprehensive think tanks on the topic. In particular, Rand authors have considered the issues confronting Colombia as it addresses civil war and reconstruction, East Asia and its economic and political development, civil-military relations in various states, military personnel, training and health in societies, and other issues that confront nations around the world as they evolve toward greater democracy. As a FFRDC, Rand works for the U.S. Air Force, U.S. Army, U.S. Navy, Department of Defense, Office of the Secretary of Defense, the intelligence community, the Unified Commands, and the Joint Staff. The Rand publications list is quite long, even in the nation-building subset of its work. With its multidisciplinary work, Rand publishes a range of reports for any topic. It produces Issue Papers outlining research questions on many topics. Research Briefs are more substantive works on the same topics. Rand also produces monographs. The most useful means of viewing its research is to look at the Web site.

Save the Children
54 Wilton Road
Westport, CT 06880
(203) 221-4030 or (800) 728-3843
E-mail: twebster@savechildren.org
Web site: http://www.savethechildren.org

Save the Children (SC) was founded in 1932 to help children in need and now operates in nineteen states domestically and more than forty-seven countries around the world. It is part of the International Save the Children Alliance. SC is a major partner with the U.S. Agency for International Development in reconstruction efforts around the world. Additionally, SC accepts support from individual donors who seek to sponsor an individual child or focus on a project for a state, such as reconstruction in Afghanistan. SC has a special program for children in Iraq facing tremendous problems after the decades of Ba'athist governing and war. SC also has projects to engage in the humanitarian side of nation-building in places such as Nepal, Ethiopia, Mali, and Afghanistan.

Stanley Foundation
209 Iowa Avenue
Muscatine, IA 52761
(563) 264-1500
Fax: (563) 264-0864
E-mail: info@stanleyfoundation.org
Web site: http://www.stanleyfoundation.org/

The Stanley Foundation, funded by C. Maxwell and Elizabeth Stanley in 1956 to help alleviate global troubles, has increasingly moved toward studying and resolving global governance concerns. One of the three major projects at the foundation involves work on humanitarian interventions, regional approaches to state concerns, refugee protection, the United Nations, U.S.-UN interactions, and postconflict resolution and rebuilding. The foundation hosts many conferences at its Muscatine site as well as in other parts of the country and then publishes the results in conference reports. The Stanley Foundation produces conference reports and a newsletter, *Courier*. Additionally, the foundation puts out a journal to illustrate how the world press covers various concerns in *World Press Review*.

Stockholm International Peace Research Institute
Signalistgatan 9
SE 169-70 Solna
Sweden
46-8-655-9700
Fax: 46-8-655-9733
E-mail: sipri@sipri.org
Web site: http://www.sipri.org

The Stockholm International Peace Research Institute (SIPRI), founded in 1966, has become one of the most respected research organizations in the world, with increasing emphasis on how to move beyond conflict to "winning the peace." SIPRI was established to commemorate Sweden's century and a half of nonin-volvement in international conflict and has proven adept at fo-cusing on methods that resolve global problems. With researchers from around the globe, SIPRI examines conflict in every part of the world. More recently, its reports have been more concerned with the building of enduring peace.

SIPRI hosts many conferences, workshops, public lectures, and scholarly assessments. The Olaf Palme Lecture, an annual event to commemorate the assassinated prime minister, draws in-ternational attention to a particular theme for a year. SIPRI's con-cerns were originally focused on Europe, but this is no longer the case. SIPRI's mission is heavily oriented toward practical solu-tions; hence publications are numerous. The *SIPRI Yearbook*, pro-duced annually since 1969 to much public acclaim, is a thorough examination of arms proliferation and transfers, moves toward resolution of conflict, military spending, and attempts at rebuild-ing societies after war. SIPRI also publishes many research reports on a wide range of themes and fact sheets on discrete concerns. All of the publications are considered impartial. While most are published in hard copy, SIPRI works are increasingly circulated on the Web.

U.S.-China Policy Foundation
316 Pennsylvania Avenue, S.E.
Suite 201–202
Washington, DC 20003
(202) 547-8615
Fax: (202) 547-8853
E-mail: uscpf@uscpf.org
Web site: http://www.uscpf.org

The U.S.-China Policy Foundation advocates for improved rela-tions among the United States, Taiwan, and the People's Repub-lic of China, including the deepening of democratic trends and nation-building. The organization hosts discussions through large public lectures, more intimate meetings, dinners, and a weekly television show, *The China Forum*, seen in several cities around the country. The *Washington Journal of Modern China*, a semiannual publication, and the *U.S.-China Policy Review* are pub-lished by the foundation to promote a better relationship between the states. Both are aimed at policymakers, scholars, and inter-ested observers in the United States, Taiwan, and the People's Re-public of China.

Washington Office on Latin America
1630 Connecticut Avenue, N.W., Suite 200
Washington, DC 20009
(202) 797-2171
Fax: (202) 797-2172
E-mail: wola@wola.org
Web site: http://www.wola.org

The Washington Office on Latin America (WOLA) is an influential think tank on nation-building and other aspects of Latin American politics and relations with the United States. It began in 1974 with an emphasis on social justice and human rights and on educating the public on why legislation in those areas is so important. It was an influential group during the 1980s conflict in Central America and in Peru in the following decade. Much of its current work concentrates on Colombia and the nation-building aspects of that society. Its work, available in many reports and statements by its staff, is considered thoughtful analysis rather than merely advocacy for its own sake. WOLA has important ties with the nongovernmental organization community in Latin America. WOLA offers internships for students in Washington, D.C., to enhance their understanding of the policy debate. WOLA publishes two newsletters, *CrossCurrents* and *Enlace*, on events in Latin America. Additionally, it publishes a number of thematic reports on issues such as human rights, democratic values, elections, and social changes, as well as reports on conditions in various states of the region. WOLA materials are increasingly available online as well as in print.

Women in International Security
Center for Peace and Security Studies
Edmund Walsh School of Foreign Service
Georgetown University
3240 Prospect Street, N.W.
P.O. 571145
Washington, DC 20057-1145
(202) 687-3366
E-mail: wiisinfo@georgetown.edu
Web site: http://wiis.georgetown.edu/

Begun in 1987 at the University of Maryland, Women in International Security (WIIS) has worked to broaden women's role in national security communities around the world, while promoting concerns of interest to women. Many of those issues fall into the category broadly called nation-building. In 2001, WIIS moved its headquarters to the Edmund Walsh School of Foreign Service at Georgetown University, enhancing its access to the policy community in Washington, D.C. With its emphasis on education, WIIS has many seminars on topics such as rebuilding after conflict, democratic governance, and military spending. Its regional concerns are global, often hosting women scholars from abroad to discuss the various topics. WIIS hosts a summer institute, usually held in Annapolis, Maryland, to help advanced graduate students understand not only international security issues around the world but the state of the international security field. WIIS also holds an annual dinner for interested scholars, both female and male, and various symposia in other parts of the world. WIIS promotes its members as speakers and experts in the security field, broadly defined, through its annual *WIIS Media Guide*, with detailed entries on members and their work.

World Policy Institute
New School University
66 Fifth Avenue, 9th Floor
New York, NY 10011
(212) 229-5808
Fax: (212) 807-1153
E-mail: DoveR@newschool.edu
Web site: http://www.worldpolicy.org

The World Policy Institute (WPI) began in 1948 as an outgrowth of the Institute for World Order, took on its independent role in 1982, and became associated with the New School University in 1991. WPI has always worked to provide an exchange between various domestic and international analysts on questions facing the global community. In the past decade, as globalization has accelerated, WPI has been even more aggressive in trying to bring together civic and business leaders, journalists, policymakers, military leaders, academics, and interested citizens to find solutions that will assist in resolving conflict. Its work has become more relevant as nation-building requirements have proliferated. With roughly a dozen projects under way, current emphases at the institute include Emerging Powers, the United States and the Islamic World, the United States in the World after September 11, Democracy and Global Governance, the United Nations, and Education on Cuba. These are carried out through publications, conferences, discussions, and other activities that promote better understanding of the nature of the problem while looking for realistic solutions WPI publishes *World Policy Journal,* a quarterly, which provides some of the most innovative thinking in the field, often with an unanticipated twist. Recent editions are available on-line, as are a number of other conference reports.

For-Profit

Abt Associates, Inc.
55 Wheeler Street
Cambridge, MA 02138-1168
(617) 492-7100
Fax: (617) 492-5219
TTY line: (617) 349-2618
E-mail: webmaster@abtassociates.com
Web site: http://www.abtassoc.com

Hampden Square Building
4800 Montgomery Lane, Suite 600
Bethesda, MD 20814-3460
(301) 913-0500
Fax: (301) 652-3618

640 North LaSalle Avenue, Suite 400
Chicago, IL 60610-3781
(312) 867-4000
Fax: (312) 867-4200

1445 East Putnam Avenue
Old Greenwich, CT 06870-1379
(203) 637-9995
Fax: (203) 698-0653

Mass Venture Center
100 Venture Way, Suite 100
Hadley, MA 01035-9462
(413) 586-8635
Fax: (413) 584-2330

181 Spring Street
Lexington, MA 02421-8030
(781) 372-6500
Fax: (781) 372-6501

1110 Vermont Avenue, Suite 610
Washington, DC 20005-3544
(202) 263-1800
Fax: (202) 263-1801

443 Leyds Street
Momentum Building, 7th Floor
Sunnyside, Pretoria 0132
Republic of South Africa
27-12-343-7000

21 El Mansour Mohamed Street, Suite 1
Zamelak, Cairo
Arab Republic of Egypt
20-2-735-2906

Abt Associates, begun in 1965, is an employee-owned company that works for improving the quality of life and health around the world, with a significant focus on encouraging nation-building at the grass-roots level of most societies. With its global presence, Abt is a major contractor for the USAID. Abt projects range from addressing HIV/AIDs in Africa, to rebuilding health systems in the former Soviet Union, to nutrition throughout the Third World. Abt has forty project offices in twenty-five nations overseas, where it works with consulting, planning, technical assistance, and other aspects of problem solving. Abt has projects in the Middle East, Eastern Europe, Southern Africa, Asia, the Caribbean, and Latin America.

Abt conducts its work through its local offices overseas and in conjunction with nongovernmental organizations, nonprofit associations and institutions, and international organizations.

Bechtel Corporation
E-mail: webmstr@bechtel.com

Bechtel is a major U.S. heavy construction corporation that has been involved in large projects around the world since its inception in 1898. Bechtel has one of the most prominent positions in the rebuilding of Iraq through contracts won from the Coalition Provisional Authority and the USAID. These contracts are heavily focused on the physical rebuilding necessary after the conflict and to get the country's economy moving again, working on bridges, in the ports, on the reconstruction of schools, on rebuilding waste treatment plants, on water facilities, at airports, and on the road system. Current projects outside of Iraq include an Algerian pipeline, an international airport in Peru, artificial islands in Kazakhstan, and a major petrochemical complex in China.

Dyncorp
c/o Computer Sciences Corporation
Corporate Headquarters
2100 East Grand Avenue
El Segundo, CA 90245
(310) 615-0311
E-mail: webmaster@csc.com
Web site: http://www.csc.com

Dyncorp, bought by the Computer Sciences Corporation in March 2003, has had a tremendous role in nation-building since its beginning in 1946. Begun by former war pilots seeking to continue their air cargo functions, Dyncorp has increasingly had a role in military logistics in parts of the world that are hard to access. Dyncorp has played a role in Colombia, Ecuador, Bosnia, and Afghanistan. Dyncorp has provided protection services to leaders, defoliation flights, and various other activities that have been contracted out for many years. Under the Computer Sciences Corporation, Dyncorp is likely to continue these activities, while enhancing the corporation's ability to take a prominent position in U.S. homeland security activities.

Creative Associates International
E-mail: webmaster@cai-dc.com

Creative Associates International (CAI) largely operates in less-developed areas of the world where unique solutions for a distinct set of social, political, and economic conditions does not allow for traditional thinking. CAI is a for-profit organization that operates in Morocco, Guatemala, El Salvador, Lebanon, Afghanistan, South Africa, Zambia, Angola, Senegal, and Jordan. It has won contracts from the USAID to improve education in Iraq and help with the massive nation-building requirements facing that state. The three main divisions of CAI include Analysis and Information Management; Communities in Transition; and Education, Mobilization, and Communication. The range of individual programs and locations in each division is impressive, and CAI's key concern is to promote peaceful approaches to these.

Halliburton
5 Houston Center
1401 McKinney, Suite 2400
Houston, TX 77010
(713) 759-2600

Halliburton, an umbrella corporation, began in oil and natural gas construction in 1919. Kellogg, Brown, and Root (KBR), a sub-section of Halliburton, has been a major construction company since World War II, when Brown Shipbuilding Company constructed its first ship for the U.S. Navy in Houston. Subsequently KBR joined Halliburton, making its headquarters in Houston and establishing offices around the world. During the U.S. role in Southeast Asia, KBR provided much of the physical construction of roads, airstrips, port facilities, and other large construction projects. KBR has also been engaged in nation-building efforts in Bosnia, Venezuela, and Guantanamo Bay, Cuba. It has been fundamental to the Department of Defense's privatization efforts since the end of the cold war, taking a prominent role in logistics in the Balkans, as an example. Vice President Richard B. Cheney was the chief executive officer for Halliburton between 1995 and 2000, and his connection with the company has raised some concerns among people who fear that the appearance of helping friends of the Bush administration might taint some of the KBR work in a postconflict Iraq. Halliburton's work, through the Government Operations Division, is contracted to the Department of Defense and Department of State, other federal level agencies, and at state and local government levels.

MPRI
1201 East Abingdon Drive, Suite 425
Alexandria, VA 22314
(703) 684-0853
Fax: (703) 684-3528
E-mail: info@mpri.L-3com.com
Web site: http://www.mpri.com
Alexandria Group: (703) 684-7114/7115 or (866) 262-4501
Alexandria Group e-mail: Patricia.Bolden@mpri.L-3com.com

MPRI focuses on education, training, and leadership around the world. It is a for-profit business, begun by eight retired army generals in 1988, which assists the U.S. government overseas, engaging in helping ministries of defense with their programming, planning, and policy development; helping militaries in transition from authoritarian to democratic governments; streamlining other militaries while working toward economically enhanced programs; and in humanitarian and peace operations around the world. While MRPI does not use the term nation-building, its list of contracts includes such work as Democracy Transition Assistance Programs, Military Stabilization, and other aspects that relate to nation-building. Other competencies include homeland security, foreign military sales, and bringing civilian and uniformed officials together to better understand the evolving international environment. In the increasing effort to privatize Department of Defense activities, MPRI contracts and expertise are increasingly important for this overall U.S. nation-building objective. MPRI recruits heavily from retiring senior military officers.

In 2000, MRPI created the Alexandria Group, a subsection of the business that focuses on law enforcement in order to expand its ability to tie law enforcement to national security issues. Along with senior army leadership, this portion of the organization has links to retired senior FBI officials.

Research Triangle Institute
P.O. Box 12194
Research Triangle Park, NC 27709-2194
(919) 485-2666
E-mail: listen@rti.org
Web site: http://www.rti.org

The Research Triangle Institute (RTI) is a major for-profit group, focusing on scientific, health, and educational resources to address nation-building needs, and is located in the area shared by North Carolina State University, Duke University, and the University of North Carolina. It has had significant connections with the USAID and has won contracts to work on many of the challenges that USAID has found in humanitarian crises and other places where meeting basic needs is the primary goal. In the immediate response to the Iraq crisis, RTI won a contract for $7.9 million, which could grow to $167 million within the first twelve months of reconstruction. The contract commits RTI to supply basic needs to the people of Iraq under the project entitled Iraq Sub-National Governance and Civic Institution Support Program. While RTI is often directly awarded contracts in nation-building efforts, it also serves as a subcontractor for Creative Research Associates for work in Iraq. Similarly, RTI is involved in

Nigeria, conducting a program called Decentralized Education Planning. Over its forty years of engaging in development around the world, twenty years of which have been spent in examining governmental and economic systems, projects have allowed RTI to participate in nation-building in El Salvador, South Africa, Indonesia, and the former Soviet republics. RTI, with its roots in this dynamic research area back to 1958, has more than 2,100 employees who specialize in health, environmental, and public service concerns.

International Organizations

International Bank for Reconstruction and Development
1818 H Street, N.W.
Washington, DC 20433
(202) 473-1000
Fax: (202) 477-6391
Web site: http://www.worldbank.org

The International Bank for Reconstruction and Development (IBRD) is commonly known as the World Bank, although that is a misnomer since the institution is not a commercial entity in any traditional sense. The IBRD and its parallel organization, the International Development Association, were created at the Bretton Woods summit in 1943, where President Franklin Delano Roosevelt hosted discussions with British officials on the architecture of the post–World War II world. The IBRD has made its mission of alleviating poverty and working toward development for political stability into a global project, with more than 180 partner nations in the UN community forming the core of the group. The IRBD was created to provide long-term development assistance for massive projects seen as too expensive for the resources of individual states, particularly those newly independent entities in former colonial areas of the world where capital flight and capital accumulation have been big problems. In 2002, the organization provided $8.1 billion in development assistance for states to borrow, in a fixed term, at a reduced lending rate, to fund 133 projects in 62 nations. Additionally, the Bank is a repository for economic information on the entire range of societal questions and is looked upon as a resource for understanding economic growth and poverty needs. The Bank has had two groups of critics, particularly over the past two decades. One group believes the organization is profligate in its loans and excessive in the behavior of its employees, and these critics demand important reforms on behalf of the citizens of states that give money to the Bank for its loan base. The other criticism is by those who fear the Bank is too quick to promote certain development paths, often to the detriment of the environment, linking it increasingly with transnational corporations seeking to exploit the weaker states of the world.

International Committee of the Red Cross
19, avenue de la Paix
CH 1202 Geneva
Switzerland
41-22-734-6001
Fax: 41-22-734-2057
E-mail: press.gva@gwn.icrc.org
Web site: http://www.icrc.org

The International Committee of the Red Cross (ICRC), three-time winner of the Nobel Peace Prize, was founded in Geneva, Switzerland, as a local organization with humanitarian principles in 1863. Four years later, built on a network in a dozen countries, the ICRC became the basic organization now so well respected for its nonpartisan, neutral humanitarian operations around the world. Unlike many humanitarian groups, the ICRC also works with victims of internal disturbances, which are not covered by the Geneva Protocols of 1949.

United Nations Education, Science and Cultural Organization
7, place de Fontenoy
75352 Paris 07 SP
France
Web site: http://www.unesco.org/unesdi/

The United Nations Education, Science and Cultural Organization (UNESCO) is one of the oldest international organizations, working toward helping societies address their problems through homegrown solutions. UNESCO recently has been actively involved in reconstruction efforts in Bosnia-Herzegovina, Iraq, and Afghanistan. Activities include enhancing educational opportunities for women, improving protection of cultural sites, improving freedom of the press, conducting humanitarian appeals from around the world, and a myriad of other projects. UNESCO was founded in November 1945 as one of the earliest offices of the new United Nations. Its goals are tied to using the mind to improve the chances for peace around the world. Though its home office is in Paris, UNESCO is truly a global body in its activities. It works in partnership with national commissions, nongovernmental organizations, parliamentarians, and UNESCO clubs around the world. UNESCO has a Web site with a wealth of publications and links to other important and useful sites in nation-building.

United Nations High Commissioner for Refugees
Case Postale 2500
CH-1211 Geneva 2 Dépôt
Switzerland
41-22-739-8111
Web site: http://www.unhcr.org

The Office of the High Commissioner for Refugees (UNHCR) of the United Nations was created in 1950 when the enormity of refugee problems in the aftermath of World War II was apparent. Its goal is to protect individual refugees and to find solutions to the problems causing their displacement. As of 1 January 2002, the commission had responsibility for 19.7 million refugees spread around the world but estimates that it has worked on behalf of more than 50 million refugees in the past half century since its creation. Because refugee settlement questions are fundamental to nation-building concerns, the commission plays a pivotal role in international resolution of this difficult problem. The commission is funded by the United Nations and accepts donations from individuals around the world. Its programs are heavily concerned with refugees in Afghanistan, Colombia, Iraq, Ethiopia, Sudan, Congo, Liberia, and other turbulent places. The commission's work is governed not only by the UN General Assembly, which created it, but also by the 1951 Convention on the Status of Refugees. The commission has a field office in virtually every country in the world. UNHCR has a vast range of publications, available in hard copy or on the World Wide Web on refugee questions.

World Bank. *See* **International Bank for Reconstruction and Development**

U.S. Government

Africa Center for Strategic Studies
Ft. Lesley J. McNair
Washington, DC 20319
(202) 685-4700
Web site: http://www.africacenter.org

The Africa Center for Strategic Studies, along with several other regional organizations at the National Defense University and elsewhere in the U.S. government, was created in the mid-1990s to promote democratic values and to help African states make the transition to sustained representational governance. This center is slightly different from its sister institutions in that its headquarters is in Washington, D.C., but all of its work is conducted in Africa where the center's academics hold numerous conferences, workshops, and seminars for civilian and military officers. Much of the work is groundbreaking, as many of these groups have never had the opportunity to interact and they view each other with much suspicion. By providing a neutral discussion venue, the center helps not only to foster better understanding of how democratic norms develop but helps to lay the foundation for genuine trust among some of the individuals in many of these states. The center is part of the National Defense University, an organization linked to the Joint Chiefs of Staff of the U.S. military, but employs mostly civilian academics and former practitioners able to explain the steps toward democracy in concrete terms.

Agency for International Development
The Ronald Reagan Building
Fourteenth Street, N.W.
Washington, DC 20523-1000
(202) 712-4810
Fax: (202) 216-3524
E-mail: pinquiries@usaid.gov
Web site: http://www.usaid.gov

President John F. Kennedy initiated the U.S. Agency for International Development (USAID) as an independent governmental arm to offer technical assistance to developing states in the Third World. The organization was a direct response to the Cuban Revolution (1959) and to the economic dependency theory postulated by general secretary Raul Prebisch of the UN Conference on Trade and Development. Some critics argued that the USAID was an instrument for spreading U.S. counterinsurgency activities during the height of the war in Vietnam. As U.S. interactions around the world have evolved over the past forty-five years, the amount of foreign assistance as a tool of U.S. statecraft has decreased, yet the responsibilities for USAID have risen dramatically. USAID focuses on technical and educational assistance in specific, targeted areas of nation-building and economic development, such as birth control, tax collection, disease prevention, good governance, and many of the other new security concerns. USAID has had programs throughout the former Third World, in states where nation-building concerns have been greatest. Today, USAID is the center point in the U.S. government for nation-building. Its work probably focuses more on the component parts of nation-building than on its grand strategy. USAID is a highly visible agency, and avoided being absorbed into the State Department in the 1990s, maintaining its independence. USAID is on the forefront of U.S. government efforts in places like Afghanistan, Iraq, and India. USAID is heavily involved in U.S. nation-building in East Timor, the former republics of Yugoslavia, Afghanistan, Iraq, Russia, states of sub-Saharan Africa, Colombia, and the Philippines.

USAID operates in more than a hundred countries around the world. Its core areas are applied in each state as required rather than as a blanket approach to development and nation-building. USAID operates in cooperation with private voluntary organizations, in partnerships in states where USAID is active, in universities, and with U.S. businesses. USAID has been key to reconstruction efforts in the Balkans, Haiti, Afghanistan, and Iraq. It lets contracts, through the competitive bidding process, to subcontracting organizations, as well as having its own staff to conduct nation-building and other relevant activities.

Asia Pacific Center for Security Studies
2058 Maluhia Road
Honolulu, HI 96815
(808) 971-8900
Fax: (808) 971-8999
E-mail: pao@apcss.org
Web site: http://www.apcss.org

The Asia Pacific Center for Security Studies (APCSS) is one of the five regional centers established in the 1990s to engage in outreach and nation-building. Under the control of the Unified Pacific Commander in Honolulu, APCSS is heavily involved in educating military and civilian leaders from the region, but also in facilitating their interaction, a key aspect to its work. The center holds numerous meetings for officials from the Asia Pacific region, while also conducting brief courses in Honolulu on issues such as civil-military relations, governance, and other topics that are new to some in the region. Contained within APCSS are the College of Security Studies, where the courses are taught, and a research arm that works on topics such as civil-military relations, defense spending, resource constraints, and transnational issues. The center also hosts visiting scholars who are engaged in research appropriate to its mission. APCSS produces a number of conference summaries, available on its Web site, and also hard copy reports such as *Asia Pacific Security Studies, Asia Pacific Occasional Papers,* and *Asia Pacific Monographs.* Each is targeted at a specific audience and has fairly limited distribution.

Center for Hemispheric Defense Studies
National Defense University
Washington, DC 20319
(202) 685-4670
Fax: (202) 685-4674
Web site: http://www3.ndu.edu/chds

The Center for Hemispheric Defense Studies (CHDS) was created in 1997 to assist military and civilian leaders in the Western Hemisphere in resolving enduring conflicts about civil-military affairs while learning about the U.S. approach to democratic governance. Students attend three-week courses on these questions. CHDS also offers seminars in other countries for those participants unable to travel to the United States and for topics relevant in a single nation. CHDS hosts many foreign visitors to discuss U.S. governance and occasionally broader conferences for those involved in nation-building efforts. CHDS has an on-line journal, *Security and Defense Studies Review,* an interdisciplinary publication in Portuguese, English, and Spanish.

Central Intelligence Agency
Office of Public Affairs
Washington, DC 20505

(703) 482-0623
Fax: (703) 482-1739
Web site: http://www.cia.gov

The Central Intelligence Agency (CIA) resulted from the Defense Reorganization Act of 1947, which also created the Department of Defense and the U.S. Air Force. The agency and many of its original personnel had ties to the World War II intelligence service, the Office of Strategic Services. The intelligence community has spread beyond the CIA into more specialized organizations, but the CIA remains the most strategic and comprehensive. The CIA is often involved in activities required for nation-building, especially in providing analyses. Stabilization actions are often covert.

The CIA has been extremely controversial throughout its history. In the 1950s, it was accused of destabilizing the regime of Prime Minister Mossadegh in Iran and then providing assistance to a move to overthrow Jacobo Arbenz Guzman in Guatemala. The agency was heavily involved in many programs in Southeast Asia and in several attempts to alter governments in Latin America and Africa. Criticisms of the agency accelerated after the overthrow of Chilean president Salvador Allende Gossens in September 1973, when hearings before the U.S. Congress verified that the agency had engaged in dubious practices at home and abroad. The CIA remains an important tool for nation-building efforts around the world.

The CIA has been important in efforts in Afghanistan and Iraq, in particular. The agency has its own specialists who do analyses of all aspects of states around the world, as well as of transnational threats. The agency also issues reports, most often only for U.S. government agencies, on specific concerns and themes. Much of the work the agency does is classified, but some is open to the public.

Coalition Provisional Authority
Web site: http://www.cpa-iraq.org

The Coalition Provisional Authority (CPA), under U.S. Ambassador L. Paul "Jerry" Bremer, began governing post-Saddam Iraq on 12 May 2003. Bremer succeeded Lieutenant General (ret.) Jay Garner, USA, who had arrived in Iraq in mid-April 2003 as the traditional military operations were being concluded. Garner's postconflict team encountered great difficulties in efforts to rebuild the basic Iraqi infrastructure. As the efforts under Garner bogged down, the Bush administration turned to Bremer to take up the task of rebuilding Iraq. Bremer's role is often compared to that of General Douglas A. MacArthur, the supreme commander and, in effect, reconstruction czar in postconflict Japan between 1945 and 1950. While the posts may have been similar, Bremer's CPA faces a much-less-settled environment because Iraq's deposed regime never surrendered to coalition forces after the 2003 operations that ousted Saddam Hussein. In mid-summer 2003, an Iraqi interim governing council was appointed, and on 1 August 2003, Ibrahim al-Jaafari was appointed the first of the rotating presidents of the interim council. In fact, Ambassador Bremer retains the most important position in Iraq, until the formal transfer of power to an Iraqi government, which has legitimacy in the eyes of its people and the capability to govern.

Congressional Research Service
The Library of Congress
The Madison Building
Washington, DC 20540
(202) 707-5000
Web site: http://www.loc.gov/crsinfo

The Congressional Research Service (CRS) is an arm of the Library of Congress and hence of the legislative branch. CRS provides a range of studies, many of them on short notice, on six major issue-based topics, including Foreign Affairs and Defense and Trade, which includes nation-building concerns. CRS specialists may study political parties, transnational crime, civil-military relations, or any other aspect of nation-building. CRS Reports are most often written only for members of Congress and their staff but can be used by the public upon request if the reports are not classified.

Department of Commerce
1401 Constitution Avenue, N.W.
Washington, DC 20230
E-mail: info@www.doc.gov
Web site: http://www.doc.gov
Iraq Task Force: (866) 352-IRAQ
E-mail for Iraq Task Force http: IraqInfo@mail.doc.gov
Web site for Iraq: http://www.export.gov/iraq
Web site for Afghanistan: http://www.export.gov/afghanistan

The Department of Commerce (DoC) is playing a much more important position in nation-building in the post–cold war world. Iraq and Afghanistan are only the last in a long line of places where the United States is attempting to use trade to help with nation-building. With the end of the cold war, the free market model took on a much clearer prominence in the administrations of presidents George H. W. Bush, Bill Clinton, and George W. Bush, since there was no alternative model. During the Clinton administration, Secretary of Commerce Ron Brown died in a plane crash on a trade mission to the Balkans, indicating the importance of trade to these efforts. Under George W. Bush's secretary of commerce Don Evans, the United States introduced the Iraq Reconstruction Task Force as well as the Afghanistan Reconstruction Task Force.

Department of Defense
The Pentagon
Washington, DC
Web site: http://www.defenselink.mil

The Department of Defense (DoD) is the most visible part of the U.S. government in nation-building because of its size and its ability to project power abroad. Nation-building has always received a tremendous contribution from the DoD, and this is even more true today. In the aftermath of World War II, General MacArthur's forces in Japan, along with U.S. forces in West Germany, were military forces. In Southeast Asia in the 1960s and 1970s, in Central America in the following decade, in Somalia, Haiti, and the Balkans in the 1990s, as well as in Afghanistan and Iraq, a DoD presence has been at the heart of U.S. nation-building efforts. In Iraq, the reconstruction efforts are concentrated under the Defense Department. One of the major concerns about the Office of Reconstruction and Humanitarian Assistance was that its leader, Lieutenant General Jay Garner, USA, was a retired general, hence putting all of the efforts in the hands of the military, rather than in those of traditional civilian humanitarian specialists. The subsequent leadership, under Ambassador L. Paul Bremer as the head of the Coalition Provisional Authority, is civilian, but the Department of Defense retains a primary role in the activities.

Department of Energy
1000 Independence Avenue, S.W.
Washington, DC 20585

(800) dial-doe
Public information inquiries: (800) 586-5575
Fax: (202) 586-4403
Web site: http://www.energy.gov

The Department of Energy (DoE) is increasingly important in
nation-building efforts as the world struggles to regularize the supplies of various resources available in a globalizing economic system. President Jimmy Carter created the DOE in 1977, believing
that the 1973–1974 petroleum embargo was proof that the United
States required a coordinated energy plan. While no administration
has in fact succeeded in that quest, the DOE plays an ever greater
role in all aspects of national security and nation-building.

Department of State
2201 C Street, N.W.
Washington, DC 20520
(202) 647-4000
Web site: http://contact-us.state.gov

The secretary of state is the senior cabinet member in stature in
case of succession. The Department of State is the elite representative of the United States in foreign affairs and has taken a paramount role in nation-building since the end of World War II.

The secretary of state is the individual most often called
upon to take the most visible public role in explaining administration actions on various activities, but members of the Foreign
Service serving overseas answer questions about U.S. policy on a
daily basis. In the second Clinton administration, Secretary of
State Madeleine K. Albright was aggressive in her justification of
U.S. nation-building efforts in the Balkans. Her successor, retired
Joint Chiefs of Staff chairman General Colin L. Powell, was no
less active in having to explain why the Bush administration engaged in campaigns against the Taliban government in
Afghanistan. He was called upon to explain why U.S. suspicions
about Saddam Hussein's weapons of mass destruction programs
merited overthrowing his regime for international security. By
contrast, George H. W. Bush's secretary of state, James A. Baker,
was instrumental in explaining why the United States sought not
to engage in nation-building efforts in the Balkans.

Drug Enforcement Agency
2401 Jefferson Davis Highway

Alexandria, VA 22301
(800) 882-9539
Web site: http://www.dea.gov

The Drug Enforcement Agency (DEA) is responsible for controlling substances deemed dangerous in the United States. This has been increasingly considered a national security issue, particularly as drug money and violence have undermined foreign governments. The DEA has agents in foreign countries, and its studies of the spread and influence of illegal drugs are crucial to a U.S. grasp of the challenges facing other states.

Federal Bureau of Investigation
J. Edgar Hoover Building
935 Pennsylvania Avenue, N.W.
Washington, DC 20535-0999
(202) 324-3000
Web site: http://www.fbi.gov

The Federal Bureau of Investigation (FBI) started in the early 1900s, with federal agents charged with investigating crimes against federal laws. Initially, these were primarily business laws; but during World War I, the bureau's activities expanded to include counterespionage. From 1924 under Director J. Edgar Hoover, the investigations focused on Prohibition violations and civil rights issues in the South. The bureau's work expanded during the Franklin Roosevelt period when the government itself grew dramatically. Director Hoover is the longest-serving figure to date in the U.S. government, serving until his death in 1972.

In recent years, and particularly after September 11, the bureau has moved toward national security concerns rather than law enforcement. Part of that includes trying to discern threats to U.S. national security in states around the world that are changing forms of government. The FBI is heavily involved in tracking transnational terror groups, drug traffickers, illegal arms dealers, and various other groups seeking to thwart the establishment and continuation of the rule of law, which is essential to the development and solidification of democratic rule and good governance. The bureau is struggling with the best ways to accomplish these evolving missions but is increasingly seeing its future in homeland security and in a greater presence overseas.

The FBI is headquartered in Washington, D.C., but has field offices across the country and in many embassies overseas. The

FBI publishes the Ten Most Wanted list for domestic lawbreakers and the Most Wanted Terrorist list for the world.

George C. Marshall European Center for Security Studies
Gernackserstrasse 2
82467 Garmish-Partenkirchen
Germany
49-8-821-750-793

Unit 24502 ECMC-PA
APO AE 09053
Web site: http://www.marshallcenter.org

The George C. Marshall European Center for Security Studies was created in 1992. It aims to educate military officials from the former Communist bloc about the challenges, opportunities, and restrictions of democratic governance. Officers and officials from across Central and Eastern Europe attend the center for a fixed period of study on a variety of topics. The center is under the jurisdiction of the U.S. European Command.

The Marshall Center has several units serving as tools of statecraft as the United States seeks to solidify the changes of the past decade. As foreign assistance decreases, the Marshall Center offers education and outreach. Like the Asia Pacific Center, the Center for Defense Studies, the Africa Center for Security Studies, and the Near East–South Asia Center, the Marshall Center is creating a broader application of how security is approached around the world.

The Marshall Center includes the College of International and Security Studies, with senior-level seminars for high-ranking officers and civilian officials to discuss issues common to states across the region, such as leadership. The college also offers considerable language training for NATO and U.S. military specialists. The Marshall Center maintains a Virtual College, which provides distance learning for those unable to travel to Germany. This college provides education to more students than the center could accommodate. The Marshall Center hosts roughly two-dozen international conferences annually to allow civilian and military officials to discuss topics like corruption and terrorism. The Marshall Center also puts much of its information on its Web site.

Institute for National Strategic Studies
National Defense University
Fort Lesley J. McNair
Washington, DC 20319
(202) 685-3838
Fax: (202) 685-3972
Web site: http://www.ndu.edu/inss/insshp.html

The Institute for National Strategic Studies (INSS), occasionally referred to as "the chairman of the Joint Chiefs of Staff's think tank," is housed at the National Defense University in Washington, D.C. INSS and the National Defense University were created in 1976 to more effectively work with existing institutions within the defense educational community in order to create a more useful analytical basis for the U.S. military. INSS works on topical and regional concerns, many of which are important in nation-building.

INSS has several sections, including the National Strategic Gaming Center, which carries out war games on topics facing the defense analytical community. The National Defense University Press publishes on topics broadly linked to nation-building. INSS has an important function in interacting with scholars and policymakers around the world, including those involved in nation-building. The INSS publication list has evolved over the years. Its best-known publication is *Joint Force Quarterly*, established in 1992 to cover the range of current issues confronting the military. The institute also publishes the *McNair Papers*, short monographs on varied areas; *Strategic Fora*, four-page assessments of current event issues; and conference reports. Its Web site makes conference papers available for some years after the meetings are held.

Iraq Reconstruction Task Force. *See* **Department of Commerce**

Near East–South Asia Center for Strategic Studies
National Defense University
U.S. Coast G2100 Second Street, S.W.
U.S. Coast Guard (Transpoint) Building, Suite 4308
Washington, DC 20593-0001
E-mail: nesa-center@ndu.edu
Web site: http://www.ndu.edu/nesa
Mailing address:
National Defense University
Fort Lesley J. McNair
Washington, DC 20319

(202) 685-4131
Fax: (202) 685-4997

The Near East–South Asia Center for Strategic Studies (NE-SACSS) is one of the regional centers established by the Clinton administration to further engagement with civilian and military officials from the Near East and South Asia. Created in the 1990s, it has been a site for discussion of nation-building issues facing states in the region and works for traditionally separated societal groups to come together in neutral territory. This center's region covers the area from Morocco east to India. The center hosts periodic conferences on important topics peculiar to this area and promotes discussions on new threats.

Office of Reconstruction and Humanitarian Assistance

The Office of Reconstruction and Humanitarian Assistance (ORHA) was created on 20 January 2003 in anticipation of Saddam Hussein's ouster in Baghdad. Its mission was to create the easiest transition from an authoritarian regime to a democratic one, thus handling all of the issues facing the post-Saddam Iraq. ORHA was organized under the Department of Defense, outlined in a 11 March 2003 news briefing, with a civilian administrator (retired Lieutenant General Jay Garner, USA, held that post from 21 April through 12 May 2003) hired by the Department of Defense, a reconstruction administrator who has been an employee of the U.S. Agency for International Development to coordinate reconstruction activities, and a humanitarian relief coordinator to handle the most immediate human needs. Additionally, ORHA activities were divided into regional functions within Iraq, recognizing that the transitions in Shi'ite, Sunni, and Kurdish areas might be somewhat different from one another. It was also envisioned that ORHA would employ Iraqis who had lived outside of the country in democratic states with the hope that they would bring that governmental style back to their homeland. ORHA, as originally conceptualized, also included civil affairs teams from within military units, Disaster Relief Teams (DARTs) from USAID, and other groups as necessary in the reconstruction effort. As the process evolved, however, it became clear that the greatest need in the immediate aftermath was the physical reconstruction of the Iraqi basic infrastructure, which proved significantly more challenging than anticipated. Because that aspect was not completed as rapidly as hoped, Garner was replaced by

Ambassador L. Paul Bremer of the Coalition Provisional Authority on 12 May 2003. The Coalition Provisional Authority superseded ORHA.

Office of the Comptroller General
441 G Street, N.W.
Washington, DC 20549
(202) 512-4800
E-mail: webmaster@gao.gov
Web site: http://www.gao.gov

The Office of the Comptroller General, also known as the General Accounting Office, was created in 1921 as an investigative arm of Congress and charged with examining the use of federal money. The office was created under the Budget and Accounting Act to guarantee that Congress knew how its money was being spent. The comptroller general's work has primarily a domestic interest, because most spending in the federal budget is domestic, but increased U.S. actions in nation-building means that more scrutiny must go into this spending. The office staff produces policy and budget audits of all aspects of nation-building, thematically and regionally. An example would be an evaluation of the effectiveness of U.S. counternarcotics assistance to Nigeria. The Office of the Comptroller General issues reports, for Congress, but distributed more broadly upon request, that thoroughly study the issues that Congress considers in doing its job.

Office of the U.S. Trade Representative
600 Seventeenth Street, N.W.
Washington, DC 20508
(888) 473-8787
E-mail: contactustr@ustr.gov
Web site: http://www.ustr.gov

The United States increasingly views trade as a vital element in nation-building. The U.S. Trade Representative (USTR) was authorized by Congress in 1963 and raised to cabinet rank in 1980. The office is increasingly important to U.S. relations around the world. As the United States seeks to solidify governments and democratic governance, trade takes on a bigger role.

Strategic Studies Institute
Department of the Army

122 Forbes Avenue
Carlisle, PA 17013
E-mail: AWCC-DPA@awc.carlisle.army.mil
Web site: http://carlisle-www.army.mil/ssi

The Strategic Studies Institute, located at the Army War College, is a key location for discussion of the complexities of nation-building. Its Web site refers to SSI as "the Army's think tank for analysis of national security policy and military strategy." The Strategic Studies Institute often holds conferences in conjunction with civilian academic institutions, on topics in this area, as well as on more traditional army themes. The Strategic Studies Institute contains the Peacekeeping Institute, created in the 1990s as it became apparent that the army would be increasingly involved in this field. In early 2003, it looked as though the institute would be closed, as some in the army tried to get out of that aspect of their duties; but the decision was reversed, with indications of the army's continued commitment to this aspect of the new strategic environment. The Strategic Studies Institute publishes a wide range of pamphlets and studies. These often examine nation-building themes and are available in hard copy. The Army War College quarterly journal, *Parameters*, often addresses nation-building themes. Finally, AWC publishes monographs and conference reports when appropriate, often under the Strategic Studies Institute imprimatur. Its Web site has a long list of the prestigious publications of the institute.

7

Print and Nonprint Resources

Print Resources

Books

Aall, Pamela, Daniel Miltenberger, and Thomas G. Weiss. 2000. *Guide to IGOs, NGOs, and the Military in Peace and Relief Operations*. Washington, DC: U.S. Institute of Peace.

As a primer on organizations for peace and humanitarian relief around the world, this book contains information on the culture, structure, approaches, and content for each.

Alden, Chris. 2001. *Mozambique and the Construction of the New African State: From Negotiations to Nation Building*. London: Palgrave MacMillan.

This is a view of Africa's work in nation-building, concentrating on Mozambique, where nation-building has been ongoing for more than thirty years.

Bacevich, Andrew J. 2003. *American Empires: The Realities and Consequences of U.S. Diplomacy*. Cambridge: Harvard University Press.

In this impressive, sober discussion of the continuity in U.S. approaches to foreign relations, with consideration of the growing role of nation-building in more recent U.S. policy, this author shows why the policy continuities are more aggressive than popular notions or politicians would indicate. This is a major work in U.S. foreign relations.

Boot, Max. 2002. *The Savage Wars of Peace: Small Wars and the Rise of American Power.* New York: Basic.

Boot writes persuasively of the costs and benefits accrued from engaging in actions around the world that appear small and relatively cost-free but that require skills and finances that are considerably more extensive than originally thought.

Clark, Wesley K. 2001. *Waging Modern War: Bosnia, Kosovo, and the Future of Combat.* New York: Public Affairs.

This highly readable memoir from the supreme allied commander during the Kosovo campaign on the frustrations of multinational as well as internal U.S. political decision making on nation-building is illuminating.

Crocker, Chester A., Fen Osler Hampson, and Pamela Aall, eds. 2001. *Turbulent Peace.* Washington, DC: U.S. Institute of Peace.

This more than 900-page volume contains seminal essays on what is involved in nation-building and the challenges the activity raises and introduces the range of actors. It has been called the bible of nation-building by some practitioners.

Darby, John. 2001. *The Effects of Violence on Peace Processes.* Washington, DC: U.S. Institute of Peace.

This series of case studies from around the world shows that violence can be devastating to the peace process and nation-building, while also illustrating how complex these issues have become.

Das, Suranjan. 2002. *Kashmir and Sindh: Nation-Building, Ethnicity and Regional Politics in South Asia.* Anthem Modern South Asian Series. London: Anthem.

A study of why ethnicity can derail nation-building, using examples from South Asia.

Dempsey, Gary T., with Roger Fontaine. 2001. *Fool's Errands:*

America's Recent Encounters with Nation Building. Washington, DC: CATO Institute.

This monograph, by the most avowedly isolationist major public policy organization in the United States, argues that attempts at nation-building and human rights protections consistently fail.

Du Toit, Pierre. 1995. *State Building and Democracy in Southern Africa.* Washington, DC: U.S. Institute of Peace.

This comparative work illustrates the development of differing political institutions in South Africa and shows the options and problems of the nation-building challenge.

Fatton, Robert, Jr. 2002. *Haiti's Predatory Republic: The Unending Transition to Democracy.* Boulder, CO: Lynne Rienner.

Fatton's book argues that nation-building and democratization are particularly difficult in Haiti, due to the nature of the political system that has been in place for almost two centuries.

Ganguly, Rajat, and Urmila Phandis. 2001. *Ethnicity and Nation Building in South Asia.* Beverly Hills, CA: Sage Publications.

This monograph looks at the interaction between ethnicity and nation-building in a region with several nation-states, some of which still have much nation-building to do.

Gottesman, Evan R. 2002. *Cambodia after the Khmer Rouge: Inside the Politics of Nation-Building.* New Haven: Yale University Press.

The volume lays out the range of problems confronting a state as it faces the vacuum left after removal of a government, no matter how brutal that government was.

Gurr, Ted Robert. 1993. *Minorities at Risk: A Global View of Ethnopolitical Conflicts.* Washington, DC: U.S. Institute of Peace.

This book, based on the Minorities at Risk project, looks at the ethnopolitical conflicts of the 1980s.

————. 2002. *Peoples versus States: Minorities at Risk in the New Century.* Washington, DC: U.S. Institute of Peace.

This volume shows the ways that ethnicity can affect nation-building and is based on an interesting study of the 275 active ethnic groups operating in the 1990s.

Hirsh, Michael. 2003. *At War with Ourselves: Why America Is Squandering Its Chance to Build a Better World.* Oxford: Oxford University Press.

This volume discusses the power struggle within the ranks of the U.S. national security elite regarding the role of nation-building, foreign assistance, and other tools of statecraft.

Huchthausen, Peter. 2003. *America's Splendid Little Wars: A Short History of U.S. Military Engagements, 1975–2000.* New York: Viking.

Although its title indicates an earlier time (the Spanish American War was the origin for the term), this book concentrates on the conflicts in the last quarter of the twentieth century. The coverage gives an interesting view of the military perspective on "operations other than war," which almost always involves nation-building in the contemporary world.

Kagan, Robert. 2003. *Of Paradise and Power: America vs. Europe in the New World Order.* New York: Knopf.

Kagan has little patience with the Europeans on many things. His view is that if they seek to lag behind he welcomes that decision as the United States has the power to move ahead.

Kagan, Robert, and William Kristol. 2000. *Present Dangers: Crisis and Opportunities in American Foreign and Defense Policy.* New York: Encounter.

Two of the prime movers behind the pressure to have the United States rethink President Bush's apprehensions about nation-building have written a sweeping assessment of what the United States has the power to do in the current international environment.

Kaplan, Robert D. 2001. *The Coming Anarchy: Shattering the Dreams of the Post Cold War.* New York: Vintage.

The original *Atlantic Monthly* article on this theme in the mid-

1990s was required reading within Department of Defense circles. This volume expands on Kaplan's somewhat apocalyptic vision of the possibility of failing states occurring across much of the highly populated, underdeveloped world.

Koonings, Kee, and Dirk Kruijit, eds. 2002. *Political Armies: The Military and Nation Building in the Age of Democracy*. London: Zed.

This book describes examples from several militaries in the developing world where their rules have had profound effects on nation-building, often to the detriment of all but the very wealthiest in those societies.

Kritz, Neil J., ed. 1995. *Transitional Justice: How Emerging Democracies Reckon with Former Regimes*. Vol. I, *General Considerations*. Vol. II, *Country Studies*. Vol. III, *Laws, Rulings, and Reports*. Washington, DC: U.S. Institute of Peace.

This is a series for use in the most extensive study of democratizing regimes.

Latham, Michael E., et al. 2000. *Modernization As Ideology: American Social Science and "Nation Building" in the Kennedy Era*. Chapel Hill: University of North Carolina Press.

This is a consideration of the role that U.S. social-science theory played during the early 1960s while "nation-building" was in vogue around the world and in U.S. strategy.

MacLaughlin, Jim. 2001. *Reimagining the Nation State: The Contested Terrains of Nation-Building*. London: Pluto.

MacLaughlin examines people's attachments in considering nation-building. He maintains that the nation-state is not as important to people as their community or geographic entity.

Mark, Susan Collin. 2000. *Watching the Wind: Conflict Resolution during South Africa's Transition to Democracy*. Washington, DC: U.S. Institute of Peace.

A first-hand account of the process in South Africa of nation-building, so particularly important because apartheid was so hideous.

Ould-Abdullah, Ahmedou. 2000. *Burundi on the Brink, 1993–1995: A UN Special Envoy Reflects on Preventive Diplomacy.* Washington, DC: U.S. Institute of Peace.

A Mauritanian diplomat treats one of the less-discussed international nation-building problems.

Perito, Robert M. 2003. *Where Is the Lone Ranger When We Need Him? America's Search for a Postconflict Stability Force.* Washington, DC: U.S. Institute of Peace.

A chronicle of U.S. expectations and experiences with peacekeeping, this book is also an exploration of the alternatives.

Shea, Dorothy. 2000. *The South African Truth Commission: The Politics of Reconciliation.* Washington, DC: U.S. Institute of Peace.

One of the most painful steps of nation-building is the truth commissions that many governments must establish to deal with torture, disappearances, and other human rights questions. This is a truthful discussion of what South Africa confronted.

Sifry, Micah L., and Christopher Cerf, eds. 2003. *The Iraqi War Reader.* New York: Touchstone.

This is a wide-ranging collection of essays on many aspects of the global intervention in Iraq throughout its history. Most relevant, however, are those portions such as that by Jonathan Schell on U.S. reasons for nation-building and engagement after the 2003 conflict.

Singer, P. W. 2003. *Corporate Warriors: The Rise of the Privatized Military Industry.* Ithaca: Cornell University Press.

A Brookings Institution scholar examines how private armies are transforming the defense scenario as well as the nation-building area of national security policy. This has a different focus from many works on the subject.

Sisk, Timothy D. 1996. *Power Sharing and International Mediation in Ethnic Conflicts.* Washington, DC: U.S. Institute of Peace.

This book considers one situation in nation-building where full democracy is extremely difficult.

Spector, Bertram, and I. William Zartman. 2003. *Getting It Done:*

Postagreement Negotiation and International Regimes. Washington, DC: U.S. Institute of Peace.

This useful case study material illustrates how tough structural change really is.

Stedman, Stephen John, Donald Rothchild, and Elizabeth M. Cousens, eds. 2003. *Ending Civil Wars: The Implementation of Peace Agreements.* Boulder, CO: Lynne Rienner.

Much of the debate on nation-building concentrates on the problems after the conflicts end. This volume considers, at least as important, how to get to that point.

Synge, Richard. 1997. *Mozambique: UN Peacekeeping in Action, 1992–1994.* Washington, DC: U.S. Institute of Peace.

This book discusses the interesting contrast between U.S. peacekeeping in southern Africa and Mozambique and shows the logistical problems involved.

Villa-Vicencio, Charles. 1992. *A Theology of Reconstruction: Nation-Building and Human Rights.* Cambridge: Cambridge University Press.

This book examines what is virtually a holy trinity—reconstruction, nation-building, and human rights—and considers whether this linkage works for the nation or inhibits civil society growth.

Woodward, Bob. 2002. *Bush at War.* New York: Simon and Schuster.

Another in a series of "inside" portrayals of a major political event, in this instance the immediate aftermath of the 2001 attacks on the United States and the move into Afghanistan. This book shows President George W. Bush's unease at walking away from his campaign pledges to avoid nation-building but at the same time the gradual realization for high-level decision makers in his administration that preventing another terrorist attack on the United States might require more nation-building than originally thought.

———. 2004. *Plan of Attack.* New York: Simon and Schuster.

This book discusses the thought the administration invested prior to March 2003 when President Bush ordered the invasion of Iraq. This volume shows how important a range of views are in getting a successful outcome to nation-building

Zakaria, Fareed. 2003. *The Future of Freedom.* New York: W. W. Norton.

This study, by an editor for *Foreign Affairs* and the international edition of the *Wall Street Journal*, describes the effects that democracy may have that are unintended or unanticipated, such as the possible election of authoritarian governments through the democratic processes being touted in the nation-building examples that the United States and international community are pushing today.

Journals

Dedicated issues
"Forum: State of the Nation." *Georgetown Journal of International Affairs* 4, no. 1 (winter–spring 2003): 3–48.

This entire issue on the nation-state contains five articles that cover the world on democracy and the creation of new regimes. This focus allows for a range of opinions on nation-state issues.

Bremmer, Ian. "Nation- and State-Building in Eurasia." Pp. 29–38.

Hutchinson, John. "The Past, Present, and the Future of the Nation-State." Pp. 5–12.

Joseph, Richard. "Nation-State Trajectories in Africa." Pp. 13–20.

Kop, Yaakov. "Nation-Building, Pluralism, and Democracy in Israel." Pp. 21–28.

Strmecki, Marin. "It's the Regime, Stupid: The Imperative of State-Building in Afghanistan." Pp. 39–48.

"The New Peacekeeping." Journal of Conflict Studies 23 (spring 2003): 5–125.

This refereed journal from the Centre for Conflict Studies at the University of New Brunswick in Canada has an interesting twist on nation-building topics and brings the Canadian view to the U.S. audience, which is often a much different perspective. The issue contains the following articles:

Morrison, Alex. "Pearsonian Peacekeeping: Does It Have a Future or Only a Past?" Pp. 5–11.

Prime Minister Pearson brought Canada to a place of primacy in neutralist peace operations. That legacy has been important for Canada but may not have much future in the new environment.

Murphy, Ray. "International Humanitarian Law and Peace Support Operations: Bridging the Gap." Pp. 12–59.

This article explores the questions that new peace operations bring in the world, not all of which are obvious.

Fitz-Gerald, Ann. "Multinational Land Force Interoperability: Meeting the Challenge of Different Cultural Backgrounds in Chapter VI Peace Support Operations." Pp. 60–85.

The ground issues of interoperability are too seldom explored in the scholarly literature.

Keeley, James F. "Willie 14:5: Commercial Satellite Imagery and UN Peacekeeping." Pp. 86–105.

New technology brings new tools to nation-building—but how is it applied?

Mays, Terry M. "African Solutions for African Problems: The Changing Face of African-Mandated Peace Operations." Pp. 106–125.

This is in the category of lessons-learned in a part of the world where problems of peace operations seem to be increasing in number.

"From Victory to Success: Afterwar Policy in Iraq." *Foreign Policy* Special Report: 51–72.

In conjunction with the Carnegie Endowment for International Peace Conference, this journal ran a series of articles on nation-building in Afghanistan and Iraq in 2003. The series included the following pieces:

Matthews, Jessica Tuchman. "Now for the Hard Part." P. 51.

Ottaway, Marina. "One Country, Two Plans." Pp. 55–56, 58–59.

Pei, Minxin. "Lessons of the Past." Pp. 52–55.

Knaus, Gerhard, and Felix Martin. 2003. **"Travails of the European Raj."** *Journal of Democracy* 14, no. 3 (July): 60–74.

This study of the Office of the High Representative in the protectorate of Bosnia-Herzegovina displays skepticism that nation-building can be useful for imposing legitimacy upon any state.

Manning, Carrie L., and Miljenko Antic. 2003. **"The Limits of Electoral Engineering."** *Journal of Democracy* 14, no. 3 (July): 45–59.

Often implied in discussions of nation-building is the thought that elections can be put into place, which will then take root and be enduring legacies. This piece outlines the results of such practices in Bosnia-Herzegovina and why elections are limited, at best, as strategies for nation-building.

Goodson, Larry. 2003. **"Afghanistan's Long Road to Reconstruction."** *Journal of Democracy* 14, no. 1 (January): 82–99.

Articles

Abramowitz, Morton. 2002. **"Dear Dubya."** *Foreign Policy* 130 (May–June): 78–79.

This retired diplomat argues that nation-building is essential to remedying the problems around the world resulting from the September 11 attacks but that public relations and diplomatic aspects of U.S. foreign policy have not been handled well.

Ackerman, Spencer. 2002. **"Drop Zone—Remember Afghanistan?"** *New Republic*, 9 September, 10.

Afghani nation-building should not be forgotten, the author argues, but has been, in the aftermath of attention on Iraq and other global threats.

Akiner, Shirin. 1997. **"Melting Pot, Salad Bowl—Cauldron? Manipulation and Mobilization of Ethnic Religious Identities in Central Asia."** *Ethnic and Racial Studies* 20, no. 2 (April): 262–409.

The wide array of ethnic groups in Central Asian states is a laboratory for nation-building students.

American Society of International Law. 2002. **"Report of Select**

Committee of Experts on Nation Rebuilding in Afghanistan, 10 December 2001." *Interest Group on International Organizations Newsletter* (spring): 1–14.

This report argues, in the immediate aftermath of the anti-Taliban campaign, that because the United States lacked a comprehensive approach to nation-building, it would experience great frustration at being unable to accomplish its goals of establishing long-term peace in Afghanistan.

Anderson, Jon Lee. 2004. **"Letter from Iraq: The Candidate."** *New Yorker*, 2 February 2004, 51–63.

The Shi'ite cleric Abdul-Aziz al-Hakim, now installed as the head of the Supreme Council of Islamic Revolution in Iraq after his brother's August 2003 assassination by a car bomb, is a prominent member of the Iraqi Governing Council. This portrayal considers his influence in the country as it works toward a post-Saddam government more representative of the Iraqi population. The author considers how this will affect the stated U.S. goal of preventing a theocratic state in the country.

Anonymous. 1993. **"'Nation-Building' in the African Arena."** *Veterans of Foreign Wars Magazine* 80, no. 6 (February): 28, 29.

Although written early in the decade, this article looks at several operations in Africa and sees the applications of counterinsurgency in nation-building.

———. 1994. **"Cambodia: Task of Nation-Building 'Monumental.'"** *UN Chronicle* 31, no. 2 (June): 38.

The secretary general of the United Nations, Boutros Boutros-Ghali, recognized that Cambodia needed much assistance to implement meaningful nation-building, but this article also indicates that the country has a long way to go before being ready for that assistance to be successful.

———. 1994. **"Mandate for UNOSOM II Revised: 'Coercive Methods' Not to Be Used."** *UN Chronicle* 31, no. 2 (June): 13–15.

The United Nations, as well as the United States, realized after the bloody experience in Somalia that the views of the Somali people are important in nation-building. This was an acknowledgment of that change in thought.

———. 2002. **"Asia: How to Rebuild a Country; Afghanistan."** *Economist* 364, no. 8288 (31 August): 30–31.

The British weekly asks whether the goal of ousting the Taliban got in the way of nation-building in Afghanistan.

———. 2002. **"Filling the Vacuum: Prerequisites to Security in Afghanistan."** *Connecticut Journal of International Law* 17, no. 3 (summer): S1–S58.

This article treats, from a legal perspective, all of the concerns that go into the construction of a new civil society.

———. 2002. **"A Model of Nation-Building?"** Available at http://www.economist.com/globalagenda. 17 April, p. 1.

This article considers whether any other options were available to the United Nations in East Timor.

———. 2003. **"Afghanistan Morass Deepens."** *New American* 19, no. 8 (21 April): 5.

An article exploring how deeply involved the United States will have to become in Afghanistan.

———. 2003. **"Special Report: The Hard Path to New Nationhood—Rebuilding Iraq."** *Economist* 367, no. 8320 (19 April): 17–19.

The reconstruction of Iraq must have political as well as economic elements. Aid is important, but so is power in the hands of local governments. The transfer of power is important if done in a meaningful way that does not appear as imperialism.

Atlas, James. 2003. **"A Classicist's Legacy: New Empire Builders."** *New York Times*, 4 May, section 4, 1.

This short assessment in the Week in Review section points to the role that the late University of Chicago professor Leo Strauss and his view of Western culture played in the thinking of prominent members of the Bush administration, most obviously deputy defense secretary Paul Wolfowitz. Although others disagree that the "Straussian" school has had that important of a role in the administration, the ties between a number of the decision makers has been noted and their attachment to rebuilding a better world is considerably different from the traditional semi-isolationism that many ascribe to the Republican Party.

Barfield, Thomas J. 2002. **"On Local Justice and Culture in Post-Taliban Afghanistan."** *Connecticut Journal of International Law* 17, no. 3 (summer): 445–450.

Transcript of a discussion on how Afghanistan differs from other states in establishing a civil society with functioning legal norms.

Barton, Frederick D., and Bathsheba Crocker. 2003. **"Winning the Peace in Iraq."** *Washington Quarterly* 26, no. 2 (spring): 7–22.

The theme of this piece is that the success of Iraq requires a number of changes to the society, which are not nearly as easy as might have been thought. It discusses the problems that have plagued the same attempts in Afghanistan and discusses how to prevent similar difficulties in Iraq.

Beinart, Peter. 2003. **"Free Form."** *New Republic*, 5 May, p. 6.

The author points out the differences between the vision of democracy that the United States seeks to promote and that understood by others in the Middle East. He focuses on what constitutes "freedom."

Bhutto, Benazir. 1996. **"Transcending Division—The Consolidation of Pakistan."** *Harvard International Review* 18, no. 3 (summer): 40–43.

The former Pakistani prime minister and daughter of a former leader argues that there are a number of lessons that Pakistan had to face in the fifty years since it became independent, all of which are important to nation-building.

Bolton, John R. 1994. **"Wrong Turn in Somalia."** *Foreign Affairs* 73, no. 1 (January–February): 56–66.

This member of President George W. Bush's state department argues that the Clinton expansion of the nation-building mission in Somalia was a mistake. His criticism proved accurate in Somalia, but will it be applicable under subsequent administrations such as the mission in Iraq?

Boot, Max. 2002. **"Liberal Imperialism."** *American Heritage* 53, no. 3 (June–July): 62–69.

This is a philosophical consideration of whether nation-building is imperialism or something else.

———. 2003. **"A Century of Small Wars Shows They Can Be Won."** *New York Times*, 6 July, Section 4, 10.

An assessment of what constitutes the phenomenon known as "small wars," which is the flip side of nation-building. Boot is one of the most provocative authors on the topic, writing as a fellow at the Council on Foreign Relations.

Boutros-Ghali, Boutros. 1994. **"Task of Nation-Building 'Monumental.'"** *UN Chronicle* 31, no. 2 (June): 38.

This was a statement by the UN secretary general on the specific task of nation-building, increasingly a function of this global body.

Brahimi, Lakhdar. 2003. **"Afghanistan's Prospects for the Future."** *Georgetown Journal of International Affairs* 14, no. 2 (summer/fall): 75–82.

The UN special representative to Afghanistan describes the issues and trade-offs that the international community will find as it works with Afghans to build an enduring democratic system in that fractured society.

Bremmer, Ian. 1994. **"Nazarbaev and the North: State-Building and Ethnic Relations in Kazakhstan."** *Ethnic and Racial Studies* 17, no. 4 (October): 619–635.

The particular ethnic makeup of this former Soviet republic makes for particularly difficult obstacles to nation-building. This article outlines President Nazarbaev's plans for confronting the challenge.

Bronson, Rachel. 2002. **"When Soldiers Become Cops."** *Foreign Affairs* 81, no. 6 (November–December): 122–132.

An important warning, this article shows why the role of nation-building is not easily taken on by soldiers who are trained for a completely different mission.

Buckley, William F., Jr. 2002. **"What Comes after V-Day?"** *National Review* 54, no. 30 (28 October): 59.

One of the loudest and most respected voices in the U.S. conservative movement argued that disposing of Hussein would not necessarily change things in Iraq and that much more thought needed to go into this course of action.

———. 2003. **"No on Liberia."** *National Review* 55, no. 15 (11 August): 50.

As the Bush administration increasingly moves toward nation-building, concerns about interventions such as in Liberia appear. The prominent conservative commentator speaks out against intervention in Liberia.

Cabe, Delia K. 2002. **"Nation Building."** *Kennedy School Bulletin,* spring, http://www.ksg.harvard.edu/ksgpress/bulletin/spring2002/features/nation_building.html (accessed 16 January 2004).

This is a discussion of the variety of requirements that the United States will have to fulfill as it embraces nation-building and questions whether this might not be done more appropriately in conjunction with allies.

Campbell, Kurt, and Celeste J. Ward. 2003. **"New Battle Stations."** *Foreign Affairs* 82, no. 5 (September–October): 95–103.

The authors believe that the new deployments of U.S. uniformed forces will have unintended consequences and warn about what needs to be done to minimize those consequences.

Carothers, Thomas. 2003. **"Promoting Democracy and Fighting Terror."** *Foreign Affairs* 82, no. 1 (January–February): 84–97.

Most observers did not expect the Bush administration's emphasis on pushing democratic systems, even in the wake of the events of September 11. This article looks at how institutionalizing democratic norms fits with fighting terrorism.

Carter, Philip. **"Faux Pas Americana."** *Washington Monthly* 35, no. 6 (June 2003): 11–13.

This article argues that the United States has a different troop-level requirement than that anticipated in Afghanistan and Iraq because winning a war requires fewer troops than keeping the peace.

Chesterman, Simon. 2002. **"Walking Softly in Afghanistan: The Future of UN State-Building."** *Survival* 44, no. 3 (autumn): 37–46.

Although the majority of articles concerns U.S. efforts at state-building, this consideration of UN activities illustrates the difficulties that the multilateral body has faced in Kosovo and East Timor, while also discussing Afghanistan. The article highlights the importance of legitimacy in the eyes of the country involved.

Chong, Terence. 2002. **"Asian Values and Confucian Ethics: Malay Singaporeans' Dilemma."** *Journal of Contemporary Asia* 32 (3): 394–406.

This is a specific instance of one ethnic group's integration into another ethnic group's nation-state and how then economic marginalization does or does not result.

Cleary, Edward L. 1997. **"The Brazilian Catholic Church and Church-State Relations: Nation Building."** *Journal of Church and State* 39, no. 2 (spring): 253–272.

The church has a crucial role in Latin American nation-building, but the applications are broader than just Latin America.

Cohen, Lenard J. 1998. **"Whose Bosnia? The Politics of Nation-Building."** *Current History* 97, no. 617 (March): 103–113.

Nation-building in Bosnia will likely be a basic consideration for future policymakers. The author hypothesizesd that the various goals in Bosnia might be incompatible.

Cohen-Almagor, Raphael. 1995. **"Cultural Pluralism and the Israeli Nation-Building Ideology."** *International Journal of Middle East Studies* 27, no. 4 (November): 461–485.

This article lays out the principal ideological bases to nation-building that have sustained Israel over its more than fifty years. It offers some interesting questions about how to protect and ensure democracy.

Collier, Paul. 2003. **"The Market for Civil War."** *Foreign Policy* (May–June): 38–45.

Thirty years ago, the answers to civil war and domestic instability questions would have revolved around gross internal inequalities. This is no longer the common answer today, and Collier harkens back to the position that economic issues are what drive these conflicts and that nation-builders must understand that.

Crock, Stan. 2003. **"Bush Is Flunking Reconstruction 101."** *Business Week Online*, 19 May. Available at http://www.businessweek.com/bwdaily/dnflash/may2003/nf20030519_0471_db056.htm (accessed 1 March 2004).

This piece argues that waging war was easy but waging peace and nation-building is far more difficult for U.S. military forces and the government guiding them.

Crane, Conrad C., and W. Andrew Terrill. 2003. **"Reconstructing Iraq: Challenges and Missions for Military Forces in a Post-Conflict Scenario."** (29 January): 1–22. Carlisle Barracks, PA: Strategic Studies Institute of the U.S. Army War College.

In the aftermath of the overthrow of Saddam Hussein, this study by two researchers in Carlisle Barracks, Pennsylvania, has received significant attention. Using World War II planning as a benchmark, as well as the 1990–1991 buildup and conflict in the Persian Gulf, these researchers asserted three months before the war began that the interagency coordination required to rebuild Iraq would be massive. Perhaps most noteworthy, it included an appendix with twenty-one categories of tasks that would need assignment. Each was not only listed but assigned a likely action office and a priority from Critical through Esssential down to Important. Many people believe that had this sort of understanding been grasped by the forces and civilians arriving in April 2003 some of the power grid and security problems that erupted could have been avoided.

Crocker, Chester A. 2003. **"Engaging Failing States."** *Foreign Affairs* 82, no. 5 (September–October): 32–45.

This former Reagan administration Africa specialist notes the contradiction of the Bush administration saying that it is concerned about "failing states" while at the same time being consumed with tracking down terrorists and weapons of mass destruction as if the two were the same. He warns of the danger in this approach.

Cullather, Nick. 2002. **"Damming Afghanistan: Modernization in a Buffer State."** *Journal of American History* 89, no. 2 (September): 512–537.

This scholarly article reviews U.S. experiences with nation-building in the 1950s and 1960s and describes how the United States repeats its behavior. Cullather believes the United States has too much faith in modernization to solve all of the nation-building turmoil around the globe.

Davis, Anthony. 1997. **"Taliban Found Lacking When Nation-Building Beckoned."** *Jane's Intelligence Review*, 1 August.

This analysis goes into considerable detail about the Taliban and what it did not accomplish in 1997 Afghanistan and considers various events in the period after the Taliban took power.

Dawisha, Adeed, and Karen Dawisha. 2003. **"How to Build a Democracy in Iraq."** *Foreign Affairs* 82, no. 3 (May–June): 36–50.

These highly respected scholars argue that there are determinable items necessary to creating a democracy in Iraq but that we are not necessarily focused on them at present.

Day, Graham, and Christopher Freeman. 2003. **"Policekeeping Is the Key: Rebuilding the Internal Security Architecture of Postwar Iraq."** *International Affairs* 79, no. 2 (March): 299–313.

Day and Freeman argue that a major consideration, too often overlooked, in nation-building anywhere around the world is the domestic security considerations often considered policing. This approach is considerably different from the view that nation-builders merely need stop conflict rather than help with developing a security structure after conflicts end within states. This has proven a powerful argument after the Iraq experience.

Democratic Principles Working Group. 2003. **"Iraqi Opposition Report on Transition to Democracy."** *Journal of Democracy* 14, no. 3 (July): 14–29.

The long-exiled Iraqi opposition has had three decades to consider what reforms are required to put their homeland on the path to democracy. This is their recipe.

Dempsey, Gary T. 2002. **"Nation Building's Newest Disguise."** *Orbis* 46, no. 3 (summer): 415–434.

This article lays out the argument that nation-building is being portrayed as fighting terrorism, but is actually a continuation of prior policy behavior.

——. 2001. **"Old Folly in a New Disguise: Nation Building to Combat Terrorism."** *Policy Analysis* 429 (21 March). Available at http://www.cato.org/pubs/pas/pa-429es.html (accessed 1 March 2004).

The CATO Institute is a Libertarian think tank in Washington, D.C., that is often opposed to any sort of intervention beyond U.S. borders and that takes a decidedly minimalist position on actions in the international system. This article argues forcefully that protecting the nation against terrorism can be handled much more effectively by other approaches.

Dettmer, Jamie. 2001. **"A House Divided on Foreign Policy."** *Insight on the News* 17, no. 26 (16 July): 16–17.

Written before the September 11 attacks, the author argues that Secretary of Defense Rumsfeld and the congressional Republican leadership of the United States were reluctant to engage in peacekeeping and associated tasks. The memories of Somalia were on their minds.

Dobbins, James, and Seth G. Jones. 2003. **"America's Record on Nation Building: Are We Getting Any Better?"** *New York Times*, 13 June, A31.

This very interesting approach contains a graphic with text on the cases that the United States has made for nation-building back to the end of World War II.

Du Toit, P. 2003. **"Why Post-Settlement Settlements?"** *Journal of Democracy* 14, no. 3 (July): 104–118.

Just because the decision to end an internal conflict is made, this study shows that subsequent political negotiation across society is often required to carry out the intent of building lasting, peaceful societies.

Dunne, Michael. 2003. **"The United States, the United Nations, and Iraq: 'Multilateralism' of a Kind."** *International Affairs* 79, no. 2 (March): 257–278.

This unusual view, worth exploring, is a different twist on why the United States is engaging in nation-building through a multilateral method.

Eid, Bassem. 1998. **"Israel at Fifty: Must Palestinians Choose?— Between Human Rights and Nation-Building?"** *Tikkun* 13, no. 3 (May–June): 61, 78.

The author, a Palestinian, challenges Israel's half-century anniversary as a valid nation-state observing human rights. This question of nation-building is important.

Eisenstadt, Michael. 2001–2002. **"Curtains for the Ba'ath."** *National Interest* 66 (winter): 59–68.

The author wrote, early in the lead-up to the 2003 conflict, that Saddam Hussein deserved to be replaced because of his behavior in Iraq and that the United States could accomplish this goal without a tremendous number of U.S. troops or financial commitment.

Fallows, James. 2004. **"Blind into Baghdad."** *Atlantic Monthly* 293, no. 1 (January/February): 52–69.

This article has attracted considerable attention as a scathing indictment of why planning for the nation-building phase in Iraq was ignored. Fallows argues that the administration did not simply misjudge but chose to ignore inconvenient facts on issues such as interagency planning and the costs involved.

Ferguson, Niall. 2003. **"The Empire Slinks Back."** *New York Times Magazine*, 27 April, 52–58.

The author, a professor at Oxford and New York Universities, does not believe the United States has the tenacity to be a true imperial power and that various problems in Afghanistan and Iraq will drive the United States away.

Friedman, Thomas L. 2003. **"It's Time to Pick Up the Pace of Nation-Building."** *International Herald Tribune*, 19 May, p. 8.

This columnist for the *New York Times* has written extensively on issues concerning U.S. involvement overseas. His arguments about nation-building often consider the contradictions in U.S. policy in a region or nation. On nation-building, his work has dealt with the popular frustration that perhaps planning for war is much easier than implementing peace.

Fukuyama, Frances. 2004. **"Nation-Building 101."** *Atlantic Monthly* 293, no.1 (January/February): 159–163.

This scholar, who received much attention for his theorizing that the globe would see fewer conflicts after the end of communist control in the cold war, takes on nation-building. He states that rehabilitating the states that are failing, collapsed, or weak will be the major task facing the United States in the near term.

Fuller, Graham E. 1997. **"The Rise of Islam in Central Asia."** *World & I* 12, no. 9 (September): 44–49.

This article explains why Islam is becoming more significant in post-Soviet Central Asia. Graham's analysis leads to thinking that this trend will continue elsewhere.

Gann, L. H. 1994. **"Beyond Apartheid: South Africa's Hazy Future."** *Orbis* 38, no. 4 (fall): 679–687.

This article appraised nation-building concerns early in President Mandela's term.

Glasser, Susan B. 2002. **"Soldiers in Civilian Clothing: U.S. Forces' Humanitarian Effort in Afghanistan Draws Ire of Aid Agencies."** *Washington Post*, 28 March, A20.

This is a compact assessment of the contradictions inherent in having civilian reconstruction as the overarching goal of many activities around the world yet conducting those reconstruction efforts through uniformed forces of the U.S. government.

Greenberger, Robert S., and Karby Leggett. 2003. **"Bush Dreams of Changing Not Just Regime but Region."** *Wall Street Journal*, 21 March.

This prescient piece, written the day after hostilities began in Iraq, described the range of issues concerning President Bush. The agenda these authors illuminate is a broader one than many in the United States thought when discussions about Iraq began in 2002.

Haider, Ejaz. 2003. **"Arc of Instability."** *World Today* 59, no. 8/9 (August–September): 24.

This author argues that Afghanistan may be important for fostering instability elsewhere in Southwest Asia or a manner of successful nation-building.

Haig, Alexander M., Jr. 1999. **"Correcting the Course of NATO."** *Orbis* 43, no. 3 (summer): 355–361.

The former U.S secretary of state and supreme allied commander of NATO argues that involving the alliance in nation-building and peacekeeping is off track for the organization and puts its future in jeopardy.

Hamayotsu, Kikue. 2002. **"Islam and Nation Building in Southeast Asia: Malaysia and Indonesia in Comparative Perspective."** *Pacific Affairs* 75, no. 3 (fall): 353–378.

The experiences of these prominent former colonial areas of Southeast Asia are strikingly different, but Islam played a unique role in each. This article considers the role of Islam, interreligious hostility, conflict, and other aspects of nation-building.

Hamburg, David. 2002. **"Preventing War through Nation-Building: A Self-Interested Approach to Peace."** *Negotiation Journal* 18, no. 4 (October): 385.

This is a different approach to nation-building, emphasizing peacemaking over retribution after September 11. The author argues in favor of self-interest.

Hamre, John, and Gordon R. Sullivan. 2002. **"Towards Postconflict Reconstruction."** *Washington Quarterly* 25, no. 4 (autumn): 4–16.

The retired comptroller of the Defense Department and former army chief of staff cogently discuss the range of issues requiring careful thought and implementation after the guns are silent in a nation-building environment.

Hayward, Allison R., Daniel Kelly, and Michael F. Williams. **"The War on Terrorism and the Commander in Chief Clause: Delegation of the President's Command Authority."** *National Security White Papers* (The Federalist Society for Law and Public Policy Studies). Available at http://www.fed-soc.org/Publications/Terrorism/commanderinchief.htm (accessed 1 March 2004).

This piece, emphasizing the president's role in the war on terrorism, argues strongly that the United States will be pushed into nation-building by the growing United Nations and popular international concern about this topic once a conflict has occurred in a sovereign state.

Helton, Arthur C. 2002. **"Rescuing the Refugees."** *Foreign Affairs* 81, no. 2 (March–April): 71–82.

Refugees play a central role in many humanitarian crises and the subsequent efforts at nation-building. This author died in the August 2003 Baghdad bomb blast while in Iraq working on refugee issues.

Henderson, Errol A. 1998. **"The Impact of Culture on African Coup d'Etat, 1960–1997."** *World Affairs* 161, no. 1 (summer): 10–22.

This article considers the question of whether culture is as important to nation-building as many believe.

Hitchens, Christopher. 2001. **"National Security?"** *Nation* 273, no. 22 (31 December): 9.

Hitchens argues that Palestine is a compelling case for nation-building; yet the United States has never formally moved in that direction.

Hyman, Anthony. 2002. **"Nationalism in Afghanistan."** *International Journal of Middle East Studies* 34, no. 2 (May): 299–316.

This article considers the role that nationalism plays in helping or stifling nation-building efforts around the world.

Ignatieff, Michael. 2002. **"Intervention and State Failure."** *Dissent* 49, no. 1 (winter): 114–123.

The author reviews the history of the past fifty years of nation-building around the world and examines the interactions between various forces in nation-building.

———. 2002. **"Nation Building Lite: The Bush Administration Is Trying to Reconstruct Afghanistan on the Cheap."** *New York Times Sunday Magazine,* 28 July, 26–34.

This author criticizes U.S. actions after the campaign ended in Afghanistan, saying that the administration was not, in the author's view, spending enough on reconstruction efforts. He focuses on the role of Special Forces in this campaign.

———. 2003. **"The Challenges of American Imperial Power."** *Naval War College Review* 56, no. 2 (spring): 53–63.

This article, written by a Harvard scholar, lays out the effects that having global reach has on strategy making for a state, in this case the United States. The author articulately illustrates that the "law of unintended consequences" too often comes into play when policymakers are not yet focused on the whole of an issue.

———. 2003. **"A Mess of Intervention."** *New York Times Magazine,* 7 September, 38–43, 71, 72, 85.

An especially incisive article on the many facets of nation-building.

Indyk, Martin. 2003. **"A Trusteeship for Palestine."** *Foreign Affairs* 82, no. 3 (May–June): 51.

The author argues that one option to nation-building would be to alter Palestine's status to give it protected status, making the transition from Arafat and the Palestine Authority to some other condition easier. The article contains much discussion on nation-building.

Institute for the Study of Diplomacy. 2003. **"Sustaining Global Democratization: Nation Building and Intervention."** *ISD Report.* Edmund Walsh School of Foreign Service at Georgetown University, February, 1–9.

The report from a panel discussion at the School of Foreign Service examines democratization in the Middle East but draws upon lessons from Iraq, Afghanistan, and the West Bank/Gaza. The panelists, Philip Wilcox, Leslie Campbell, William Zartman, and Phyllis Oakley, have all participated in democratization efforts around the world.

Jehl, Douglas. 2003. **"U.S. Considers Private Iraqi Force to Guard Sites."** *New York Times*, 18 July, Internet edition, A1.

Questions about the use of private firms for nation-building efforts have grown since the mid-1990s as demands for U.S. forces have grown in number, while force levels have either stayed the same or fallen. This illustrates the quandary, which would force any decision makers to rely on private entities created of U.S. or other foreign nationals.

Kagan, Robert. 2002. **"Iraq: The Day After."** *Washington Post*, 21 July, B7.

Kagan, a prominent member of the intellectual community supporting nation-building as practiced by the Bush administration, discusses that the challenges after Saddam is ousted would be important and long-term and debunks the argument that there was no credible thought of what to expect once the conflict ended.

Kamaara, Eunice. 2000. **"The Role of the Christian Church in Socio-Economic and Political Development in Kenya."** *Journal of Third World Studies* 17, no. 1 (spring): 165–176.

This article shows the significant role that religion is playing in the nation-building process of this East African state, an aspect of nation-building that is ignored in much of the conventional and scholarly literature.

Kaplan, Robert D. 1994. **"The Coming Anarchy."** *Atlantic Monthly*, February, 44–65.

Written by one of the most influential writers from the popular press, this was a widely cited article in national security circles because of its dire predictions of nation-state collapse and the resulting lawlessness that would require international intervention to repair. Along with his reports from Afghanistan and Iraq, Kaplan's writings address the basic issues of nation-building

———. 2003. **"Supremacy by Stealth."** *Atlantic Monthly*, July/August, 66–80.

Kaplan argues that the United States has an undisputed empire and lays out how we are making this less than clear to the public. Particularly useful is a list of the U.S. military operations from 1993 to the present: eighty-six separate operations by his count.

Kasper, Sara, and Minxin Pei. 2003. **"Lessons for the Past: Examining America's Record in Nation-Building."** *Policy Briefing.* Washington, DC: Carnegie Endowment for International Peace.

These Carnegie scholars argue that the U.S. record has not been all that good in the nation-building business and suggest methods to improve that record.

Kinsley, Michael. **"Thanks for Nothing."** *Slate: The Online Magazine.* Available at http://slate.msn.com/toolbar.aspx?action=print&id=2081640 (accessed 16 January 2004).

This author argues that nation-building is as deeply linked to the opportunities for U.S. companies in the reconstruction of Iraq as it is to the desire to create a better world for post-Saddam Iraq.

Kitfield, James. 2002. **"Beyond Arafat."** *National Journal* 34, no. 30 (27 July): 2228–2233.

This piece notes that the Bush administration strategy of trying to get rid of Yasir Arafat makes it difficult to choose a path other than nation-building for Palestine.

Kolsto, Boris Tsilevich. 1997. **"Patterns of Nation Building and Political Integration in a Bifurcated Postcommunist State: Ethnic Aspects of Parliamentary Elections in Latvia."** *East European Politics and Societies* 11, no. 2 (spring): 366–392.

The post-Soviet states offer many lessons on nation building. This article describes how the ethnic aspects play out.

Kolsto, Pal. 1996. **"Nation-Building in the Former USSR."** *Journal of Democracy* 7, no. 1 (January): 118–133.

The successes and failures of nation-building in Russia are crucial for the future. Russia's experience is a barometer of any global change in the process.

Korb, Lawrence. 2000. **"Money for Nothing."** *Foreign Affairs* 79, no. 2 (March–April): 149–153.

This article describes the differences between the Clinton and Bush administrations in their levels of military readiness and effects of this difference on the ability to do nation-building, among other issues.

Kritz, Neil. 2002. **"Promoting a Formal System of Justice in Post-Taliban Afghanistan."** *Connecticut Journal of International Law* 17, no. 3 (summer): 451–459.

The author lays out precisely what steps the Afghanis must take to create an enduring justice system in their country.

Kym, Will. 2000. **"Nation-Building and Minority Rights: Comparing West and East."** *Journal of Ethnic and Migration Studies* 26, no. 2 (April): 183.

The author does a comparative analysis showing why nation-building has a different focus in the West than in Asia for minorities.

Lande, Carl H. 1999. **"Ethnic Conflict, Ethnic Accommodation, and Nation-Building in Southeast Asia."** *Studies in Comparative International Development* 33, no. 4 (winter): 89–117.

In this scholarly article examining what the author has determined are four types of ethnic conflicts in independent Southeast Asia, the reader is shown why nation-building is so difficult.

Leibstone, Marvin. 1988. **"Creating the Military Element: A US Provision and Its Quandary."** *Military Technology* 22, no. 11 (November): 6.

On a topic that is more discussed now than when this article was written, the author examines the U.S. proclivity to use private forces for nation-building rather than enhancing the militaries in the states involved.

Levin, Michael. 1997. **"The New Nigeria."** *Journal of Asian and African Studies* 20, no. 6 (June): 134–145.

The author catalogs the nation-building efforts of the Nigerian government.

Lewis, Peter. 2003. **"Nigeria: Elections in a Fragile Regime."** *Journal of Democracy* 14, no. 3 (July): 131–144.

Consolidation, a vital phase of nation-building, has proven exceedingly difficult for Nigeria. This is an analysis of the pitfalls the country has encountered along its path.

Lieven, Anatol. 2002. **"The Wilsonian Veneer of US Foreign Policy."** *Financial Times*, 15 July, 9.

This piece argues that the Clinton approach to Wilsonian values in foreign policy may not be all that different, in practice, from the Bush approach.

Lloyd, John. 2002. **"The Case for Intervention: How Politics, Morality and Economics Are Framing Debate on Iraq's Postwar Future."** *Financial Times*, 27 December, 14.

This article is a brutally frank discussion of the difficulties characterizing various nation-building efforts prior to the Iraq conflict.

Loescher, Gil, and James Milner. 2003. **"The 'Missing Link': The Need for Comprehensive Engagement in Regions of Refugee Origin."** *International Affairs* 79, no. 3 (May): 595–618.

Loescher, an employee at the United Nations, was seriously injured in the Baghdad U.N. bombing in 2003, where he was working on refugee issues. He and Milner argue that refugee issues will continue to bedevil nation-building until they are adequately addressed.

Lorenz, Rick. 1996. **"Nation Building in the Balkans: U.S. Efforts to Promote the Rule of Law in Bosnia and Herzegovina."** *Washington State Bar News* 50, no. 10 (October): 28–59.

The lessons from the former Yugoslav republics also apply elsewhere, according to this article, which gives special emphasis to the legal implications.

Looney, Robert. 2002. **"Rebuilding Afghanistan."** *Strategic Insights* 1, no. 4 (June). Available at http://www.ccc.nps.navy.mil/si/june02/southAsia.asp (accessed 12 February 2002).

This piece in a new electronic journal by a frequently cited scholar specializing in defense economics estimates what nation-building is likely to cost in Afghanistan in the aftermath of the Taliban ouster.

Lowry, Rich. 2001. **"Two Cheers for Nation Building."** *National Review Online*, 22 October. Available at http://www.nationalreview.com/lowry102201.shtml (accessed 3 March 2003).

This article from the on-line version of this conservative weekly supports the nation-building concept.

Lyons, Terrence. 1997. **"The Lessons of Somalia for Eastern Zaire."** *Brookings Review* 15, no. 1 (winter): 47.

The disintegration of Zaire in the mid-1990s raised some of the same questions that had arisen nearly a decade earlier in attempting nation-building for Somalia. This article argues for the need to stick to humanitarian efforts and not go into broader activities.

MacGinty, Roger. 2003. **"The Pre-War Reconstruction of Post-War Iraq."** *Third World Quarterly* 24 (4): 601–617.

This is a fascinating study of the actions that preceded the conflict, perhaps shaping it as well as the subsequent environment.

MacKinlay, James N. 1995. **"Zaire: The Positive Role of Religion in Nation-Building."** *Brigham Young Law Review* 2: 671–690.

The article argues that Zaire's nation-building was greatly affected by the role of the Catholic Church, which remained the most important functioning institution as this state began disintegrating.

Makiya, Kanan. 2003. **"A Model for Post-Saddam Iraq."** *Journal of Democracy* 14, no. 3 (July): 5–12.

This author argues that the new Iraq must be demilitarized and given a strong federal system and liberal values. An Iraqi exile teaching at Brandeis University, Makiya originally presented this article as a speech at an American Enterprise Institute conference on planning for an Iraq after Saddam in early October 2002. He advocated a federal system for Iraq with its ethnic and religious diversity.

Mallaby, Sebastian. 2002. **"The Reluctant Imperialist."** *Foreign Affairs* 81, no. 2 (March–April): 2–7.

Mallaby argues that the Bush administration is pushed by circumstances to try nation-building, although the candidate promised to not engage in this activity.

Mandela, Nelson. 1995. **"Building Together: A Plan for National Reconstruction."** *Harvard International Review* 17, no. 4 (fall): 10–13.

The challenges facing South Africa have rarely been higher for any other nation. Mandela laid out plans and programs to avoid greater problems as the state tried to make the transition from a highly divided state into a more unified one.

Marquis, Jefferson P. 2000. **"The Other Warriors: American Social Science and Nation Building in Vietnam."** *Diplomatic History* 24, no. 1 (winter): 79–105.

This is an exploration of the way that counterinsurgency and social science applications were used during the conflict in Southeast Asia.

Marx, Anthony W. 1996. **"Race-Making and the Nation-State."** *World Politics* 48, no. 2 (January): 180–209.

Race is intimately linked to other aspects of nation-building, and this article tries to show the reader that pattern more clearly.

———. 2002. **"The Nation-State and Its Exclusions."** *Political Science Quarterly* 117, no. 1 (spring): 103–126.

This is a social-science interpretation of nation-building and its applicability and is far more scholarly than other items contained here.

McCloskey, Donald N. 1987. **"The Rhetoric of Economic Development."** *Cato Journal* 7, no. 1 (spring–summer 1987): 249–254.

This traditionally anti-interventionist think-tank journal expresses the concerns that nation-building efforts are actually quite different than they appear on the surface.

McFaul, Michael. 2003. **"Since Sept. 11, Nation-Building is Ascendant Again in White House: Dueling Ideologies Make Justification for War Unclear."** *San Jose Mercury News*, 19 January, Internet edition.

This author reiterated the reasons that the nation was confused about justification for the Iraq conflict, emphasizing how liberals differed from conservatives on this issue.

Metzl, Jamie Frederic. 2001. **"Let Private Firms Aid UN Nation-Building."** *Christian Science Monitor*, 13 August, Internet edition.

This piece argues that the United Nations would benefit from private assistance in place of government help, which is now largely from the United States, in addressing increasingly common requests for nation-building.

Moore, David. 2001. **"Neoliberal Globalisation and the Triple Crisis of 'Modernisation' in Africa: Zimbabwe, the Democratic Republic of Congo and South Africa."** *Third World Quarterly* 22, no. 6 (December): 909–932.

How modernization is linked to nation-building in Africa is explored in this article.

Morrell, James R., Rachel Neild, and Hugh Byrne. 1999. **"Haiti and the Limits to Nation-Building."** *Current History* 98, no. 626 (March): 127–132.

This article paints a bleak picture in discussing the five years of nation-building in Haiti.

Mousavizadeh, Nader. 1996. **"Washington Diarist: Bosnians."** *New Republic* 214, no. 26 (24 June), 1 p.

This author argues that Bosnia-Herzegovina, in the mid-1990s, became the most important place for nation-building in the world.

Nagata, Judith. 1997. **"Ethnonationalism versus Religious Transnationalism: Nation-Building and Malaysia."** *Muslim World* 87, no. 2 (April): 129–151.

For many Muslims, nationalism conflicts with religious values. This article contemplates how this affects nation-building efforts.

Neal, Terry M. 2003. **"Bush Backs into Nation Building."** *Washington Post*, 26 February. Available at http://www.washingpost.com/ac2/wp-dyn/A6853-2003Feb26?language=printer (accessed 23 May 2003).

This brief newspaper article discusses the differences between what the president proposed in a speech before the American Enterprise Institute in 2003 and what he argued as a candidate in the

2003 campaign. It also describes the positions of Gore's advisers on the new Bush commitment to nation-building.

Nye, Joseph S., Jr. 2003. **"U.S. Power and Strategy after Iraq."** *Foreign Affairs* 82, no. 4 (July–August): 60–73.

This is a challenging essay about what the United States will face as it continues down this path that was originally scorned. Nye points out that there will be increasing demands on the United States to engage in similar activities but that the United States most likely will more frequently look to the United Nations for assistance.

Ottaway, Marina. 2002. **"Think Again: Nation Building."** *Foreign Policy* (September–October): 16–22.

There are many reasons that nation-building appears far simpler than it becomes once activities start on the ground. Ottaway explains these reasons in a seminal piece on nation-building.

Owen, John M., IV. 2002. **"The Foreign Imposition of Domestic Institutions."** *International Organization* 56, no. 2 (spring): 375–409.

In this somewhat theoretical piece, the author outlines what would today be called nation-building, from 1500 to 2000. Comparing experiences over a long period of time, the author comes to the conclusion that using force to impose democratic institutions is not very successful, as indicated in the existing data.

Peel, Quentin. 2002. **"Caught in the Web of Nation-Building: Quentin Peel."** *Financial Times*, 16 October, 21.

This is a brief analysis on the causes and effects of nation-building efforts around the globe.

Pei, Minxin. and Sara Kasper. 2003. **"Lessons from the Past: The American Record in Nation-Building."** *Carnegie Endowment Policy Brief No. 24*, 1 May. Available at http://www.ceip.org/files/Publications/2003-04-11-peipolicybrief.asp?from=pubdate (accessed 1 March 2004).

This critical assessment argues that nation-building is a much tougher undertaking for the United States than is generally believed and that, when approached unilaterally, even harder. The *Brief* argues that this is exceptionally difficult for outsiders.

Peterson, V. Spike. 1996. **"The Politics of Identification in the Context of Globalization."** *Women's Studies International Forum* 19, nos. 1–2 (January–April): 5–16.

In one of the earlier articles on globalization, the author examines its ties to nation-building, seemingly contradictory concepts.

Ponnuru, Ramesh. 2001. **"Get Realist."** *National Review* 53, no. 25 (31 December): 17–19.

This article is an assessment of the realist and antirealist theoretical approaches to nation-building in the Bush administration.

Posz, Gary, Bruce Janigian, and Jong Jun. 1994. **"Redesigning U.S. Foreign Aid."** *SAIS Review* 14, no. 2 (summer–fall): 159–170.

The author makes a wide-ranging appraisal of whether foreign assistance would be useful for U.S. strategy of the future.

Prosper, Pierre-Richard. 2002. **"On Respect for the Rule of Law in Post-Taliban Afghanistan."** *Connecticut Journal of International Law* 17, no. 3 (summer): 433–436.

This is a transcript of a discussion of what is required to establish rule of law.

Reeves, Phil. 2003. **"Afghanistan after the War Bodes Ill for Iraq."** *Washington Report on Middle East Affairs* 22, no. 3 (April): 30–31.

Fears have been growing in Afghanistan that the international system as the donor community is forgetting its commitment, and that these problems are possibly applicable to Iraq.

Remnick, David. 2003. **"Comment: After the Battle."** *New Yorker*, 31 March, 29–32.

This brief piece discusses not only the link between imperialism and nation-building in the U.S. psyche but also the discomfort that nation-building generates when it involves the potential for tremendous profits for U.S. corporations.

Rice, Condoleezza. 2000. **"Promoting the National Interest."** *Foreign Affairs* 79, no. 1 (January–February): 45–63.

This widely cited article from prior to the 2000 presidential election indicated the skepticism with which candidate George W. Bush approached nation-building.

Rice, Susan E. 2003. **"The New National Security Strategy: Focus on Failed States."** *Brookings Policy Briefing #116*. Washington, DC: Brookings, February.

This former Clinton National Security Council staffer on Africa concentrates her analysis on the role of failed states in our future responsibilities and interests.

Rock, Michael T. 1993. **"'Twenty-Five Years of Economic Development' Revisited."** *World Development* 21, no. 11 (November): 1787–1802.

Economic development is closely tied to nation-building. This reviews the last quarter of a century of this economic theory and history, challenging prior conclusions and predicting new understandings of the phenomena.

Roman, Peter J., and David Tarr. 1998. **"The Joint Chiefs: From Service Parochialism to Jointness."** *Political Science Quarterly* 113, no. 1 (spring): 91–112.

This article is an important consideration of how the members of the Joint Chiefs of Staff approach nation-building.

Rubin, Barnett R. 2002. **"A Blueprint for Afghanistan."** *Current History* 101, no. 654 (April): 153–157.

Rubin believes that Afghanistan proved an important lesson in the September 11 tragedy and argues that stability is crucial to the world, regardless of the costs.

———. 2003. **"Transitional Justice and Human Rights in Afghanistan."** *International Affairs* 79, no. 3 (May): 567–582.

Rubin argues that Afghanistan's transitional period, especially in issues of the application of justice, shows the role of human rights in nation-building.

Saikal, Amin. 2000. **"Afghanistan after the Loya Jirga."** *Survival* 44, no. 3 (autumn): 47–56.

This article, unlike many others, advocates nation-building for Afghanistan and neighboring states.

Saletan, William. 1999. **"Humanitarian Hawks."** *Mother Jones* 24, no. 4 (July–August): 29–31.

The author discusses the ways in which various political groups in the U.S. political system supported and rejected the international intervention in the Balkans in the late 1990s.

Schneider, William. 2001. **"Not Exactly a Bush Flip-Flop."** *Atlantic Online*, 31 October. Availablet at http://www.theatlantic.com/politics/nj/schneider2001–10–31.htm (accessed 16 January 2004).

In this discussion of the clear differences between President Bush's positions during the campaign of 2000 and the aftermath of September 11, Schneider explains why he believes that the president set certain norms for this activity rather than having merely abandoned a campaign promise.

Schnell, Izhak. 2001. **"Transformation in Territorial Concepts: From Nation Building to Concessions in Israel."** *Geojournal* 53, no. 3 (March): 213–217.

This is an extremely political science–oriented consideration of territory in the Israeli-Palestinian conflict.

Schwartz, Stephen. 2002. **"How Not to Nation-Build."** *Weekly Standard* 8 (6): 11–13.

This piece argues that the current nation-building efforts of the United States and the international community are not working as desired. Schwartz argues that U.S. views must be separate from those of Europe.

Shahrani, Nazif. 2002. **"War, Factionalism, and the State in Afghanistan."** *American Anthropologist* 104, no. 3 (September): 715–723.

An anthropologist discusses the reasons why nation-building has proven so illusive in Afghanistan historically and why this will happen again.

Shaw, Timothy M. 2003. **"Conflict and Peace-Building in Africa: The Regional Dimensions."** *Discussion Paper No. 200310.* New York: United Nations University, February, 1–20.

This prominent western scholar on Africa argues that peace-building (hence also nation-building) must have a regional component because the conflicts are increasingly regional in orientation. With the growing international attention to the turbulence in Liberia, this is a timely assessment with potential immediate applicability.

Shikaki, Khalil. 1996. **"The Peace Process, National Reconstruction, and the Transition to Democracy in Palestine."** *Journal of Palestine Studies* 25, no. 2 (winter): 5–20.

This article looks at various peace approaches, issues crucial to the nation-building that cannot be ignored for Palestine.

Slim, Hugo. 2003. **"Why Protect Civilians? Innocence, Immunity and Enmity in War."** *International Affairs* 79, no. 3 (May): 481–502.

The author gives a sobering discussion of the people who are completely vulnerable in wars.

Slocomb, Margaret. 2001. **"The K5 Gamble: National Defense and Nation Building under the People's Republic of Kampuchea."** *Journal of Southeast Asian Studies* 32, no. 2 (June): 195–210.

This case study of the various forces that had to be controlled and then entreated to join the political system in the post-Khmer Cambodia (Kampuchea) provides an excellent example of how nation-building proceeds and what it requires.

Spencer, William H. 2002. **"Establishing the Rule of Law in Post-Taliban Afghanistan."** *Connecticut Journal of International Law* 17, no. 3 (summer): 445–450.

A transcript of discussion of what is required to institutionalize the rule of law in the often-lawless Afghanistan.

The Stanley Foundation. 2003. **"Who Rebuilds After Conflict?**

38th Conference on the United Nations of the Decade." 15–20
June, Loch Lomond, Scotland, 1–32.

This conference report illustrates the problems that anyone will
face in responding to structural turmoil within a state. The two
dozen participants, some from Europe while others from the
United States, included practitioners, retired military, and theo-
reticians. The conclusion is that the United Nations, in conjunction with its member states, will be required to accomplish rebuilding in any foreseeable case.

Starobin, Paul. 2002. **"Marching into the Unknown: Georgia
Will Be a Test Case of the New U.S. Policy to Shore Up Strategic but Failing States."** *Business Week* 3804 (21 October): 58–59.

Georgia, on the southern periphery of the former Soviet Union, is
far from completed in its nation-building but increasingly important to the type of concerns the United States has around the
world.

Steele, Jonathan. 2002. **"Nation Building in East Timor."** *World
Policy Journal* 19, no. 2 (summer): 76–88.

In this summary of some of the more recent challenges facing the
world in nation-building prior to September 11, the author describes how hard the UN Transitional Administration in East
Timor worked but with what problems resulting.

Stephens, Andrew. 2003. **"America."** *New Statesman* 16, no. 765
(14 July): 11–12.

In this short article, the author argues that nation-building looked
like an easy issue for presidential candidate Bush but that now it
appears a necessary step for the Bush administration.

Stephens, Joe, and David B. Ottoway. 2003. **"Postwar Reconstruction Efforts Have Had Dicey History."** *Washington Post*, 28
April, A13.

The authors discuss a study by the Center for Strategic and International Studies on various nation-building efforts and how they
have worked out.

Strohmeyer, Hansjorg. 2001. **"Collapse and Reconstruction of a
Judicial System: The United Nations Misses Kosovo and East**

Timor." *American Journal of International Law* 95, no. 1 (January): 46–63.

The author considers the judiciary in the process of nation-building for two new states in the international community.

Sundhaussen, Ulf. 1995. **"Indonesia's New Order: A Model for Myanmar?"** *Asian Survey* 35, no. 8 (August): 768–781.

Myanmar has had tremendous problems in creating a civil society. This author advocates examining Indonesia for possible application to Myanmar.

Tan Chwee Huat. 1989. **"Confucianism and Nation Building in Singapore."** *International Journal of Social Economics* 16, no. 8 (August): 5–17.

This author considers the role that a religious/ethical system plays in nation-building and the creation of a civil society in one of the world's most "successful" states.

Tang, Anthony. 1988. **"Why Does Overcrowded, Resource-Poor East Asia Succeed? Lessons for the LDCs?"** *Economic Development and Cultural Change Supplement* 36, no. 3 (April).

This article preceded the "Asian values" debate that appeared early in the 1990s, and argues that East Asia's Confucian history and culture was able to sustain development better than the democratic, individual-rights model. The type of model does not relate to nation-building success of failure.

Tharoor, Shashi. 2003. **"Why America Still Needs the United Nations."** *Foreign Affairs* 82, no. 5 (September–October): 67–80.

This veteran UN diplomat and civil servant argues that the United Nations is crucial to legitimacy for nation-building efforts around the world.

Tolz, Vera. 1998. **"Conflicting 'Homeland Myths' and Nation-State Building in Post-Communist Russia."** *Slavic Review* 57, no. 2 (summer): 267–287.

This author asks the question of whether the myths of nationhood help or are significant in nation-building efforts of the modern era.

————. 1998. **"Forging the Nation: National Identity and Nation-Building in Post-Communist Russia."** *Europe-Asia Studies* 50, no. 6 (September): 993–1123.

The question of nation-building is considered in arguably the greatest national collapse of all time in this, the largest successor state of the Soviet Union.

Traub, James. 2000. **"Inventing East Timor."** *Foreign Affairs* 79, no. 4 (July–August 2000): 74–89.

The nation-building process for East Timor went more smoothly than many people ever believed possible. The United Nations' commitment to this small, targeted project was intense, but it still proved a significant challenge.

Tronvoll, Kjetil. 1998. **"The Process of Nation-Building in Post-War Eritrea: Created from Below or Directed from Above?"** *Journal of Modern African Studies* 36, no. 3 (September): 461–482.

This discussion of Africa's newest state considers what the requirements are for nation-building in the post–cold war era.

Tully, Andrew F. 2003. **"Iraq: Analysts Disagree about U.S. Postwar Objectives, Strategies."** Available at http://truthnews.com/world/2003010016.htm (accessed 16 January 2004).

This brief analysis illustrates how complicated and contradictory U.S. objectives can be in the whole of strategy, particularly in Iraq.

Von Hippel, Karin. 2000. **"Democracy by Force: A Renewed Commitment to Nation Building."** *Washington Quarterly* 23, no. 1 (winter): 95–112.

This UN official with experience in Kosovo provides a sophisticated assessment of what we have learned over the past decade about the operations now broadly called nation-building. Von Hippel defines nation-building, explains how its interpretations differ in the United States and Western Europe, and shows why this is likely to continue, regardless of the political party in power.

Vuong, Quynh-Nhu. 2003. **"U.S. Peacekeeping and Nation-Building: The Evolution of Self-Interested Multilateralism."** *Berkeley Journal of International Law* 21, no. 3 (winter): 804–824.

The article argues that the United States has no interest in handling nation-building without multilateral support from the Europeans, but this has been an evolution over the past few years.

Walker, William O., III. 2001. **"A Reprise for 'Nation Building':** **Low Intensity Conflict Spreads in the Andes."** *Nacla Report on the Americas* 35, no. 1 (July–August): 23–28.

Walker makes a compelling argument that the United States is not engaged in antidrug efforts in Colombia but is really conducting nation-building.

Watrous, Steve. 1994. **"Nobody Here But Us Roadbuilders."** *Progressive* 58, no. 10 (October): 30–33.

The rubric of nation-building has been used in Central America to justify joint exercises between the U.S. and Salvadoran militaries. This article asks whether these operations aren't something more than humanitarian operations.

Wilkin, Peter. 2003. **"Revising the Democratic Revolution—Into the Americas."** *Third World Quarterly* 24 (4): 655–669.

This article considers the ways that the push toward democratization has been applied in Latin America.

Wisner, Frank G., II, Nicholas Platt, Marshall Bouton, Dennis Kux, and Mahnaz Ispahani. 2003. **"Afghanistan: Are We Losing the Peace?"** *Council on Foreign Relations Working Paper,* June, 1–31.

The thesis of these authors is that the United States should pressure the states surrounding Afghanistan to support Hamid Karzai's government rather than the country's warlords. The nineteen months since the defeat of the Taliban regime have not proven sufficient to give Karzai any more than nominal control over Kabul, and the authors say that more direct pressure is crucial.

Woodward, Susan. 1997. **"Bosnia."** *Brookings Review* 15, no. 2 (spring): 29–31.

Woodward has been one of the most prolific authors on the long-running conflict in the Balkans. She argues, in an article from several years ago, that the successes of nation-building cannot always be guaranteed but must be revisited to keep the success

going. She also goes into much detail about the interactions between civilian and military officials in nation-building activities.

Young, Craig, and Duncan Light. 2001. **"Place, National Identity
and Post-Socialist Transformations: An Introduction."** *Political
Geography* 20, no. 8 (November): 941–956.

Another discipline of social science, political geography, considers the questions of nation-building.

Zeller, Tom. 2003. **"Building Democracy Is Not a Science."** *New
York Times*, 26 April, Section 4, 2.

An interesting text and set of charts compares multilateral and
U.S. unilateral actions to install democracy in various places
around the world, based on the Polity IV Project at the University
of Maryland.

Nonprint Resources

National Public Radio

National Public Radio, with its wide range of shows, frequently
covers topics on nation-building. Following is information for ordering transcripts of NPR programs:

NPR
c/o Burrelle's Transcripts
P.O. Box 7
Livingston, NJ 07039–0007
(877) 677–8398
Fax: (801) 343–3707
Web site: http://www.npr.org

All Things Considered, the afternoon news magazine, regularly
produces analyses on nation-building questions. These tend to be
relatively brief but timely interviews by scholars or policymakers.
Relevant examples include:

"U.S. Forces' Nation-Building in Afghanistan under Criticism for
Deficiency in Security against Bandits and Warlords" (8 May
2003)

"Iraqis React to U.S. Nation-Building Efforts" (28 April 2003)

"Private Interests and Military Policy" (11 March 2003)

"NPR Profile: Bush Administration and Pentagon Planners Consider What Type Operations Would Be Needed to Change the Iraqi Government" (30 July 2002)

"New Afghan Government" (6 December 2001)

"Afghanistan and Nation-Building" (26 October 2001)

"Afghan Refugee Crisis and Hunger" (11 October 2001)

"Nation-Building" (8 October 2001)

"U.S. Military Response" (24 September 2001)

"U.S. Aid to Colombia" (14 August 2000)

"Peacekeeping Operations" (28 February 2000)

"U.S.–Colombian Relations" (10 January 2000)

"Kosovo Liberation Army" (21 June 1999)

"Kosovo" (7 June 1999)

"Kosovo Refugee Crisis" (5 April 1999)

"Military Strike in Kosovo" (30 March 1999)

"Bosnian Elections" (11 September 1998)

The Diane Rehm Show is a production of member station WAMU in Washington, D.C., and has been nationally syndicated for about ten years. Rehm interviews many public policy figures, and nation-building has been a frequent focus. Tapes for both *The Diane Rehm Show* and *The Kojo Nnamdi Show* are available at

American University
WAMU 88.5 FM
Washington, DC 20016–8082
(877) 677–8398
Web site: http://www.wamu.org/cassettes.html

Relevant segments of *The Diane Rehm Show* have included:

"Nation-Building" (1 April 2003)

"Liberia, Peacekeeping, and Humanitarian Operations" (11 August 2003)

"Iraq Update" (21 July 2003)

"Iraqi Donors Conference" (22 October 2003)

"Liberia Update" (14 July 2003)

"Guerrilla Warfare in Iraq" (8 July 2003)

"Rebuilding Iraq" (2 July 2003)

"U.S. Rebuilding of Iraq" (12 June 2003)

"Nation-Building" (21 April 2003)

"Road to Democratic Iraq a Daunting Task" *Morning Edition* was produced by NPR to discuss the cost and long-term nature of the nation-building project under way after the end of Saddam Hussein's regime in Iraq (originally aired 18 April 2003).

"Post-War Iraq," (7 April 2003)

Fresh Air with Terry Gross is a nationally syndicated program on NPR stations. In one segment from 8 May 2003, Terry Gross interviewed former NPR reporter Sarah Chayes about the challenges of nation-building in Afghanistan. Chayes now works for a nongovernmental organization, Afghans for Civil Society, which is dedicated to rebuilding civil society in the remote state. Chayes's remarks illustrate the serious threat that warlords present to the entire project. Audio tapes or transcripts of this show are available on-line at http://www.burrelles.com.

The Kojo Nnamdi Show, also produced at WAMU public radio in Washington, D.C., is a formerly nationally syndicated hour-long show that often deals with nation-building. These shows tend to challenge the conventional wisdom somewhat more than many other programs available through NPR, perhaps because Nnamdi himself was born outside of the United States and he does not seek easy answers. Topics in nation-building that are covered include:

"Liberia/Zimbabwe and the Congo" (5 June 2003)

"Reconstructing Iraq" (28 May 2003)

"Emerging Democracy" (17 April 2003)

"Exporting Democracy" (16 April 2003)

"Humanitarian Issues in Iraq" (14 April 2003)

"Nation-Building" (20 February 2003)

"U.S. Military Training Abroad" (3 June 2002)

"The Peace Corps at 40" (13 April 2001)

"Iran and Democracy" (21 January 2000)

"Operations Other Than War" (1 March 1999)

Weekend Edition and *Morning Edition* often do somewhat more extended pieces to give context to events in the international system. "Romans as Nation Builders" on *Weekend Edition* illustrates similarities and difficulties facing the Roman Empire as it sought to create various portions of its wide-ranging political empire, some of which are applicable, while others are not, for the United States as it considers its goals and responsibilities around the world (originally aired 28 April 2003). Other shows have included:

"Interview with Secretary of Defense Donald Rumsfeld," *Morning Edition* (19 August 2003)

"U.N. Nation-Building Mission in Kosovo Moving Slowly," *Morning Edition* (19 May 2003)

"The Real 'Lawrence of Arabia,'" *Weekend Edition Saturday* (3 May 2003)

"Roman Nation-Building," *Weekend Edition Saturday* (19 April 2003)

"The Road to Democracy in Iraq Is a Daunting Task," *Morning Edition* (18 April 2003)

"Pentagon Official Outlines Postwar Plans for Iraq," *Morning Edition* (11 April 2003)

"Nation-Building," *Morning Edition* (9 April 2003)

"Nation-Building," *Morning Edition* (15 March 2002)

Other NPR segments relevant to nation-building:

"L. Paul Bremer and the National Press Club," *National Press Club* (23 July 2003)

"Nation-Building in Afghanistan," *Talk of the Nation* (28 November 2001)

"Afghanistan Update," *Talk of the Nation* (26 November 2001)

Television

British Broadcasting Corporation (BBC)

The BBC has a worldwide reputation for investigative reporting on wide-ranging topics. The resources are listed by type.

BBC News

"Afghanistan: Is Reconstruction Working?" (26 February 2003)
This program argues that the citizens of Afghanistan are free from the Taliban but not necessarily living in a significantly improved environment.

"Saddam Courts Iraqi Nationalism" (4 January 2003)

Saddam Hussein has been involved in trying to link himself to Iraqi nationalism.

"Afghanistan's New 'Heroes'" (13 August 2002)

In the aftermath of the campaign against the Taliban, the Northern Alliance is a tremendous influence on Afghanistan.

"Head to Head: South Africa's Mega-Merger" (28 November 2001)

The political evolution of South Africa in the aftermath of a decade of black rule is examined.

"Women's Vital Peace Role" (8 November 2001)

The head of the UN Population Fund argues that women have a major part in nation-building.

"Afghanistan: The Hazards of Nation-Building" (4 October 2001)

The United States had a tremendous task as it considered the steps necessary to develop a democratic Afghanistan.

BBC On-line On the Record Interviews

"Professor Fred Halliday," at http://www.bbc.co.uk/otr/in-text/20011125_whole.html (25 November 2001)

A professor at the London School of Economics examines the deep problems of nation-building in Afghanistan.

"Francesc Vendrell," at http://www.bbc.co.uk/otr/intext/20011014_int_1.html (14 October 2001)

The head of the UN Special Mission to Afghanistan posits that the future for the country is both positive and quite workable.

"On the Record Special War Report," at http://www.bbc.co.uk/otr/intext/20011014_whole.html (14 October 2001)

This is a British transcript on the initial moves into Afghanistan in October 2001.

Other BBC Programs

"The Talk Show: Kenneth Kaunda: A New Deal for Africa," at http://www.bbc.co.uk/bbcfour/talkshow/features/kenneth-kaunda-transcript.shtml (17 June 2002)

"World Lectures: Dr. Hana Ashrawi: Humanizing Globalization?" at http://www.bbc.co.uk/worldservice/people/features/world_lectures/ashrawi_lect.shtml

C-Span

Book TV is a weekend presentation by the public service network, C-Span, on cable television. Videos of various segments are available:

Book TV
C-Span
400 North Capitol Street, Suite 650
Washington, DC 20001
(202) 737–3220
E-mail: booktv@c-span.org

As an example, discussion of nation-building in Iraq occurred on 15 June 2003, featuring several authors of the *Iraqi War Reader*. In June 2003, U.S. Agency for International Development director Andrew Natsios and a team toured much of Iraq to see what reconstruction requirements would be. C-Span recorded this tour and replays its periodically. With two networks, C-Span replays its wide variety of shows, but determining the somewhat irregular schedule for those replays is sometimes difficult. C-Span is an important source of information on nation-building.

Public Broadcasting System (PBS)
The American Experience

American Experience is an occasional program that covers history topics of general interest. "The American Experience: Vietnam," originally aired in 1983, was an example of a program on nation-building.

Frontline

Frontline, the award-winning PBS investigative series, has frequent hour-long shows that deal with public policy issues relating to nation-building. The initial airing date of some specific titles is shown where available. Videotapes of many of the shows are available (noted in brackets). Ordering information follows:

PBS Video
P.O. Box 751089
Charlotte, NC 28275
(877) 727-7467
Fax: (703) 739-8131
Web site: http://www.pbs.org/wgbh/pages/frontline/shows/military/etc/script.html.

"Crisis in Central America," 4 parts

"Liberia: American Stepchild" [$29.98 for 90 minutes]

"Vietnam: A Television War" [$99.95 for 780 minutes on 7 tapes]

"The War behind Closed Doors"

"Blair's War" (April 2003)

"The Long Road to War" (17 March 2003)

"Campaign against Terror" (8 September 2002) [$29.98 for 120 minutes]

"The Future of War" (24 October 2000)

"Survival of Saddam" (25 January 2000)

"The Long Walk of Nelson Mandela" (25 May 1999)

"Give War a Chance—Nation-Building in Bosnia" (11 May 1999)

"Hunting Bin Laden" (13 April 1999)

"Saddam's Killing Fields" (31 March 1992)

"The War We Left Behind" (27 October 1991)

"War and Peace in Panama" (9 April 1991)

"Battle for Salvador" (12 April 1988)

"Revolution in Nicaragua" (11 April 1988)

"Castro" (10 April 1988)

"Yankee Years" (9 April 1988)

"Operation URGENT FURY" (2 February 1988)

"Ambush in Mogadishu" (1998) [$14.95 for 60 minutes]

"War on Nicaragua" (21 April 1987)

"Standoff in Mexico" (1 April 1986)

"The American Way of War" (30 April 1985)

"Retreat from Beirut" (26 February 1985)

The Newshour with Jim Lehrer

The following lists of segments from this program, perhaps the most highly respected public policy forum on U.S. television, illustrate its depth of coverage. This program takes different forms, grouped together below according to type. The *Newshour* Web site, http://www.pbs.org/newshour, has a wealth of information. The index feature can isolate the stories relating to a single large concern or by region. For example, Liberia is found at http://www.pbs.org/newshour/bb/africa/liberia/index.html, Nigeria is at http://www.pbs.org/newshour/bb/africa/nigeria/index.html, and Iraq is located at http://www.pbs.org/newshour/bb/middle_east/iraq/index.html.

Online Newshour: "Governing Iraq" (22 July 2003)

This is a general discussion of what Ambassador Bremer faces in trying to assemble and implement a strategy for nation-building in Iraq. Three months after major hostilities were thought to be over, governing Iraq looked considerably more challenging than originally envisioned.

Online Newshour: "Guerrilla War" (8 July 2003)

Continuing attacks on coalition forces raised the possibility of guerrilla forces, a possibility that Secretary Rumsfeld rejected.

Online Newshour: "The President Abroad" (5 June 2003)

The extent of President Bush's travels abroad raised the issue of how committed he is to nation-building around the world.

Online Newshour: "Historical Perspectives" (15 May 2003)

This segment examines the difference between colonialism and nation-building.

Online Newshour: "Rebuilding Shakeup" (12 May 2003)

This is a discussion of whether the United States adequately planned for the post-conflict necessities of Iraq.

Online Newshour: "Winning the Peace" (9 April 2003)

The segment discussed what will be required to build the Iraqi nation as we hope to see it.

Online Newshour: "After the War" (8 April 2003)

The reasons to involve the United Nations versus using U.S. forces only for nation-building in Iraq are explored.

Online Newshour: "Plans for a Postwar Iraq" (11 February 2003)

A variety of views is presented of what is required and in place to rebuild Iraq after the war finally begins.

Online Newshour: "Words of War" (29 January 2003)

Statements by U.S. government officials as to why this conflict is necessary in Iraq are reviewed.

Online Newshour: "GOP Platform 2000" (31 July 2000)

The position that candidate George W. Bush had on nation-building is important to the 2000 GOP Platform, trying to intervene more selectively that President Clinton.

Online Newshour: "Building a Nation" (19 May 2000)

Nation-building efforts in Kosovo and elsewhere are analyzed.

Online Newshour: "War in the Caucasus" (29 September 1999)

The problems of the former Soviet republics remain crucial to the study and implementation of true nation-building.

Online Newshour: "Bosnia Update" (22 December 1997)

How nation-building efforts were going in Bosnia, two years after the Dayton Peace Accords, are investigated.

Online Newshour: "Generals on Bosnia" (21 December 1995)

Several retired senior U.S. officers give their analyses of the possibilities for nation-building in the Balkans, in the aftermath of the Dayton Peace Accords.

Online Newshour: "U.S. and Bosnia" (14 December 1995)

The challenges and opportunities for nation-building in the period immediately following the Dayton Peace Accords on Bosnia-Herzegovina are analyzed.

Online Newshour: "Albright Interview" (11 December 1995)

This focuses on the Dayton Peace Accords and their implementation.

Online Newshour: "Interview with Nelson Mandela" (6 October 1994)

The South African leader faced one of the most difficult challenges in nation-building.

"Building a Nation: Foreign Minister of Afghanistan" (25 July 2000)

An interview with the new forreign minister of Afghanistan in Kabul.

"Building a Nation: Violence and Internal Strife Continue" (20 August 2002)

"Threat and Response: Iraq and Nation Building" (7 August 2002)

Newshour Extras provide background on nation-building issues and are usually narratives without interviews, noted on the Web as aimed at student audiences. There are many of these added regularly. Two that are particularly relevant are:

Newshour Extra: "Building a Nation" (19 May 2000)

Newshour Extra: "Building and Breaking Nations" (5 August 2002)

"Rebuilding Shakeup: Did the U.S. Prepare for Nation-Building?" (12 May 2003)

"Mr. Bush's Press Conference" (11 October 2001)

"Historical Perspectives" (15 April 2003)

"After the War" (8 April 2003)

"Assessing Mr. Bush's News Conference" (11 October 2001)

"Plans for a Post-War Iraq" (11 February 2003)

Online Newshour International Background Reports can be accessed at http://www.pbs.org/newshour/bb/international/international.html. Topics relating to nation-building include:

"Governing Iraq" (22 July 2003)

"Turmoil in Liberia" (21 July 2003)

"Update: On the Ground" (12 June 2003)

"Postwar Perspective" (11 June 2003)

"Ravaged Land" (9 June 2003)

"Ravaged Land" (28 May 2003)

"Prisoners' Status" (7 February 2003)

"Afghanistan's Money" (14 January 2003)

"Keeping the Peace" (21 November 2002)

"Newsmaker: Hamid Karzai" (28 January 2002)

"Rebuilding Afghanistan" (23 January 2002)

"Prospects of Peacekeeping" (9 January 2002)

"Helping Hand for Argentina" (7 January 2002)

"Relief Efforts" (11 December 2001)

"Afghanistan's Future" (30 November 2001)

"Shaping the Future" (27 November 2001)

"Aid for Afghanistan" (22 November 2001)

"Conversation: Lakhdar Brahimi" (25 October 2001)

"Holy War?" (11 October 2001)

"Relief Efforts" (2 October 2001)

"Making Peace" (22 August 2001)

"Peace Prospects" (9 July 2001)

"Update: Balkan Troubles" (15 March 2001)

"Conversation: Sierra Leone" (25 January 2001)

"Congo's Uncertain Future" (23 January 2001)

"Reaching Out to Refugees" (21 July 2000)

"Human Cargo" (20 June 2000)

"Conversation: Catherine Bertini" (9 June 2000)

"Peacekeeping Perils" (9 May 2000)

"Crisis in Sierra Leone" (4 May 2000)

"Rebuilding Haiti" (11 January 2000)

"The Mission to Haiti" (21 December 1999)

"Chechnya at War" (8 December 1999)

"The Chechen Conflict" (18 November 1999)

"The Continuing Chechnya Conflict" (25 October 1999)

"U.N. Secretary General Kofi Annan" (18 October 1999)

"James Obinski" (15 October 1999)

"Seeking Refuge" (22 July 1999)

"Tortured Souls" (14 July 1999)

"Assessing the Costs" (13 March 1998)

"Your Bills Are Past Due" (11 March 1998)

"U.N. Secretary General Kofi Annan" (4 March 1998)

"Policing the World" (26 February 1998)

"Violence Returns" (7 January 1998)

"Annan: Man with a Plan" (16 July 1997)

"State of Human Rights" (30 January 1997)

"Kofi Annan" (16 December 1996)

"U.S. Plans Zaire Mission" (13 November 1996)

"Zaire" (11 November 1996)

Online Newshour Latin America Background Reports can be accessed at http://www.pbs.org/newshour/bb/latin_america/latin_america.html.

"Free Market Backlash" (31 December 2003)

"Colombia's Struggle" (6 October 2003)

"Venezuelan Power Struggle" (17 January 2003)

"Troubled Nation" (17 December 2002)

"Leftist Landslide" (28 October 2002)

"Bailing Out Brazil" (8 August 2002)

"New Leader" (7 August 2002)

"Widening Worries" (5 August 2002)

"Assault on Drugs" (29 July 2002)

"Divided Nation" (31 May 2002)

"Back in Power" (15 April 2002)

"Foreign Aid" (22 March 2002)

"Confrontation in Colombia" (25 February 2002)

"Helping Hand" (7 January 2002)

"Upheaval" (21 December 2001)

"White Powder, Black Gold" (6 July 2001)

"Drug War" (30 August 2000)

"War on Drugs" (22 June 2000)

"Nation Building" (19 May 2000)

"Chile: Confronting the Past" (13 March 2000)

"Drug War Update" (15 February 2000)

"U.S. Involvement in Colombia" (11 August 1999)

"Democracy in Central America" (10 March 1999)

"The Road to Recovery" (30 November 1998)

"Hungry for Aid" (13 November 1998)

"Andres Pastrana" (6 October 1998)

"The Rebirth of Chile" (17 April 1998)

"Massacre in Mexico" (24 December 1997)

"Confronting History" (27 October 1997)

"Helpful Ally?" (3 September 1997)

"Summit of the Americas" (8 May 1997)

"Partner in Crime" (27 February 1997)

"Chile's Recipe for Success" (26 February 1997)

"Ecuador's Succession Crisis" (10 February 1997)

"Nicaragua: Favoring Capitalism" (22 October 1996)

"Mexican Uprising" (4 October 1996)

"Haiti's New President" (21 March 1996)

"Columbia's [sic] Samper and the Drug Link" (20 March 1996)

Online Newshour White House Background Reports are viewable at http://www.pbs.org/newshour/bb/white_house/white_house. html. A partial list of the topics relating to nation-building includes:

"Situation Report" (16 July 2003)

"Who Should Rebuild Iraq?" (30 April 2003)

"The New Iraq" (28 April 2003)

"Islam and Democracy" (28 April 2003)

"Moving towards an Interim Government" (15 April 2003)

"Reshaping Iraq" (15 April 2003)

"Historical Perspectives" (15 April 2003)

Online Newshour International Reports, at http://www.pbs.org/
newshour/bb/international/international.html, are yet another
source of analysis on the nation-building question. Topics covered include:

"Governing Iraq" (22 July 2003)

"Saddam's Sons" (22 July 2003)

"Turmoil in Liberia" (21 July 2003)

"Update: On the Ground" (12 June 2003)

"Postwar Perspective" (11 June 2003)

"Ravaged Land" (9 June 2003)

"Rebuilding Iraq" (13 May 2003)

"Life in Basra" (12 May 2003)

"Stabilizing Iraq" (12 May 2003)

"New U.S. Administration in Iraq" (12 May 2003)

"Lifting Sanctions" (9 May 2003)

"Lessons of War" (1 May 2003)

"Who Should Rebuild Iraq?" (30 April 2003)

"The New Iraq" (28 April 2003)

"Islam and Democracy" (28 April 2003)

"Crime and Punishment" (25 April 2003)

"Coping with Change" (16 April 2003)

"Historical Perspectives" (15 April 2003)

"After the War" (8 April 2003)

"The Humanitarian Effort" (21 March 2003)

"Closing Thoughts from Brzezinski and Mead" (21 March 2003)

"Truth and Justice" (23 January 2003)

"Venezuelan Power Struggle" (17 January 2003)

Online Special Reports can be found by individual topic or through http://www.pbs.org/newshour/special_projects/international_coverage.html, which then aggregates the regional coverage. Most are linked to nation-building:

10 February 2003: Experts examine the deepening divide between European leaders and the United States over conflict with Iraq.

6 February 2003: Three Middle East experts discuss Saddam Hussein's options.

5 February 2003: Experts assess Secretary Powell's case against Iraq.

4 February 2003: The secretary of state's role in the Iraq debate is examined.

31 January 2003: Iraq's ambassador to the United Nations discusses his country's response to U.N. weapons inspections.

23 January 2003: Turkey's ambassador to the United States discusses regional concerns over a potential war with Iraq.

20 January 2003: Experts discuss the possibility of Saddam Hussein going into exile.

16 December 2002: Attempts by Iraqi opposition groups to form a government to administer a post-Saddam Iraq are discussed.

19 March 1999: The president discusses the Kosovo situation in his press conference.

11 March 1999: Congress debates U.S. troops in Kosovo.

23 February 1999: National security advisor Samuel Berger discusses the Kosovo peace talks.

22 February 1999: While peace talks stall, a new round of fighting erupts in Kosovo.

18 February 1999: Secretary of state Albright discusses the negotiations meant to bring a peaceful end to the Kosovo crisis.

4 February 1999: Secretary Albright discusses the prospects for peace in Kosovo.

26 January 1999: NATO's supreme allied commander on Kosovo is interviewed.

18 January 1999: Fighting in Kosovo continues.

27 October 1998: U.S. special envoy Richard Holbrooke discusses the latest troop withdrawals from Kosovo.

14 October 1998: U.S. special envoy Holbrooke discusses the Kosovo crisis.

7 October 1998: NATO threatens air strikes against Serbian forces.

2 October 1998: National security advisor Samuel Berger discusses the Kosovo crisis.

1 October 1998: Two senators discuss possible U.S. involvement in Kosovo.

23 September 1998: Yugoslav president Slobodan Milosevic is the focus.

5 August 1998: Charges of ethnic cleansing surface in Kosovo.

15 July 1998: A look at the Kosovo Liberation Army.

7 July 1998: U.S. special envoy Holbrooke discusses the situation in Kosovo.

12 June 1998: NATO increases pressure on Yugoslavia over Kosovo.

Newshour: "Rebuilding Shakeup" (12 May 2003)

This discussion considers the problems Lt. Gen. Garner encountered in Iraq and what Ambassador Paul Bremer brings to the table in nation-building.

Newshour: "Building a Nation" (19 May 2000)

This is an extended view of the processes involved in carving out the new state of East Timor from its former master, Indonesia. This, along with the former Yugoslav states, represented the biggest challenges of nation-building before September 11 focused world attention on terrorism.

NOW

NOW, on PBS, considers public policy questions such as nation-building with host Bill Moyers.

NOW: "Reconstruction Resources," 14 November 2003, http://pbs.org/nov/politics/contractsites.html

NOW: transcript, 25 April 2003, http://www.pbs.org/now/transcript/transcript217_full.html

Superpower Global Affairs Television

Another show, the half-hour *Superpower Global Affairs Television,* devotes a significant portion of its work to nation-building. It is funded by Azimuth Media, which focuses on international security. Most of this show appears on DISH television and PBS stations around the nation, including Toms River, New Jersey; Washington, D.C.; Chicago; Brooklyn, New York; Claremore, Oklahoma; Denver, Colorado; San Bernadino, California; and College Station, Texas. It has produced more than two hundred separate segments, including ones on the reconstruction of Iraq, SARS pressures in China, reaction to war in Iraq, and a range of other topics. Transcripts are free from info@superpowertv.org, and email messages on programming are available through subscription: weekly@superpowertv.org.

Speeches

Carafano, James Jay. 2003. **"The U.S. Role in Peace Operations: Past, Perspective, and Prescriptions for the Future."** *Heritage Lectures,* no. 795, 13 August (delivered as speech 24 July 2003).

Carafano discusses the history of U.S. involvement in peace operations and describes why this is such a difficult task.

Center for Defense Information Eye on Iraq. **"Iraqi Reconstruction Updates No. 1 through No. 4: A Rough Start."** Available at http://www.cdi.org/program/issue/index.cfm?ProgramID=69&issueid=142 (accessed 1 March 2004).

This periodic assessment by analysts at a nonpartisan this describes the evolution of nation-building in Iraq.

Clinton, William J. 1999. **"Address to the Nation."** 24 March.

Available at http://www.pbs.org/newshour/bb/europe/jan-june99/address_3-24.html (accessed 1 March 2004).

This speech presented the argument that the United States needed to push NATO for air strikes to penalize the Serbs for their human rights abuses in Kosovo. Ultimately, NATO did just that, and peacekeepers are now in Kosovo and other parts of the Balkans.

CNN/AllPolitics. 2000. **Presidential Debates Transcript.** 11 October. Available at http://www.cnn.com/ELECTION/2000/debates/transcripts/u221011.html (accessed 16 January 2004).

President Bush's supposed opposition to nation-building as a policy came mainly from this debate with Vice President Gore. The transcript illustrates why President Bush's decisions, first in Afghanistan, then in Iraq, seem to contradict his campaign promises.

Joseph, James A. 1997. **"Nation-Building in South Africa: An American Perspective."** Presented before South African Jewish Board of Deputies, Capetown, South Africa, 18 April. Available at http://pretoria.usembassy.gov/wwwhjj7.html (accessed 3 March 2004).

The ambassador to South Africa explains why the United States believes that values are so crucial to any attempts at nation-building, especially in a country such as South Africa, where racial hatred and legal issues have been so ingrained. He also discusses the role of both civil society and nongovernmental organizations in such an important effort.

Perle, Richard. 2002. **"Next Stop Iraq."** Remarks delivered at the annual Foreign Policy Research Institute (FPRI) dinner in Philadelphia on 14 December. Available at http://www.fpri.org/enotes/americawar.20011130.perle.nextstopiraq.html (accessed 12 February 2004)

These remarks came from this private-sector advocate of the Bush administration approach to ousting Saddam Hussein.

Rumsfeld, Donald H. 2003. **"Beyond Nation Building."** Speech from 14 February. Available at http://www.defenselink.mil/speeches/2003/sp20030214-secdef0024.html (accessed 16 January 2004).

The secretary of defense explained, before Operation IRAQI FREE-DOM began in mid-March 2003, why nation-building would be an easier task in Iraq than in Afghanistan. Citing experiences in East Timor, Haiti, Somalia, and other locations, he attempts to dispel concerns that this might be a much tougher problem than as presented by the president.

Transcripts

Abrams, Eliott, and Charles Rangel. 1998. **"U.S. Policy towards Cuba: Is It Time for Change?"** 2 February. Available at http://www.cfr.org/publication.php?id=61 (accessed 12 February 2004).

This is a discussion by a former Reagan and George W. Bush administration official and then New York Democratic congressman about whether the United States ought to alter its more than thirty-five-year policy of embargoing and ignoring Cuba with the hope of toppling Fidel Castro.

Cohen, Jerome. 1999. **"Reflections on the Chinese Constitution and Its Relation to the Basic Law of the Hong Kong Administration Region."** 15 September. Available at http://www. cfr.org/publication.php?id=3234 (accessed 15 March 2004).

Cohen, a Council of Foreign Relations member, is a prominent jurist who has been involved in protecting the human rights of many Chinese citizens and is perhaps the leading expert in the United States on the Chinese Communist constitution.

Council on Foreign Relations. 1998. **"Democracy: Is It for Everyone?"** 19 May. Available at http://www.cfr.org/publication. php?id=47 (accessed 12 February 2004).

This is a discussion of whether the world ought to be more actively pushing democratic systems in states with poor records in that area. It offers an assessment of the problems as well as opportunities.

————. 2002. **"Toward a Greater Democracy in the Muslim World."** 4 December. Available at http://www.cfr.org/publication.php?id=5300 (accessed 12 February 2004).

This discussion, from the months leading up to the second Iraq war, illustrated the split opinion on whether democracy is workable in the Muslim world.

Videos

Afghanistan: From Ground Zero to Ground Zero
From the series America at War.
Type: Mini DVD
Length: 52 minutes
Date: 9 September 2002
Source: DCTV
87 Lafayette St.
New York, NY 10013-4435
(212) 966-4510
Fax: (212) 219-0248
Web site: http://www.dctvny.org
Cost: $325

This video describes the evolution of life in Afghanistan between the end of the Soviet period (late 1980s) when the Taliban and more secular groups began fighting for control. It evolves into the post-Taliban Afghanistan of today where the NATO forces, primarily with U.S. assistance, are still working to stabilise a nation-state out of the tribal system in place.

Index

319

About the Author

Cynthia A. Watson is a professor of strategy and director of faculty development at the National War College in Washington, DC, where she has been on the faculty since 1992. Dr. Watson earned her M.A. in economic history/Latin American studies at the London School of Economics and her doctorate in government and international studies at the University of Notre Dame. She has also worked for the U.S. House of Representatives and the General Accounting Office as well as at Loyola University and Ithaca College. Dr. Watson is a member of the International Institute for Strategic Studies and a fellow of the Inter-University Seminar on Armed Forces and Society, and she serves on the editorial board of *Third World Quarterly*. Dr. Watson is also certified as fluent in Spanish for Recording for the Blind and Dyslexic, a national resource for people with reading disabilities.

Dr. Watson has written on political violence, civil-military relations, and national security in Latin America, Asia, and the United States for her entire career. She authored *U.S. National Security Policy Groups* (1990), *U.S. National Security* (2002), and was a contributing co-editor, with Constantine Danopolous, to *The Political Use of the Military* (1996). Her more recent work has focused on transnational issues relating to China, China and Taiwan in Latin America, and the nation-building turmoil of Colombia.